Geopolitical Exotica

BORDERLINES

A BOOK SERIES CONCERNED WITH REVISIONING GLOBAL POLITICS
David Campbell and Michael J. Shapiro, series editors

Volume 30 Dibyesh Anand, *Geopolitical Exotica: Tibet in Western Imagination*

Volume 29 Prem Kumar Rajaram and Carl Grundy-Warr, editors, *Borderscapes: Hidden Geographies and Politics at Territory's Edge*

Volume 28 Louiza Odysseos, *The Subject of Coexistence: Otherness in International Relations*

Volume 27 Denise Ferreira da Silva, *Toward a Global Idea of Race*

Volume 26 Matthew Sparke, *In the Space of Theory: Postfoundational Geographies of the Nation-State*

Volume 25 Roland Bleiker, *Divided Korea: Toward a Culture of Reconciliation*

Volume 24 Marieke de Goede, *Virtue, Fortune, and Faith: A Genealogy of Finance*

Volume 23 Himadeep Muppidi, *The Politics of the Global*

Volume 22 William A. Callahan, *Contingent States: Greater China and Transnational Relations*

Volume 21 Allaine Cerwonka, *Native to the Nation: Disciplining Landscapes and Bodies in Australia*

Volume 20 Simon Dalby, *Environmental Security*

For more books in this series, see page 192.

Geopolitical Exotica

Tibet in Western Imagination

DIBYESH ANAND

BORDERLINES, VOLUME 30

 University of Minnesota Press

Minneapolis

London

Published by the University of Minnesota Press
111 Third Avenue South, Suite 290
Minneapolis, MN 55401-2520
http://www.upress.umn.edu

Library of Congress Cataloging-in-Publication Data

Anand, Dibyesh
    Geopolitical exotica : Tibet in western imagination / Dibyesh Anand.
        p.   cm. — (Borderlines ; v. 30)
    Includes bibliographical references and index.
    ISBN: 978-0-8166-4765-1 (hc : alk. paper)
    ISBN-10: 0-8166-4765-8 (hc : alk. paper)
    ISBN: 978-0-8166-4766-8 (pb : alk. paper)
    ISBN-10: 0-8166-4766-6 (pb : alk. paper)
    1. Tibet—History.   2. Tibet—International relations.   3. Group
identity.   4. Geopolitics.   I. Title.
    DS786.A6753 2007
    951'.5—dc22
                                                                    2007034924

Printed in the United States of America on acid-free paper

The University of Minnesota is an equal-opportunity educator and employer.

12 11 10 09 08 07   10 9 8 7 6 5 4 3 2 1

Wherever the wind blows from
Its rage always falls upon me.
O, please, my dear flagstaff, do excuse me
I the poor flag must pray for leave

—TIBETAN VERSE

(TRANSLATED BY W. Y. EVANS-WENTZ,

MODERN POLITICAL PAPERS)

Contents

Acknowledgments   ix

Introduction   xiii

1. Postcoloniality, Representation, and World Politics   1

2. Imagining the Other   17

3. Poetics of Exotica Tibet   37

4. The West and the Identity of "Tibet"   65

5. The Politics of Tibetan (Trans)National Identity   87

6. Postcoloniality and Reimag(in)ing Tibetanness   109

   Conclusion   129

   Notes   133

   Bibliography   151

   Publication History   183

   Index   185

Acknowledgments

Writing this book has been an intimate experience for me.

It would not have been possible without the generous support received from the University of Bristol Postgraduate Scholarship, Overseas Research Scholarship Award Scheme, Economic and Social Research Council Postdoctoral Fellowship Programme, British International Studies Research Award; British Academy Society for South Asian Studies Travel Grant, University of Bath Centre for Public Economics Grant, Chiang Ching-Kuo Foundation Library Grant, and British Academy Small Research Grant.

The Tibetan government-in-exile's Department of Information and International Relations at Dharamsala provided valuable information during my fieldwork. St. Stephen's College (Delhi) and especially its inspiring history lecturers (including David Baker, Aditya Pratap Deo, Sangeeta-Luthra Sharma, Upinder Singh, and Tasneem Suhrawardy) instilled an academic curiosity in me that changed the direction of my life.

I thank Jutta Weldes for her encouragement, support, guidance, and patience during my doctoral research. She is the best supervisor and colleague one can have. I also express appreciation to the Department of Politics at the University of Bristol for supporting me and setting a high standard—thanks to Richard Little, Vernon

Hewitt, Andrew Wyatt, Liz Grundy, Anne Jewell, and, especially, Judith Squires. I met Juha Jokela and Johanna Kantola while we were doing our PhDs in the department and we remain friends. Thanks to Rob Walker and Richard Little for the valuable comments on my project in their role as PhD examiners.

The shift from Bristol to Bath at the postdoctoral stage could not have been smoother. Geof Wood, as a good mentor, ensured I built on my existing strengths and expanded to new areas. Thanks to John Sessions, Andy McKay, Allister McGregor, and many others for continuing support. Without the timely grant from the department's Centre for Public Economics, the book would have been incomplete; thanks to Colin Lawson for this. Stefan Wolff is a model senior academic colleague who never failed to help. My gratitude to my students for maintaining my illusion that they find my frequent use of Tibet examples as fascinating as I do.

The intellectual journey of which this book is a product has been enriched by comments and encouragement at various stages by more people than I can recall. My appreciation to Robbie Barnett, Costas Constantinou, Philip Darby, Clare Harris, Barry Hindess, Nitasha Kaul, Christiaan Klieger, Mark Laffey, Jan Magnusson, Martin Mills, Dawa Norbu, Barry Sautman, Tsering Shakya, Michael J. Shapiro, and several other discussants of my conference papers. If I forgot someone, my apologies! Christiaan made me feel at home in the community of Tibetan studies and is a true friend. Mike Shapiro's encouragement helped give me direction at crucial times.

The editorial staff at the University of Minnesota Press has been fantastic in their support. Thanks to Mike Shapiro and David Campbell for editing a series, Borderlines, that new multidisciplinary academics could look to and aspire to be part of. William Callahan provided extremely useful and helpful comments and supported me in more than one way. I remain indebted to him.

My parents, Runa Jha and Namo Nath Jha, always made me believe in myself; I never felt the need to conform. I could not have asked for more understanding parents. The list of family members is long, and it feels odd to "thank" them for what we in any case expect to do in a family: be there for each other without having to ask.

How do I even begin to verbalize my dependence on one person who has made this journey worthwhile? I can say she was always there for me, to support me, to nurture me. But I would be wrong—she was always ahead of me, never letting me rest in illusory professional successes, reminding me not to confuse professional with intellectual. I would like to dedicate this book with love to Nitasha Kaul, my intellectual and life companion, for traveling together with me, for being different, for being herself.

Introduction

I am not erudite enough to be interdisciplinary, but I can break rules.
—GAYATRI CHAKRAVORTY SPIVAK,
A CRITIQUE OF POSTCOLONIAL REASON

Though critical international theories have questioned mainstream International Relations (IR) on epistemological, ontological, and methodological grounds, they remain largely focused on the "West." I contend that the parochial character of IR can be effectively challenged by a postcolonial IR based on conversations between critical international theories and postcolonialism. Adopting a historical analytical perspective, I examine "Exotica Tibet" (henceforth used as a shorthand for Western exoticized representations of Tibet and Tibetans) and its constitutive significance for the "Tibet question."[1] Exotica Tibet is interrogated in terms of its *poetics* (how Tibet is represented) and its *politics* (what impact these representational regimes have on the identity discourses of the represented). While Tibet excites the popular imagination in the West, it has been treated cursorily within political studies. I contextualize the empirical study of the Tibet question to put forward more general arguments that may apply to other parts of the postcolonial world and provide new insights into themes of representation and identity.

GEOPOLITICAL EXOTICA:
IR, POSTCOLONIALITY, AND THE TIBET QUESTION

Mainstream IR remains preoccupied with the "big" issues of war and order, power and security. In the process, it ignores, marginalizes, and trivializes issues that affect the everyday lives of a majority of the world's population living mostly, though not exclusively, in the so-called third world. This has status quoist implications. In the spirit of the Western Enlightenment, IR's parochialism takes on the garb of universalistic pretensions. However, thanks to the various critical international theories, it is no longer possible to speak with confidence of a single discipline called IR. Voices of authority are now continuously engaged by the voices of dissent. While various strands of the "third debate" (see Lapid 1989) have critiqued the conventional theories and widened the self-definition of IR, it still remains mainly "Western" in orientation. Insularity in the guise of universalism remains strong. Reconceptualizing IR away from its moorings in realist and liberal paradigms involves questioning its ontological, epistemological, and methodological concerns while at the same time combating conspicuous elements of its geographical parochialism. In order to go "beyond the dominant rituals of International Relations theory and practice" (George 1996, 70), we must foreground political concerns from "beyond" the West while at the same time recognizing the West's contested and constitutive role in shaping that which lies beyond it. This can be done through adoption of *postcoloniality* (a postcolonial critical attitude) that involves inter- as well as antidisciplinarity.

IR should no longer be seen as merely the study of particular kinds of political relations because it also involves intercultural and intersubjective relations. A postcolonial international theory based on conversations of critical IR with antidisciplinary intellectual endeavors like postcolonialism will make this possible. How exactly such conversations take place would differ according to the themes and contexts involved. I do not provide a blueprint for such a dialogue. Instead, the focus is on the themes of representation and identity, especially those involving the West–non-West dynamics. Postcoloniality offers a means to talk about world politics without "political evacuation and disciplinary incorporation" (Weber 1999, 435).

But the task is not only to look at concerns and issues affecting people in the non-Western world. It also entails examining old themes of state, power, war, and peace from new and different perspectives. For example, within the rubric of conventional IR Tibet is mostly considered in terms of its role in Sino-Western relations or Sino-Indian border disputes (see Lamb 1986), thus effectively denying subjectivity to the Tibetans themselves. This resonates with the early-twentieth-century British preoccupation with Tibet's role in the "Great Game"—the imperialist rivalry between the British and the Russians in Central Asia. The analysis of the Tibet question using postcolonial IR theory entails scrutinizing the vocabulary afforded by conventional IR and considering hitherto undertheorized issues such as imperialism, history, diaspora, representation, and identity.

Postcoloniality politicizes culture and encultures politics. In this work, the case for a postcolonial IR is made by looking at the general theme of representation (and its productive relation with identity) and the specific issue of Western representations and Tibetan identity discourses. What Doty writes about representation of the South (the non-West) by the North (the West) reflects my use of the term "representation" here:

> By representation I mean the ways in which the South has been discursively represented by policy makers, scholars, journalists, and others in the North. This does not refer to the "truth" and "knowledge" that the North has discovered and accumulated about the South, but rather to the ways in which regimes of "truth" and "knowledge" have been produced. (1996b, 2)

Even though the issues raised by the Tibet question are international in scope and there is an increasing recognition that it remains one of the unsolved problems in world politics, Tibet rarely figures in the international politics literature. When it does come up, it is either as a footnote to the Cold War (see Conboy and Morrison 2002; Knaus 1999; Shakya 1999), or as a pawn in Sino-Western (see Sautman 1999; Xu Guangui 1997) or Sino-Indian relations (see Addy 1984; Ghosh 1977; Ginsburgs 1960; Mehra 1979, 2005; Norbu 1997). This neglect reflects a web of strategic interests of major Western and regional powers, IR's focus on relations between states, and, finally, its ethnocentrism.[2] All this was clearly evident after 1959, when China acquired complete control over Tibet, giving up the uneasy accommodation with the Dalai Lama–led Tibetan government that had lasted for less than a decade. Despite the international condemnation of Chinese action in both strongly worded representations such as those of the International Commission of Jurists and feeble statements in the United Nations General Assembly,[3] the states of the world accepted the Tibet question as an "internal" Chinese matter.

Realist and liberal strands of IR theory seem incapable of engaging with the complexity of the Tibet question, though the emergence of critical schools within the field suggests the potential for a better understanding. The Tibetan issue can be studied in terms of sovereignty/suzerainty, imperialism, human rights, representation, identity, nationalism, diaspora, and transnationalism. An approach that highlights the interlinkages between these and also emphasizes the need for some sort of dialogue between critical IR and postcolonialism better addresses the complexity surrounding it. Critical international theories provide sophisticated investigations of some of these themes, notably sovereignty, representation, and nationalism. But themes of imperialism, diaspora, Western representational practices, and transnational identity require insights from postcolonial theory.

Thus, within the wider argument for a postcolonial approach to IR, I seek to theorize Western cultural representations of Tibet and their constitutive (both enabling and constraining) and performative roles in two crucial elements of the Tibet question—the framing of the debate over political status of Tibet and Tibetan identity discourses. If we are to redefine IR as a discourse of world politics that appreciates the importance of issues of power in a postcolonial world, we have to take on board concerns such as the ones expressed here. After all, Tibetanness is a typical postcolonial/post-colonial narrative of identity politics combining processes of migration with the human desire for fixity.

A critical engagement with "Exotica Tibet and world politics" presents its own problems in disciplinary terms. IR has not dealt with postcolonialism and the Tibet question sufficiently; postcolonial studies has ignored IR as well as Tibet; and, although Tibetan studies has some encounter with postcolonial theory (see Bishop 1989, 1993; Korom 1997a, 1997b; Lopez 1998), it has had little contact with IR theory. So, in borrowing from IR, postcolonial theory, and Tibetan studies, I move beyond all three to set up a theoretical framework within which to understand the poetics and politics of Exotica Tibet. Not only does this framework entail recognizing the cultural underpinnings of world politics, but it also politicizes our understandings of culture. In the spirit enunciated by the first collection of poststructuralist writings in IR, here is a book "that is theoretical (but not methodological), that is empirical (but not empiricist), that problematizes (but does not problem-solve) world politics" (Der Derian and Shapiro 1989, xi).

CHAPTER OUTLINE

Chapter 1 highlights the ethnocentrism of IR and outlines a critical approach to the *international* informed by postcoloniality. It then focuses on representation of the Other as an international political practice. After examining the treatment of representation within critical IR, its limitations are highlighted and the stage is set for analysis of the poetics and politics of Exotica Tibet in the subsequent chapters.

Cultural representation of the non-Western Other lies at the core of Western colonial and neocolonial discourses. A critical political analysis of the Western imagination of the Other involves a recognition at two levels—the practices of essentializing and stereotyping that provide the backbone as well as various strategies (such as infantilization, eroticization, debasement, idealization, and self-affirmation) that put flesh on the imagined Other. The strategies are not fixed ahistorically but nevertheless remain stable over a period of time. In chapter 2 I identify significant rhetorical strategies that characterize Western representations of the (non-Western) Other, focusing mainly on Western colonial representations, and substantiate the argument through the empirical study of Exotica Tibet.

In chapter 3 I further delve into the poetics through an in-depth analysis of a selection of prominent cultural sites within which Exotica Tibet has operated in the twentieth century. This includes novels, travelogues, memoirs, films, and images. The idea is not to provide an exhaustive list of the cultural sites that have contributed to the creation of the *imagin-o-scape* of Exotica Tibet but to lay bare the representational strategies operating within them.

After this encounter with poetics, in the next three chapters I shift attention to the politics of Exotica Tibet—examining the impact of the representational regimes on the *identity of Tibet* as well as *Tibetan identity*. Exoticized representation has had a very significant effect on identity discourses among the Tibetans. Tibet is not some prediscursive geographical entity but a place that is discursively constructed through the imaginative practices of the various actors involved.[4] Similarly, Tibetanness is not some essence of Tibetan life but is the politicized articulation of themes of identity and difference, of commonality and distinctiveness. And indeed the representational regimes, even though productive, tend to restrict and contain the options available for self-expression. This productive-cum-restrictive impact of Western representations on the identity of Tibet as well as on Tibetan identity reflects a trait of modern representational regimes in general.

Through a historical analysis of the crucial role played by British imperialism in the framing of the Tibet question in terms of sovereignty, suzerainty, autonomy, and independence, chapter 4 explores how sovereignty relates to the conjunction of international relations, imperialism, and Orientalism. This provides a sound basis for understanding contemporary political problems contextually and challenging the prevailing view of political problems of international standing as intractable nationalist and long-standing historical conflicts. I bring to relief the destructive/constructive role of imperialism in shaping the contemporary world (thus challenging the historical amnesia or a simplistic use of history that characterizes much of the IR scholarship).

In chapters 5 and 6 the specific case of Tibetanness (Tibetan national identity) as articulated in the diaspora will be taken up to highlight the politics of representation and thus support the case for a postcolonial critical approach to world politics. As I will argue, Exotica Tibet is an important but not an exhaustive determining factor of Tibetanness. I will examine the articulations of Tibetanness in political (chapter 5) and cultural (chapter 6) spheres, argue for new ways of theorizing these identities, and interrogate the constitutive role of Western representations in these identity discourses. In chapter 5, I highlight various dynamics of political Tibetanness and foreground the crucial role played by the poetics of Exotica Tibet. In chapter 6, I offer new ways of theorizing cultural facets of Tibetanness through an innovative postcolonial analysis of the symbolic geography of Dharamsala (the seat of the Dalai Lama–led Tibetan government-in-exile). This retheorization exemplifies ways in which postcoloniality can challenge conventional disciplinary endeavors and offer new ways of doing IR. In this sense, my endeavor is as much antidisciplinary as it is interdisciplinary. While looking at cultural and political identities separately, the chapters emphasize the intermeshing between both, thus highlighting the need for enculturing political analysis and politicizing cultural analysis.

The conclusion sums up the arguments made in the different chapters and underlines that postcolonial IR offers an effective means to appreciate the political and productive effect of Western representational practices, especially on non-Western people. The poetics and politics of Western representations are legitimate areas of enquiry for IR not only because these support particular foreign policy regimes (as highlighted by critical IR) but also because they have a productive effect on the identities of political actors. Postcolonial IR appreciates the importance of popular culture for our understanding of world politics.

1

Postcoloniality, Representation, and World Politics

Every established order tends to produce (to very different degrees and with very different means) the naturalisation of its own arbitrariness.

— PIERRE BOURDIEU, *OUTLINE OF A THEORY OF PRACTICE*

Whoever studies contemporary international relations cannot but hear, behind the clash of interests and ideologies, a kind of permanent dialogue between Rousseau and Kant.

— STANLEY HOFFMAN, *THE STATE OF WAR: ESSAYS ON THE THEORY AND PRACTICE OF INTERNATIONAL RELATIONS*

Non-Western peoples, and sometimes even states, have been ridden roughshod over both literally and figuratively in IR. One such people are the Tibetans. It is surprising that even as several critical theories have challenged the dominant IR paradigms on ontological, epistemological, and methodological grounds in the last two decades, geographical parochialism has continued relatively unabated. My contention is that a postcolonial critical attitude, *postcoloniality*, offers an effective means of challenging this. The rejection of positivism (see Ashley and Walker 1990a, 1990b; Campbell 1998a, 1998b; Campbell and Dillon 1993; DerDerian and Shapiro 1989; George 1994; Lapid 1989; Shapiro 1988; Sjolander and Cox 1994; Smith et al. 1996; Walker 1993) and a reengagement with culture within IR (see Chay 1990; Lapid and Kratochwil 1996; Shapiro and Alker 1996; Weldes et al. 1999) has opened up space for a postcolonial IR

1

endeavor. The encounter of postcolonialism with IR, that is, *postcolonial international relations,* is a new phenomenon[1] and remains neglected by most IR textbooks (for an exception, see Baylis and Smith 2005).

POSTCOLONIALIZING THE INTERNATIONAL IN IR THEORY

The engagement of critical IR with postcolonialism is partly an attempt to estrange the basics of IR, partly a call for dialogue and bridge building with critical discourses of IR, partly a critical review of existing critical discourses in (or at the edge of) IR, partly a call for appropriating the discursive space of IR for the play of hitherto silenced and marginalized voices, and partly *an undoing of* IR. It is through an interaction with non-Western context, material, and agents of knowledge that the dominant "Occidental" theories of interpretation can be challenged and redrawn (Spivak 1990, 8), and IR is no exception. This involves dealing not only with what has been spoken in IR but more importantly with what has not been said. For as Walker points out, power is often most persuasive and effective amid the silences of received wisdom (1993, 13).

IR's Parochialism

Hoffman's quote from 1965 in the epigraph, which reduces IR to a debate between two white, privileged, European males, neatly reflects the parochial character of IR. In 1985 Holsti writes that hierarchy seems "to be a hallmark of international politics and theory," and since the domination of the United States and the United Kingdom is overwhelming, IR is "a British-American intellectual condominium" (102–3). Fifteen years on, Buzan and Little point out that "there is no doubt that IR has been studied from a very Eurocentric perspective with a concomitant failure to come to terms with how non-European 'others' understood international relations or organized their world" (2000, 21). A cursory look at the literature of IR shows that there are relatively few works on issues facing the third world.

This would not be a problem had IR recognized its own narrow character and not claimed to have universal applicability.[2] *International Studies Quarterly,* one of the most prestigious journals in the field of IR, claimed in 2002 that it publishes "the best work being done in the variety of intellectual traditions included under the rubric of international studies," and yet articles challenging the mainstream and addressing the concerns of third world peoples are rare in it. Mainstream IR theories are Western in terms of their origin,[3] inspiration, priorities, and political biases and yet they claim to be universal (see Ling 2002).

Even when various "global" voices and dialogue are sought to be promoted (as in Rosenau 1993), the third world is either ignored[4] or spoken for by some Westerner,[5] revealing the will to universalize within IR's insular thinking. When IR scholars speak of the Cold War as a period of "long peace" (Gaddis 1987) and give reasons for "why we will soon miss the cold war" (Mearsheimer 1990), they completely ignore that "[f]or the overwhelming majority of the world's peoples, global politics since World War II has been anything but peaceful" (Klein 1994, 15). When IR scholars write about the third world in "prestigious" IR journals, they usually do so from the vantage point of the West. The West (particularly the United States; see Gibbs 2001) and its security concerns seem to dominate the IR literature. Various powerful countries see the non-West mainly as a playground for their "power politics." The realist paradigm is entrenched especially within works dealing with the third world and the "[c]onventional IR with its focus on great power politics and security, read narrowly, naturalizes . . . global hierarchies and thus reproduces the status quo" (Chowdhry and Nair 2002, 1). IR has, in general, not encouraged an intimate knowledge of non-Western countries. Issues central to the lives of common people in the third world have been largely marginalized and silenced in IR.

The project of deparochializing IR thus entails recognition of its Eurocentrism[6] and the poverty of IR when it comes to matters concerning the majority of the world's people who live in areas formerly under direct or indirect colonial rule of Western European states. These people(s) and places have been variously worlded as "the third world," "the South," "the East,"[7] "the developing world," and so on. Here I use "worlding" in a Spivakian sense to denote the giving of a "proper name to a generalized margin" (Spivak 1997, 199), to refer to the way colonized space is brought into the world, that is, made to exist as part of a world essentially constructed by Eurocentrism. The self-image of the West is often implicated in and produced by the process of naming—for instance, posing the non-West as "developing" makes the West the "developed" and hence superior (see Escobar 1995). This does not mean that non-Westerners have only been victims, lacking any agency. In fact, often the non-Westerners have catachrestically appropriated the Western (politics of) naming. We will see this in the context of Tibetans in subsequent chapters.

The Postcolonial Enterprise

In contradistinction to mainstream IR's unquestioned acceptance of modernity, postcolonialism seeks to combine participation in a progressive agential politics of identity with a metacritique of modernism for its parochial ideas and exclusionary practices disguised as universalism.[8] The primary focus here is on issues affecting people living in the third world as well as minorities in the West. I use "postcolonial" to signify a position against imperialism and Eurocentrism. Western ways of knowledge production and dissemination in the past and present are not taken for granted but put under scrutiny. Postcolonialism does not signal a closing off of that which it contains (colonialism), or even a rejection (which would not be possible in any case), but rather an opening of a field of inquiry and understanding following a period of relative closure. It involves engaging with issues and experiences that have influenced significantly the lives of peoples in the third world.

The focus within postcolonialism is on micropolitical concerns, on the politics of everyday life, as it is here that the real effects of knowledge regimes are felt. While postcolonialism foregoes the idea of some grand emancipation, it remains an empowering discourse for gendered and racialized subjectivities, hitherto marginalized by the dominant discourses. However, such a retheorization of politics does not necessarily imply the jettisoning of macropolitical questions. Though the specificity of "big" political issues is negotiated and resisted at an individual and local level, they often have a containing and constraining influence. One such macropolitical question is related to the issue of self-determination. While skepticism of nation- and state-building projects within postcolonialism (see Prakash 1995) is understandable, it cannot be denied that there are many groups, such as the Tibetan or Palestinian diasporas, who seek to define their collective identity in terms of nation and collective aspirations in terms of state. The *inter-national* (in practice, inter-state) character of world politics circumscribes means of collective political self-expression. While the postcolonialists have contributed substantially by studying resistance to state-building projects from the perspectives of gender and indigeneity, there is also a need to take into account resistance coming from those identifying themselves as distinct nations or as distinct ethnic groups. The discrediting of nationalism as a liberating ideology does not mean that all those who mobilize themselves in the name of nationalism now are operating under some sort of "false consciousness," for often it is done strategically. For instance, Tibetans adopt different vocabularies keeping in mind the audience, ranging from the rhetoric of human rights to the right of self-determination, from autonomy to secession. Postcolonial theory needs to take such issues into account to be more meaningful to many people living within the third world. As Scott has argued, the thrust of the argument now should be to move away from postcoloniality's politics of theory to a new theory of politics where "the accent is on *political* rather than cultural criticism" (1999, 19, emphasis in original).

As critical theories going under the name of feminism, poststructuralism, and constructivism have already challenged the dominance of conventional IR theories, a postcolonial IR becomes a real possibility. This possibility itself shows how far IR has changed in the last two decades since the disciplinary/intellectual histories of IR and Postcolonial Theory have been very distinct.

IR and Postcolonial Theory: Divided Skies, Divided Horizons?

A brief comparison of IR, an established *discipline-in-crisis,* and Postcolonial Theory, an *antidiscipline,* gives us an idea of how these two diverge. Here I begin with mainstream IR theory,[9] especially its realist and liberal strands, before moving on to critical IR in the next section. IR emerged as a discipline in its own right in the Anglo-American world at a time when the authority of Western imperialism was more or less secure. The proponents concerned themselves with the "big" issues of war and peace that affected the relations between "civilized" nation-states. Theoretical antecedents were traced to thinkers and states*men* of the Western world. While Thucydides' and Machiavelli's works were being invented as antecedents of realism, writings from non-Western history such as Kautilya's *Arthashastra* (a treatise on statecraft written, allegedly, by a pundit in ancient India) were ignored. Due to their focus on narrowly defined big questions, the debates between idealists and realists conveniently ignored the issues that were central to the everyday lives of people of the colonizing countries as an "internal" matter and by the very same logic refused to see any link between the international system and colonized places. Exclusive concentration on state-as-actor meant no attention was given to the people under colonial rule. The imperial powers ensured that their relationships with their colonies remained an internal matter (Darby and Paolini 1994, 384), outside the purview of IR.[10] The distinction between international relations and imperial relations was identified and asserted. Denial of the Wilsonian principle of self-determination to places outside Europe after the First World War illustrated the double standards of Western powers. They conferred the badge of civilization only on the European countries, the United States, and later on Japan—revealing that the label was related more to the political influence of the state than anything else.

Given the close links between the emerging IR discipline and foreign policy–making bodies of government, it would not be wrong to state that IR as a knowledge formation was complicit with existing power structures from its inception. The close linkage between IR and policy-making authorities continues today, especially in the United States (see Hoffman 1977; Smith 2000). This close association with the decision-making process coupled with the theoretical underpinnings of positivism, empiricism, and the search for "objectivity" ensured IR's status as a status quoist discourse par excellence.

This inherent conservativeness of IR ensured that even with formal decolonization after the Second World War there was no major shake-up in the theoretical underpinnings of the discipline. Significantly, when decolonization was at its peak in the 1960s and the third world was asserting itself through the Non-Aligned Movement (NAM), IR was self-referentially engaged in its own debate over methodological issues—the "second debate" between traditionalism and behaviorism. Any serious analysis of imperialism was eschewed as it breached the neat and artificial distinction between the external and the internal—something central to the IR enterprise (see Walker 1993). The concepts remained unchanged, still rooted in "Western notions of self and sovereignty [that] have been grounded in claims of superiority, a higher knowledge of civil institutions, and a mission to elevate the other" (Grovogui 1996, x). Ontologically, decolonization was looked upon merely as an expansion of international system/society from its original home in Europe to the rest of the world, as the addition of new members into the preexisting international community. Epistemologically too, there was little change as scientistic and positivistic assumptions were held to have universal application. State-as-actor remained the focus of analysis; sovereignty, power, national interest, and state rivalry were seen as defining international relations. While at a theoretical level all states were considered to be sovereign and thus legally equal, the hierarchical character of this relationship was often implicitly recognized[11] as most of the works in IR concentrated on East-West relations and the Cold War. Though at a pedagogical level IR acquired a global audience, its theoretical parsimony continued unabated.

The newly independent states, now worlded as the "third world" or "developing countries" were the subject of analyses in IR primarily in two ways: first, as a playground for the rivalry of the powerful countries; and second, when they defied the logical authority of the powerful states (and also the theoretical authority of IR by acting "irrationally"), as was the case with Iran (see Chan and Williams 1994).[12] What went earlier under the name of imperial relations now became a subject matter for imperial history. Instead of studying developments in the third world in the wider historical context of a long period of brutal colonization and a structurally truncated form of decolonization, imperialism was deemed a thing of the past. This general neglect of history (or often an adoption of a reified view of history) should not come as a surprise, for IR always had tendencies toward taking ahistoricized positions. Within realist and liberal IR that accounts for the bulk of the discipline, there is hardly any recognition or analysis of the legacies of colonialism and neocolonialism. The absence of any consideration, be it crude or sophisticated, of neocolonialism in mainstream IR is conspicuous.

Also significant is the lack of a serious effort to deal with themes such as culture, identity, and representation. Mainstream IR has ignored that world politics is a product of wider processes of identity construction in which the Self and the Other are constituted (Connolly 1991). Darby points out that the story of IR "[tells] of how power was exercised, not of how it was experienced" (1997, 23). This has led to a depersonalizing and dehumanizing of the discipline. Wars are studied in terms of strategy and rarely in terms of human consequences.

Mainstream IR's theoretical and empirical closure and lack of self-reflexivity stand in stark contrast to Postcolonial Theory, which remains largely undisciplined. While drawing theoretical inspirations from critical thinkers of both Western and non-Western traditions, a conscious oppositional stance is adopted vis-à-vis the dominant discursive systems in place. Thus, a reflexive criticality is the hallmark of postcoloniality. Imperialism and its impact on peoples and cultures are given a due importance (see Bhabha 1994; McClintock 1995; Richards 1993; Sharpe 1993; Suleri 1992). While problematizing categories such as third world, the voices of third world peoples are promoted, their agency and subjectivity asserted (see Spivak 1988; see also Mohanty et al. 1991). Contemporary problems are historicized, while at the same time "history" as it has come to be commonly understood is put under interrogation (see Chakrabarty 2000; Guha and Spivak 1988; Prakash 1995). Diversity of theoretical input[13] gels with a wide range of issues brought under the label "postcolonial." Postcolonial Theory is certainly multi/trans/interdisciplinary. In fact, it is antidisciplinary.

As pointed out earlier, rather than being confined to "big" issues, postcolonialism concentrates on the politics of everyday life. Universal ideas and their unproblematic implementation globally are eschewed. While acknowledging the relationship of complicity between the production of explanations and the violence and injustices associated with the structures of imperialism and capitalism, a deconstructive scenario of the kind emphasized by postcolonial theorists like Spivak involves paying attention to critics' complicity with the object of critique, a "disclosure of complicity" (1988, 180). Elsewhere, Spivak suggests two methods to confront the situation— overtly marking one's positionality as an investigating subject and laying bare one's inescapable institutional interests (1993, 56). This kind of self-reflexivity is absent from mainstream IR.

Darby surmises that the contrast between the mobile and variegated nature of the postcolonial discourse and the conservative character of mainstream IR reflects a general situation that exists between established disciplines and new formations of knowledge (1997, 13). I find this contentious. While there is no doubt that new disciplines informed by feminism and cultural and postcolonial theories are more radical, the surmise seems to suggest that it is only a matter of time before the disciplinary establishment would blunt their critical edge. As a corollary, one may also take the implication that when IR was a new formation of knowledge it was radical. Certainly this does not seem to be the case.

A basic difference exists between the established disciplinary knowledge formations such as IR and some of the new ones, a difference that cannot be accounted for by temporal factors only. It is not a question of academic incorporation or assimilation but of metatheoretical differences. Self-reflexivity regarding theoretical stances and empirical agendas was not a prominent feature of older disciplines even when they were new. Claims were not made on behalf of the unprivileged. Justification for disciplinary endeavors was given in the name of methodological correctness. Right from its inception, IR has, on the whole, been a status quoist discipline with limited debate over strategies of maintaining a good international order. On the other hand, many new hybridized disciplines have adopted a critical and oppositional stance vis-à-vis the established discursive and material structures. Not only do they involve a critiquing of the existing norms and structures but they also promote a constant questioning of their own shifting positionalities. While the older disciplines like IR were informed by a heady confidence in the Enlightenment ideas of Progress, Reason, and Emancipation, the new knowledge formations' attitudes to these ideas vary from skepticism to outright rejection. The latter argue that the Enlightenment ideas have sought to universalize particularistic, ethnocentric, and masculinist notions. Unlike older disciplines, which emerged to carve out an exclusive niche for themselves, the new ones seek to challenge disciplinary compartmentalization and circumvent it, and they are often antidisciplinary. While IR emerged as a corollary to the study of politics, Postcolonial Theory's emergence within humanities and social sciences has come as a challenge to various disciplinary boundaries. Its challenging nature offers interesting opportunities for the adoption of a postcolonial approach to world politics, in alliance with critical IR.

Critical IR, Postcolonial IR

Given the potential critical edge in the discourse of postcolonialism, it is surprising that even the more radical endeavors in the field of IR, with the exception of feminism,[14] have generally ignored it. For instance, in the pioneering postmodern work *International/ Intertextual Relations* (Der Derian and Shapiro 1989), the long bibliography does not include works that move beyond the confines of the "West." Even when the term "postcolonialism" is used in IR, for instance in Clapham's work on Africa and the international system (1996), it is devoid of postcoloniality (that is, a postcolonial criticality) and is used in the simplistic periodizing sense of postcolonial times. "[E]ven works embarking from professedly critical postmodern and poststructural perspectives often replicate the Eurocentric ecumene of 'world politics'" (Krishna 1999, xxix).

Why this lack of engagement of critical international theories with a potential ally (postcolonial theory)? Krishna brought attention to this as early as 1993 when he highlighted the fact that some postmodern theorists commence from a remarkably self-contained and self-referential view of the West and are often oblivious to "the intimate dialogue between 'Western' and 'non-Western' economies, societies, and philosophies that underwrite the disenchantment with modernity that characterizes the present epoch" (Krishna 1993, 388). Cautioning against a blanket critique of subjectivity and agency, which he alleges to be a feature of some postmodernist works, Krishna prefers a postcolonial perspective that entails sensitivity to hierarchical relations between races, genders, and classes while also challenging the ethnocentricity of IR.

While I agree that the critical insurgencies in general and postmodern/poststructuralist writing in particular have tended to ignore the concerns of the non-West, I do not accept Krishna's caricature of postmodern writings in IR as depoliticizing. For not only do these endeavors create space for imagining alternatives (a fact Krishna recognizes) but they also accept the need to formulate ironic, provisional, and yet politically enabling essentializing of subjectivity (something that Krishna accuses them of ignoring). What critical theories like critical social constructivism, feminism, postmodernism, and poststructuralism have exposed is International Relations as a discursive process, a process that constitutes the world we live in. Conceptualizing the *international* as discursive allows for contestation and recognition of different possibilities of being *international*.

In his critique, Darby claims that both postmodern and conventional IR share a sense of remoteness from the phenomena under analysis; both look at an essentially depeopled landscape where ethics and intentions do not rate highly (admittedly from very different perspectives) and do not pursue consequences in human terms (1997, 15–17). This comparison underemphasizes the politicizing potentialities of postmodern IR (for instance, Campbell 1998a, 1998b; Shapiro 1988; Walker 1993). Darby also critiques the postmodern influence within Postcolonial Theory as depoliticizing and rejects the concept of "strategic essentialism" for lacking a cutting edge and for inscribing the secondary status of the third world in the thinking of the first world. In contrast, he argues that we need to give much more weight to the problems of the third world, rather than continuing to tailor our approach to the issues in hand in line with the requirements of an often resistant body of theory (1997, 15–17). These arguments not only repeat the positivist fallacy of making a distinction between theory and practice but they also contrast material structures with discursive practices as if they do not perform a mutually constitutive role. Darby ignores the fact that the constitutive paradox of essentialism and antiessentialism is irreducible. Spivakian *strategic essentialism*—"a strategic use of positivist essentialism in a scrupulously visible political interest" (in Landry and MacLean 1996, 214)[15]—still seems to be the best way forward for it enables while at the same time it is humbling (a characteristic noticeably absent from the often arrogant pronouncements of mainstream IR).

IR's third debate has seriously charged the discipline of IR with promoting the status quo and a lack of self-consciousness and reflexivity. The "truths" of IR have been revealed as effects of regimes of truth, knowledge as complicit with power, pursuit of objectivity as a chimera, hitherto universal concepts as ethnocentric and particularistic. Let me then recapitulate some of the commonalities that can provide a contingent ground for conversations between existing critical international theories and postcolonialism in order to come up with a postcolonial IR that seeks to deparochialize the discipline of IR. Both endeavors seek to provide a critique of dominant discourses for being the typical products of Western modernity. They reveal the silences of the disciplines by exposing philosophical closures and the underlying power-knowledge nexus. Both are marked by constitutive paradoxes. Challenge to the sovereignty of subjectivity goes along with an assertion of subjectivity. Resurgence of identity accompanies the deconstruction of identity as constructed and processual. The universalistic pretensions of the mainstream are revealed as particularistic and ethnocentric. Emphasis on the local and particular go hand in hand with attempts at more inclusive understandings. The strategy involved includes *rereading*[16] and *rewriting* the canonical texts, as well as constructing an alternative and different archive. Reality is no longer seen as an objective fact but as a series of representations.

WORLD POLITICS AS THE POLITICS OF IMAGINATION

Social and cultural identities by their very nature have always been discursively constructed. What is new and peculiar to modernity is the desire and ability to construct a bounded identity based on a fixed and autonomous idea of self. This has been paralleled by the power of representations to construct identity and by highly unequal access to discursive and representational resources at a global level. Representational practices feed the dominant knowledge regimes and structures and shape the very identities they seek to represent. The best-known example of this is the ideational construct of Orientalism, which reflects the close connection between particular modes of cultural representations, anthropology, and European imperialism (see Said 1978). In the process it also creates the categories of "Oriental" and "Occidental" people.

Representation and Critical IR

Within IR, it is important to look at Western cultural representations of non-Western people. This is so for various reasons. Representations populate the world with specific subject positions within which concretized individuals are then interpellated (see Weldes 1999). Identity claims of various non-Western communities thus operate within power relations put in place by the West. This does not deny non-Westerners their agency, for there is always space for resistance and accommodation. But it emphasizes differential access to the creation and molding of discursive (both material and nonmaterial) resources. It offers ways of challenging and denaturalizing modes of representation that abet domination by "making it acceptable and coherent within the dominant ethos that constructs domestic selves and exotic Others" (Shapiro 1988, 122–23). Recognition of the productive dimension of representation implies that the very basis of world politics—identity—is challenged. The recognition of the salience of Western representations of the non-West in world politics also questions the conventional view of international studies as a social "science" that has little to do with culture, morality, society, and the like. It underlines the importance of culture as a factor in molding, sustaining, and questioning political practices. It recognizes world politics as a process of cultural interactions in which the identities of actors (including their values and visions) are not given prior to or apart from these interactions. Instead, they are shaped and constituted in the complexes of social practices that make up world politics. Rather than denying the importance of actors in enacting and reshaping the social practices in which they are embedded, it focuses our attention also on the social construction of actors. Thus, representation is an inherent and important aspect of global political life and therefore a critical and legitimate area of inquiry.

"A whole range of analyses in IR have taken this [Said's] idea up and mapped the different ways in which the West constructs the non-western world" (Diken and Laustsen 2001, 768). This comment is surprising given that IR, including critical IR, with few exceptions (see Biswas 2001; Doty 1996b; Gusterson 1999) has more or less ignored the questions raised by Orientalism critique. The question of representation has historically been excluded from the academic study of international relations and the "price that international relations scholarship pays for its inattention to the issue of representation is perpetuation of the dominant modes of making meaning and deferral of its responsibility and complicity in dominant representations" (Doty 1996b, 171).

The focus on representation within critical IR has been mainly on the constitutive function of representation in generating and sustaining particular policy regimes (see Doty 1996b) and on the identity politics of the representer. For instance, Campbell argues that the inscription of otherness was linked to American foreign policy and the enframing of American identity:

> At one time or another, European and American discourse has inscribed women, the working class, Eastern Europeans, Jews, blacks, criminals, coloreds, mulattos, Africans, drug addicts, Arabs, the insane, Asians, the Orient, the Third World, terrorists, and others through tropes that have written their identity as inferior, often in

terms of their being a mob or horde (sometimes passive and sometimes threatening) that is without culture, devoid of morals, infected with disease, lacking in industry, incapable of achievement, prone to be unruly, inspired by emotion, given to passion, indebted to tradition, or . . . whatever "we" are not. (1998b, 89)

In Weldes (1999) as well as Weldes et al. (1999), representation is analyzed as a central concept of international relations and foreign policy. As in Campbell, it is the foreign policy regime sustained by particular representational practices and the identity of the representer (the United States) that is under investigation. Doty (1993, 1996a, 1996b) provides effective analysis of representation as foreign political practice. Similarly, Neumann studies the "*use* of 'the East' as the other" (1999; emphasis added) as a general practice in the identity formation of Europe; Klein examines NATO "as a set of [representational] practice by which the West has constituted itself as a political and cultural identity" (1990, 313); and Dalby (1988) analyzes how the Soviet Union was constructed as a dangerous Other in order to produce an ideological rationale for the U.S. national security state.

In all these studies of Western representation of the Other, the focus is on either its rationalizing role in some foreign policy regime or on its productive effect on dominant identity discourses within the West. These works have not dealt with the poetics and politics of Western representations of the non-West from the vantage point of the latter. The focus has remained largely on a critique of Western practices, not on its productive and restrictive impact on the non-West. This is at best an incomplete step in the right direction. While recognizing the significance of representation of the Other for the representer, we must identify and analyze the impact on the identity of the represented. Chapters 4–6 focus on the productive dimension of representations vis-à-vis the represented through the empirical study of the identity of Tibet and Tibetans. My emphasis is on the ways in which particular encounters between the West and the non-West have shaped the latter. Representations support not only particular politics of the representer toward the represented but, significantly, they construct the very identities of the actors involved, especially the Other. Representations are productively linked with identity discourses of all kinds. The conventional idea that representation draws upon a pregiven identity is turned on its head, for it is identity that is fashioned out of particularized representations. In the case of Exotica Tibet, then, representational discourses are not reflective of, but actually productive of, Tibetan identity. Within critical IR, the paucity of serious consideration of the "how," "why," and "what impact" questions of Western representations of/on non-Western communities shows that the task of provincializing the West has only just begun.

Theorizing Representation

Constructionist theories (Hall 1997b, 15–74) are best suited for a contextualized understanding of social and political concepts like representation and identity. They do not argue that the material world does not exist but that it acquires meaning only through the mediation of language and discursive systems. Though such a discursive approach characterizes the work of many scholars, no one has been more prominent than Foucault (1970, 1972, 1980, 1984, 1986) in shaping it. Foucault is concerned with the production of knowledge and meaning not through language but through discourse. Discursive practices have their own inclusionary and exclusionary aspects.

> Discursive practices are characterised by the delimitation of a field of objects, the definition of a legitimate perspective for the agent of knowledge, and the fixing of norms for the elaboration of concepts and theories. Thus, each discursive practice implies a play of prescriptions that designate its exclusions and choices. (Foucault 1986, 199)

Foucault's reformulation of discourse also calls for recognition of the explicit linkage between knowledge, truth, and power. Identification of the knowledge-power *(pouvoir/savoir)* nexus reveals the linkage of truth claims with systems of power:

> Truth isn't outside power, or lacking of power: contrary to a myth whose history and functions would repay further study, truth isn't the reward of free spirits, the child of protracted solitude, nor the privilege of those who have succeeded in liberating themselves. Truth is a thing of the world: it is produced only by virtue of multiple forms of constraint. (Foucault 1980, 291)

The recognition of the constructed character of truth facilitates a critical political positioning. Nothing is sacrosanct. However, this does not undermine the impact of truth claims on the lives of people.

All knowledge, once applied in the "real" world, has real effects and in that sense becomes true.[17] This Foucauldian identification and exploration of the link between power, knowledge, and truth is radical in its implication. It shifts the terrain of inquiry from the question "What is truth?" to the question "How do discursive practices constitute truth claims?" In terms of representation, we may see the implication as a shift in the focus from some core reality beneath/behind representations to the modalities of their functioning. The question is no longer whether a representation is true or false but what discursive practices operate to render it true or false. It is not about how representations reflect some subjects but, more crucially, how subjectivity itself is constructed within discursive practices, how representational regimes are productive of subjectivity. Discourses then are "practices which form the objects of which they speak" (Foucault 1972, 49). Adopting this approach to Tibetan identity, the pertinent question shifts from "How far do representations (both Western and self-) of Tibetans *reflect* their identity?" to "How do representational regimes affect the discursive production of Tibetanness?" This helps us look at Tibetanness as a politicized identification process, instead of some pregiven, essentialized, fixed object.

It is important for my analysis to underline a two-pronged approach I will be taking. First, I will explore the *poetics of representation*—how is Tibet as the Other represented, how is Tibet produced within representations about it. This entails examining how Tibet is imagined within Western culture by looking at literature (both fiction and nonfiction), films, travel accounts, and so on. Second, I will analyze the *politics of representation*—effects and consequences of representation on the identity of Tibet and Tibetans. The latter places expositions on Tibet in the context of power, imperialism, neocolonialism, (trans)nationalism, and Orientalism. Chapters 2 and 3 will discuss the poetics while chapters 4, 5, and 6 will deal with the politics of Western representations of Tibet.

2

Imagining the Other

Within the context of European imperialism, the issue of the representation of natives was often considered as belonging to the realm of scientific objective ethnography, journalistic commentaries, or fiction (Spurr 1993). A clear boundary was said to exist between fiction and nonfiction writing. It was presumed that, unlike fiction, nonfiction writing such as literary and popular journalism, exploration and travel writings, memoirs of colonial officials, and so on are unmediated by the consciously aesthetic requirements of imaginative literature. Emphasis was on the recording of observed facts. However, as argued by scholars from fields as diverse as postcolonial theory (Bhabha 1983; McClintock 1995; Said 1978; Shohat 1995; Spurr 1993), anthropology (Clifford 1988; Clifford and Marcus 1986; Fabian 1990; Van Maanen 1995), and international relations (Campbell 1998b; Doty 1996b; Weldes et al. 1999), such views are no longer tenable. Starting with Said (1978) the enterprise of postcolonial theory has unpacked the notion of neutral academic expertise and highlighted how Western knowledge and representations of the non-Western world are neither innocent nor based on some preexisting "reality" but implicated in the West's will to power and its imperial adventures. The image of a scientific, apolitical, disinterested, knowledge-seeking "gentleman" braving all odds to study non-Western cultures has been revealed as hollow.

The mask of objectivity in the colonial discourse hid relations of inequality and domination. Fiction as well as nonfiction writings were permeated with various strategies of representation. These were not epiphenomenal but central to the ways in which the Other was sought to be known. What Kabbani points out about travel writing holds true for nonfictional writings in general: during imperialism, it ultimately produced "a communal image of the East," which "sustained a political structure and was sustained by it" (1986, 10).

Various forms of representing the non-West—visual (films, television, photographs, paintings, advertisements, and so on) as well as textual (such as fiction, travelogue, journalism, ethnography, and anthropology)—were closely linked to the production of imperial encounters. Asymmetry of productive power is a common trait shared by these encounters. The contemporary neocolonial world too "bears witness to the unequal and uneven forces of cultural representation involved in the contest for political and social within the modern world order" (Bhabha 1994, 171). It is not only the represented (here the colonized, the third world, the South) who are subjects of and subjected to the process; even the representer (the colonizer, the first world, the West) is constructed by representational practices. This in no way implies similar experiences for the colonizer and the colonized (the representer and the represented). It only indicates that though everyone is subjected to representational practices, the impact differs according to the existing power relations. To illustrate this point, while both the West and Tibetans are subjects of Exotica Tibet, and the latter are not mere victims but exercise their agency through creative negotiations, the West does not have to construct its identity according to the perception of Tibetans. Westerners exoticize Tibet, and in turn, Tibetans exoticize the West. But while Western exoticization has a defining productive impact on Tibetan identity discourse (as discussed in detail in chapters 5 and 6), the same cannot be said of Tibetan exoticization of the West. This reflects the asymmetry in their power relations.

A concentration on Western representations does not deny the fact that representational practices were prevalent in non-Western societies too. In fact, historically all cultures and civilizations have had their own particular representational practices for perceiving those they considered as Other. But—and this is a crucial qualification—it was only with modern European imperialism that the capacity to convert these representations into *truth* on a systematic and mass scale emerged. What makes such representational practices distinctly modern is their productive capacity. Production of knowledge about the Other through representations goes hand in hand with the construction, articulation, and affirmation of differences between the Self and Other, which in turn feed into the identity politics among the representer as well as the represented.

ESSENTIALIZING AND STEREOTYPING THE OTHER

The practices of essentializing and stereotyping the Other underlie different strategies of Western representations. Essentialism is the notion that some core meaning or identity is determinate and not subject to interpretation. Inden writes that essentialist ways of seeing tend to ignore the "intricacies of agency" pertinent to the flux and development of any social system (1990, 20). In the colonial context, we find essentialism in the reduction of the indigenous people to an "essential" idea of what it means to be "native"—say, Africans as singing-dancing-fighting, Chinese as duplicitous, Arabs as cruel and oppressors of women, Tibetans as religious, and so on. Imperialism drew its strength from representations of natives as quintessentially lazy, ignorant, deceitful, passive, incapable of self-governing, and the native rulers as corrupt and despotic. Therefore, it should come as no surprise that the British officials involved during the 1903–4 invasion of Tibet saw it as something welcomed by "ordinary" Tibetans seeking deliverance from their Chinese and monastic overlords. Captain Cecil Rawling in a military report in 1905 wrote: "It seems to be the general wish of the inhabitants of that country (Tibet) that they should come under British administration" (in Lamb 1960, 296). Curiously, Lamb's own assessment that "when dealing with the *primitive* peoples of Central Asia, the problem often was not how to expand one's power but how to prevent its indefinite expansion" (101; emphasis added) also puts the onus of responsibility for imperial expansion on the victims themselves. This is made possible by their essentialist representations as requiring paternal imperialism—an alternation of iron fist and velvet glove.

A stereotype is a one-sided description of a group/culture resulting from the collapsing of complex differences into a simple "cardboard cut-out," seeing people as a preset image and "more of a formula than a human being" (Gross 1966, 2). It reduces people to a few, simple characteristics, which are then represented as fixed by nature. "Stereotyping reduces, essentialises, naturalises and fixes 'difference'" (Hall 1997a, 257–58). Stereotypes function as a marker between norm and deviancy (see Gilman 1985), between "us" and "them." As Said argues, stereotypical images of the Orient's separateness—"its eccentricity, its backwardness, its silent indifference, its feminine penetrability, its supine malleability"—have been part of Western discursive practices for a long time (1978, 4). Such images flourished to justify imperialism as a civilizing mission—the restless, honest, active, exploratory, masculine, enlightened, modern spirit of the "white man" stood in contrast to the laziness, deceit, passivity, fatalism, femininity, backwardness, and traditional spiritlessness of the natives. For example, Captain John Noel's films *Climbing Mount Everest* (1922) and *The Epic of Everest* (1924) developed the "contrast between the extroverted, aggressive, and manly British climbers with the introverted, passive, and squalid but mystical Tibetans" (Hansen 2001, 92–93).

Stereotyping is a simplification because it freezes what is otherwise a fluid, contested, complex always-in-motion identity. Let me illustrate this with an example from the story of the first two men to reach Mount Everest—Tenzing Norgay and Edmund Hillary. Reaching the summit, Tenzing Norgay says he felt the warm presence of the mountain, buried an offering to the gods, and said in prayer: "I am grateful, Chomolungma" (in Hansen 1998); Hillary took photographs to survey the area, urinated on the summit, and later told one of the other climbers, George Lowe: "Well, George, we knocked the bastard off" (Outside Online 1999). This difference in attitude may be due to cultural factors. But to interpret humility as passivity and fix the identity of Tenzing Norgay (read as representative of Sherpas and other natives) as essentially passive in contrast to adventurous, scientific Hillary (read as white man) leads to a reified and fixated form of representation (excluding those who do not "fit" in the image—women, for instance). Stereotyping is not about expressing cultural difference but fixing it in a pregiven sociocultural milieu with extreme power differentials.

Stereotyping served imperialism at both representational and psychic levels—supporting the idea of paternal domination and acting as a kind of perceptual blinder protecting the colonizers from the discomforting consciousness of either poverty or guilt (Lebow 1976, 22). It allowed the participants in the massacre of Tibetans at Guru (31 March 1904) that took place during the British invasion of Tibet to blame it on the "crass stupidity and childishness of the Tibetan general" (Mehra 1979, 223), malevolent "thorough-going obstructionist" (IOR: MSS EUR/F197/105 n.d., 6) monks, superstitious Tibetan soldiers—everyone except themselves. We *must* liberate the ordinary natives from their brutal leaders—this sentiment can be seen in Colonel Francis Younghusband's account of the 1903–4 expedition to Tibet where, after criticizing Tibetans for being crafty, immoral, overreligious, dirty, and lazy, he talks about the role of the British in providing enlightened guidance to ordinary Tibetans (Younghusband 1910, 321). Younghusband argued for a permanent settlement at the end of the invasion "which would prevent the Lhasa Lamas from ever again usurping monopoly of power to the detriment of British interests and to the ruin of their own country" (IOR: MSS EUR/F197/106 n.d., 2).

Though in everyday conversation we tend to use stereotypes only for negative images, stereotyping has within it dualism and ambivalence (Bhabha 1983; Chow 1993; Hall 1997a). As Hunt in his study of hierarchy of race and American foreign policy points out, the Americans created for "Orientals" two distinctly different images: "a positive one, appropriate for happy times when paternalism and benevolence were in season, and a negative one, suited to those tense periods when abuse or aggrandizement became the order of the day" (1987, 69). While sometimes a positive stereotype may be politically and socially helpful for a group, in the long run it reifies and imprisons the represented subjects in their own arrested image. This problem can be seen most clearly in the case of Tibetans, who seem to be prisoners of their stereotyped images. Alluding to the real effects of the language of stereotype about Tibet, Lopez points out that it "not only creates knowledge about Tibet, in many ways it creates Tibet, a Tibet that Tibetans in exile have come to appropriate and deploy in an effort to gain both standing in exile and independence for their country" (1998, 10). However, these stereotypes legitimize only certain goals and actions geared toward achieving them—the prevalent stereotypes paint Tibetans mainly as passive victims requiring outside help. And this outside support comes at a price.

STRATEGIES OF REPRESENTATION

In spite of commonalities and consistencies, it is complexity, oppositionality, and ambivalence that lie at the heart of Western colonial representations. Imaginative practices through which the imperial West came to represent the Other can be interrogated through the various strategies of representation involved. Though there was always a will to reify the represented, this was undermined by the nature of representation—it was not a singular act but one necessitating repetition. There always was a paradox in the Western representations of other cultures—an unresolvable tension between transparency and inscrutability, desire and disavowal, difference and familiarity. Therefore Exotica Tibet is not a distinct phenomenon devoid of contrariety; rather, it is defined by a "true *complexio oppositorum,* a rich complexity of contradictions and oppositions" (Bishop 1989, 63, emphasis in original). So near, yet so far! As Žižek puts it:

> The very inconsistency of this image of Tibet, with its direct coincidence of opposites, seems to bear witness to its fantasmatic status. Tibetans are portrayed as people leading a simple life of spiritual satisfaction, fully accepting their fate, liberated from the excessive craving of the Western subject who is always searching for more, AND as a bunch of filthy, cheating, cruel, sexually promiscuous primitives . . . The social order is presented as a model of organic harmony, AND as the tyranny of the cruel corrupted theocracy keeping ordinary people ignorant. (2001, 64–66; emphasis in original).

The following section of the chapter analyzes the most common discursive strategies marshaled in the representation of the non-Western Other in the context of Western imperialism and uses Exotica Tibet as the main empirical site of investigation.

Gaze

Surveillance is a technique through which, under an overpowering gaze, the non-Western subject is rendered "a knowable, visible object of disciplinary power" (Doty 1996b, 11). The gaze is not mere innocent curiosity: "to gaze implies more than to look at—it signifies a psychological relationship of power, in which the gazer is superior to the object of the gaze" (Schroeder 1998, 208). Through observation, examination, and interpretation objects are differentiated, categorized, identified, and made ready to be acted upon. Objectification (fixing the essence) of the gazed goes hand in hand with its subjectification—gaze and surveillance are productive of the identity of the gazed.

Surveillance as a strategy for representing the Other and rendering it disciplined is characterized by the all-knowing gaze of a white "man," the colonial master, the West. It enables both the visual possession of the body of the gazed and an interposition of technique that safely conceals the body of the gazer (Spurr 1993, 22). Observations then are presented as dispassionate, objective facts. The gaze is disembodied—statements are made as if there is no seer behind the observations.

This is not to say that non-Westerners are visually impaired, powerless to gaze back at the West. But the authority of imperialism for a large part of the modern period ensured that mastery and control remained a possession of Western "man." The "monarch of all I survey" rhetorical gesture remained peculiar to the West (Pratt 1992, 201). Establishment of mastery through surveillance, gaze, and observation was accompanied by consolidation of shades of political dominance over the object of the gaze. Appropriation was done in the name of scientific curiosity, ethnographic material gathering, protection of simple masses from their own despotic rulers, or the spread of progress.

British colonial and military officials who went inside Tibet often wrote their accounts as scientific exploration or as exciting adventure (see Bailey 1957; Forman 1936) or as "everyday" observation (Gordon 1876, v). Behind their innocent-sounding descriptions of travel—for example, "[a] narrative of a plant hunter's adventures and discoveries" (Ward 1934)—lay the violence of imperialism. Though their gaze might be considered by Europeans as that of the adventurer or romantic, its effect on the natives was the same as that of some steely-eyed militarist's gaze—the establishment and institutionalization of control through political rule and knowledge formation. To know is a prelude to possessing, especially if there is a huge asymmetry of power. Such asymmetry led to situations where it was perfectly acceptable for a participant in the Tibet mission of 1903–4 to say, "In fact the visible riches and treasures of Lhasa fairly made our mouths water. The Tibetans however would not sell, and to our honour be it said; although *Lhasa was a fair object to loot*, and lay in our power, not a farthings worth was *forcibly* [author adds this word in pen in a typed text] taken from it" (IOR: MSS EUR/C270/FL2/E/1/144, 6; emphasis added; see Carrington 2003 for an analysis of the predatory nature of the mission). Securing priceless artifacts through coercion and displaying them in the private and public collections in the West was an essential feature of Western imperialism.

Paradoxically, the project of rendering the Other knowable and the image of it as primitive and simple went hand in hand with the recognition that there are elements of inscrutability and mystery that eluded complete understanding of the Other. While discussing his own failure to fathom the unease of Phuntsog, a Tibetan who is no longer considered an "authentic" native as he has learned the language of the imperialist, Candler, an early example of embedded reporter (a *Daily Mail* reporter accompanying the British invasion of Tibet in 1903–4), calls him a "strange hybrid product of restless western energies, stirring and muddying the shallows of the Eastern mind. Or are they depths? Who knows? I know nothing, only that these men are inscrutable, and one cannot see into their hearts" (1905, 206).

Frustrated with the inaccessibility, invisibility, and inscrutability of "the Orientals," Western desire subjects them to a relentless investigation. Veil becomes a metaphor for all that invites, titillates, and yet resists Western knowing. It is "one of those tropes through which Western fantasies of penetration into the mysteries of the Orient and access to the interiority of the other are fantasmatically achieved" (Yegenoglu 1998, 39).

Surveillance and gaze facilitate other representational strategies that fix the Orient and the Other, particularly those that seek to classify, differentiate, and provide identity to the Other (and in turn to the Self).

Differentiation—Classification

Differentiation and classification, two crucial factors in the formation of the modern subject (Foucault 1984, 7–11), are also evident in Western representations of the Other. The ideational differentiation between the West and the Rest underpins these representations. The need to articulate one's personal and collective self in terms of identity comes from an internalization of this principle of differentiation. Classification occupies a central place in any account of non-Western people. It polices discourses, assigns positions, regulates groups, and enforces boundaries (Spurr 1993, 63). Given the taxonomizing predilection and conceit of Western imperialism, we can hardly disagree with Rampa's conjecture about the fate of the yetis: "[If] Western Man had his way, our poor old yetis would be captured, dissected, and preserved in spirit" (1956, 220).

While some classifications may be essential for understanding, often the classification of non-Western peoples was a corollary of the hierarchization and racialization of cultures. Classifying the Other as barbarian or savage validated its dehumanization and was seen as justification for the use of violence to impose European norms (Keal 2003; Salter 2002). At the top were the white Europeans and at the bottom were "primitive" Africans and aboriginal populations in the "new world." Chinese, Arabs, Indians, and others occupied different positions in the hierarchical table. The nineteenth- and twentieth-century obsession with racializing culture can be seen in the case of Tibetans too where different commentators sought to identify characteristics of the Tibetan "race." A typical example was Sandberg, who was unflattering in his comments about the "'Tibetan race' as 'a weak and cowardly people, their pusillanimity rendering them readily submissive'" (in Bonnington and Clarke 2000, 209). The fact that racism has less to do with color and more to do with power relations becomes evident in the British treatment of the Irish as "colored," as "white negroes" (McClintock 1995, 52; Lebow 1976) during the nineteenth century. Captain William Frederick O'Connor's observation at the start of the twentieth century about Tibet is illustrative: "Common people are cheerful, happy-go-lucky creatures, absurdly *like the Irish* in their ways, and sometimes even in their features" (in Sharma and Sharma 1996, 191; emphasis added). On the other hand, the French traveler Alexandra David-Neel finds that *dobdob*, the Lhasa monk "police," looks like a "real negro" (1936, 105). Differentiation, classification, and identification, when combined with racialization, evolutionism, and hierarchization, lead to the debasement of most non-Western natives and idealization of some.

Debasement—Idealization

The seemingly opposite techniques of debasement (and its corollary negation) and idealization (and its corollary affirmation) have similar rhetorical structures; these involve processes of decontextualization and othering. In terms of Western representations of the non-West, the binary of the noble/ignoble savage has been a product of such discursive practices. The ease with which writers and observers have switched between highly negative and eulogizing appraisals of Tibetan culture is illustrative. Throughout the nineteenth and twentieth centuries Tibetans were seen as either "backward and barbaric or noble and charming" (Dodin and Rather 2001a, 397).

Natives have been debased and associated with filth and dirt numerous times. The discourse of contamination and disease was used to enforce colonial oppression and to inculcate a sense of inferiority in the colonized peoples. This has particularly been the case with the representations of Tibet and Lhasa where physical dirt was seen as symbolically standing for an inherent weakness in Tibetan character. Thomas Manning, the first Englishman to visit Lhasa, noted in 1811:

> There is nothing striking, nothing pleasing in its appearance. The inhabitants are begrimed with dirt and smut. The avenues are full of dogs, some growling and gnawing bits of hide which lie about in profusion and emit a charnel-house smell; others limping and looking livid; others ulcerated; others starved and dying, and pecked at by ravens; some dead and preyed upon. In short, everything seems mean and gloomy, and excites the idea of something unreal. Even the mirth and laughter of the inhabitants I thought dreamy and ghostly. (in Chapman 1992, 146–47)

The British Foreign Office, in its report of 1920 in the section on "geography," felt under compulsion to allude to the poor sanitary conditions and the "gruesome custom" of the disposal of the dead by cutting them into pieces and leaving them to be devoured by vultures, dogs, and pigs (Foreign Office 1920, 22). George Knight, the leader of the 1922–23 British expedition to Tibet "affirms" the truth of various labels attached to Tibet: "It is a land of mountains, monasteries and monks, land of women, dogs and dirt, country of the great unwashed" (1930, 25; see also Knight 1894). However, the unequivocal condemnation of Tibetans for being "dirty" began to change as some visitors starting reevaluating the dominant Western stance. Chapman, visiting in the late 1930s, amended his preconceived conclusions about Lhasa: "It is true that the common people do not wash, that their houses are, by our standards, filthy, and that they live in a state of serfdom—but what a delightful folk, nevertheless" (1992, 146).[1]

Debasement of the natives often accompanied the strategy of negation by which Western writings conceive of the Other as absence, emptiness, nothingness, thus denying Other its agency, its history, and, often, its language. Negation serves to erase what one sees in order to clear "a space for the expansion of the colonial imagination and for the pursuit of desire" (Spurr 1993, 92–93). This, in colonial times, led to ground clearing for the expansion of colonial rule in places including the Americas, Australia, and parts of Africa.

Idealization and self-affirmation often exist along with negation and debasement as evidenced in the present-day positive exoticization of Tibet in the Western popular imagination. Paradoxically, despite its difference, Tibet was often seen as the non-Western culture with which Europeans could identify (see Kaschewsky 2001). While early Christians sought traces of a forgotten community of Christians here, theosophists looked for the lost brotherhood of wise hermits. In the mid-nineteenth century, Joseph Wolff popularized the idea of a long-lost population of Jews in the Himalayas (Feigon 1996: 14–15; see also Kamenetz 1995; Katz 1991). On the other hand, the Nazi SS sent an expedition in 1938–39 to ascertain whether Tibet was an abode of true Aryans or not (Hale 2004). Thus, we can see that there are various ways in which often conflicting desires of the West got invested in Tibet. One such set of conflicting desires is expressed through the strategies of eroticization/moralization.

Eroticization—Moralization

Eroticization and moralization are central to Western representations of the Other. Reference to the licentiousness and voracious sexual appetite of Arabs/Africans, the feminization of Asian males, the availability of docile and yet elusive Oriental women—such motifs are conspicuous in many Western fiction and nonfiction writings and in films. The Orient becomes the "fertile" ground on which the sexual fantasies of Western "men" (mainly though not exclusively; for a discussion of gender and imperialism, see Blunt and Rose 1994; Lewis 1996; McClintock 1995; Midgley 1998; Sharpe 1993) is played out. The ideas of sexual innocence and experience, sexual domination and submissiveness play out a complex dance in the discourse of "the West and the Rest" (Hall 1992, 302; also see Schick 1999).

One important reason for eroticization, of course, has been to escape from conventional censorship in metropolitan societies. Association is made between the Orient and the "freedom of licentious sex" and "escapism of sexual fantasy" (Said 1978, 190). Contemporary incarnations of such images can be seen in a range of places, from sex tourism at Thai beaches to the standardization of "Oriental" sex as a commodity in the "red light" districts of Europe. At the same time, the Orient also provides opportunities for the play of "forbidden" desires of same-sex love, especially male homosexuality, as evident in the works of William Beckford, Lord Byron, T. E. Lawrence, Edward Carpenter, and E. M. Forster (see Parsons 1997), to name a few. Investment of these "forbidden" desires in the non-West may be a resistance to the hegemonic masculinity of metropolitan culture, but it does not challenge the unequal power relations between the Western representer and the non-Western represented.

The very language of exploration was marked by strong gender distinctions and drew much of its subconscious force from sexual imagery. Discovery of America was often seen literally as *dis-covering* of the unknown land, un-covering of the naked, available, desirable, and primitive female body of America by the clothed, civilized European man (for instance, Jan van der Straet's 1575 depiction *The Discovery of America*; see Gallagher 1997).

The intent to subjugate indigenous people can be seen as the male's mastery of the female. The feminization of colonial space is an act of epistemic as well as corporeal violence. The feminized landscape titillated and provoked explorers and discoverers to take control of her, to possess her—this was a common sentiment expressed in exploration literature from the fifteenth century onward. Edward William Lane described his first sight of Egypt in 1825 thus: "As I approached the shore, I felt like an Eastern bridegroom, about to lift the veil of his bride, and to see, for the first time, the features that were to charm, or disappoint, or disgust him" (in Kabbani 1986, 67).

These erotics of imperial conquest evident in the evocation of feminized space were linked to the Enlightenment's pursuit of truth. After all, "study, understanding, knowledge, evaluation . . . are instruments of conquest" (Said 1978, 309). European consciousness is encoded as masculine and the object of knowledge as feminine. The combination of knowledge and eroticization is illustrated strongly in Bell's description of Lhasa as practically "untouched by white men"—"Shut off from their outer world by their immense mountain barriers, Tibet still presented a *virgin field of inquiry*" (1928, viii; emphasis added). Grenard regrets Tibet's closure, her foiling of attempts by Europeans to pry her open: "In truth, the Tibetans are one of the nations that have changed the least in the course of the centuries and it is greatly to be regretted that they are so difficult to access and so obstinately opposed to enquiries" (1904, 373). This resonates with Said's analysis of the Middle East in the Western imagination: "The Middle East is resistant, as any virgin would be, but the male scholar wins the prize by bursting open, penetrating through the Gordian knot despite the 'taxing task'" (1978, 309).

Not surprisingly, after the British invasion of Lhasa in 1903–4, Lord Curzon wrote, "I am almost ashamed of having destroyed the virginity of the bride to whom you aspired, viz. Lhasa," in a letter addressed to Sven Hedin (a famous Swedish explorer) as the latter described the expedition as "the rape of Lhasa" (in Schell 2000, 201). For his part, Hedin lost "the longing that had possessed [him] to penetrate the Holy City" (in Bishop 1989, 176). These writers and commentators draw upon a long tradition of what McClintock calls "European porno-tropics" treating "male travel as an erotics of ravishment" in which uncertain places were figured as "libidinously eroticized" (1995, 22). The most prevalent metaphor for the British invasion of Tibet was that of "unveiling."[2] Candler (1905) titled his account *Unveiling of Lhasa*. The attitude of European travelers to Tibet was "almost voyeuristic," the most commonly expressed aim being to "get a 'peep' at Tibet, or at Lhasa" (Bishop 1989, 177).[3] Millington, who later wrote his book as "a man in the street," described going to Lhasa as "assisting in drawing aside a purdah" and departure as the "show was over" (1905, 77, 199). Writing about Lhasa, Waddell says that the enigma has been solved (virginity lost!) for the

> fairy Prince of "Civilisation" has roused her from her slumbers, her closed doors are broken down, her dark veil of mystery is lifted up, and the long-sealed shrine, with its grotesque cults and its idolised Grand Lama, shorn of his sham nimbus, have yielded up their secrets, and lie disenchanted before our Western eyes. Thus, alas! Inevitably, do our cherished romances of the old pagan world crumble at the touch of our modern hands! (1905, 2)

This triumphalism (of civilization over obstinacy) was mixed with regret and a sense of inevitability with a feeling of betrayal. For "Shangri-la" (most commonly associated with Tibet, as discussed in the next chapter) is conceptualized as "a virginal state: once defiled by foreign invasion, modernization or internal political strife, it is as if some kind of betrayal has taken place" (Hutt 1996, 52). Candler expresses these mixed emotions when he says, "To-morrow, when we enter Lhasa, we will have unveiled the last mystery of the East. There are no more forbidden. Why could we have not left at least one city out of bounds?" (in Sharma and Sharma 1996, 119).

Eroticization was not the only representational technique deployed by the West when gendering the Orient. Moralization was also an effective tool. Morality was seen as a sign of progress, and European bourgeois standard came to represent the pinnacle of civilization. This was contrasted with a "lack" of morality among natives, "Orientals," and the domestic working classes. The policing of morality primarily involved policing women's bodies. Hence, cultures (like that of Tibet) where this sort of policing was negligible were seen as inferior. A common idea among travelers and commentators was that Tibetans ranked low in terms of morality and the "freedom" accorded to women was both a cause and an effect of this low standard. A discourse of filth and contamination was attached to that on morality and the status of women. In the words of a member of the British expedition to Lhasa in 1903–4: "Tibetan morals are not of a very high order and there seems to be a good deal of promiscuousness in the relations of the lay population. I twice came across parties of men and women bathing together in a small stream behind the Potala, which struck me as most unusual as the majority of Tibetans are filthy and grimy to a degree" (IOR: MSS EUR/C270/FL2/E/1/144 n.d., 8).

Macdonald contended that in Tibet women have much influence and, compared with the West, morals are lax (1929, 133–34). Those who showed admiration for Tibetan society were not exempt from passing judgments about the Tibetans—Riencourt argued that Europeans and Americans can learn a lot from the Tibetans because among them women are "perfectly free" and equal; however, a laxity in sexual relations was a sore spot as it led to rampant sexually transmitted diseases (1950, 152–53). In contrast to European (and Japanese, in the case of a Japanese traveler to Lhasa, Ekai Kawaguchi) women, Tibetan women are unclean, disrespectful to their husbands, and lacking character and hence are "objects more to be loved and pitied not respected and adored" (Kawaguchi in Sharma and Sharma 1996, 175). Thus, we see that eroticization and moralization often went hand in hand as representational strategies.

Chronopolitics

Chronopolitics, or the politics of time, has played an important role in Western representations of the non-Western Other. The Other has been imagined as socially and culturally backward (in time)—medieval (feudal), archaic (like ancient Egyptians or Mesopotamians), prehistoric (primitive), or simply beyond the matrix of time (timeless). The colonial journey and travel of contemporary Western commentators is often figured as proceeding forward in geographical space but backward in historical time. This technique rendered nondominant groups out of the present and legitimized control in the name of modernity. That natives were backward, requiring the rule/control/guidance/assistance of more advanced "foreigners" to enter the modern era, was taken as uncontested fact.

The Other is both a prisoner of time (frozen in a certain stage of history) and an escapee (outside the time grid, timeless, outside history). The West is the present, the now, and it has the duty/right to bring progress to the Other. The entire range of timeframe available under chronopolitics can be illustrated through European representations of Tibet and Tibetans at the turn of the nineteenth century. The world is divided into chronological reserves, and when we enter Tibet, we reach a different age, as if the "tracts of past time persisted here and there which could be visited" (Spufford 1996, 212).

The most prevalent representation of Tibet was that it was medieval. Candler's impression about Tibet being medieval was "confirmed" as a result of the only incident in 1904 in Lhasa, when a Tibetan monk attacked the soldiers of the occupying British Indian force. He described how a lama "ran amuck outside the camp with the coat of mail and huge paladin's sword concealed beneath his cloak, a *medieval* figure who thrashed the air with his brand like a flail in sheer lust of blood. He was hanged *medievally* the next day within sight of Lhasa" (Candler 1905, 246, 265; emphases added).

The monk was hanged in full public view to act as a deterrent to any other Tibetan contemplating resistance. It is interesting that the British justified their own barbarity by blaming it on the medieval quality of their field of operation, by putting the responsibility on the victims. We see ambiguity and nostalgia as the twentieth century unfolds. Chapman muses in his account first published in 1940, "Tibet is in the position of European countries in the Middle Ages—in many ways a position which we are bound, nowadays, to envy" (Chapman 1992, 193).

Apart from medievalism, Tibet also was imagined as parallel to the ancient archaic world. Potala palace, for Landon, was "an image of that ancient and mysterious faith which has found its last and fullest expression beneath the golden canopies of Lhasa" (1905, 262). As in the writings of theosophists, precursors to New Age movements, Tibetan Buddhism began to be imagined as forming a direct connection with ancient Egyptian religion. The Western imagination of Tibet also flirted with the prehistoric and the primitive (see Bishop 1989, 156). Grenard was reminded of "American Redskins" (1904, 72), while Chapman wrote, "I sang an Eskimo folk-song and Norbhu [a Tibetan companion] said it was exactly like Tibetan music—a doubtful compliment, but interesting, seeing that the Eskimos and Tibetans are, ethnologically speaking, fairly closely related" (1992, 52). One significant emblem of Tibet's association with the prehistoric in the Western imagination is the figure of *Yeti*, made popular through works such as *Tintin in Tibet*.

Chronopolitics entails not only a fixing of cultures and groups of people in particular chronological reserve but also detemporalizing, releasing the imagination from the confines of time and history. In Western representations, places such as the Potala palace of Lhasa represent the timelessness of Tibetan life: "To me the Potala represents the very essence of the Tibetan people. It has a certain untamed dignity in perfect harmony with the surrounding rugged country; a quality of stolid unchangeableness—it seems to say: 'Here I have been for hundreds of years, and here I intend to stay for ever'" (Chapman 1992, 7).

The idea of Tibet as located back in time and hence lower on the scale of evolution, as well as timeless, offered space for two mutually contradictory representations—Tibet as irrational and childlike and Tibet as repository of wisdom.

Infantilization—Gerontification

The Orient is the space for the "wisdom of the East" in some representations, while in others it is essentially irrational, emotional, uncivilized, childlike. Infantilization is a crucial representational strategy through which the Other is rendered incapable of making decisions for itself. Not surprisingly, Rudyard Kipling, exhorting Americans to take up their "responsibility" of civilizing the Philippines, wrote in "The White Man's Burden" (1899): "Your new-caught, sullen peoples, Half-devil and *half-child*" (in San Juan 2000, 99; emphasis added). As Doty points out, complementary to the childlike attributes attached to the Filipinos in the American counter-insurgency discourses were ineptitude and inefficiency (1993, 313). Infantilization justifies guardianship, patronage by the adult, more enlightened, rational West. Tibetans would prosper "under British auspices and assistance" (Sandberg 1904, 14)—such sentiments were rife during the time of the British invasion.

During lengthy negotiations preceding and accompanying the British invasion of Tibet in 1903–4, Tibetans were commonly compared to obstinate, illogical children. Younghusband found them "very much like big children" (Uncovered Editions 1999, 105, 148). While discussing the Tibetan attitude during the pre-Lhasa negotiations, Fleming observed in 1904 that "logic was a concept wholly alien to the Tibetan mind." The Tibetans' "power of reasoning did not even extend to that of a child"; they did not evade issues but simply declined to recognize their existence (1961, 221). Landon qualified this by saying that Tibetans had their own sense of morality in that they were industrious and capable of "extraordinary physical activity" though "it is true that this activity finds its vent rather in the muscles of the legs than in those of the fingers, *but this is only to be expected*" (1905, 45; emphasis added).

A good illustration of the effectiveness of infantilization in clearing the conscience of European imperialists as aggressors, as perpetrators of violence, comes from the massacre of Tibetans at Guru. Younghusband found "Tibetans huddled together like a flock of sheep" (Younghusband 1910, 177) and later put the blame on the Lhasa priest: "Ignorant and arrogant, this priest herded the superstitious peasantry to destruction" (178–79). The imagery of Tibetans as children or as dumb animals (sheep) allowed the British to visualize that had it not been for some "selfish" elite (priests in the case of Tibetans), ordinary people would have welcomed European dominance.[4]

The Orient is not only a place where the mental development of people is arrested at the level of a child; it is also a place of sages, an old place. As Žižek writes, "What characterizes the European civilization is . . . its *ex-centered* character—the notion that the ultimate pillar of Wisdom, the secret *agalma,* the spiritual treasure, the lost object-cause of desire, which we in the West long ago betrayed, could be recuperated out there, in the forbidden exotic place" (2001, 67–68; emphasis in original).

Association of the East with wisdom and spirituality, through the technique that may be called *gerontification,* is well exemplified in the case of Tibet. It is often the place, not the people, that is rendered wise on account of its age. Though Madame Blavatsky (1892) and Kipling (through his lama figure in *Kim*) were instrumental in bringing together the idea of Tibet with the search for wisdom and spirituality, it is in the twentieth century that this association gathered a momentum of its own. After living the life of Tibetan mystic for a few years, David-Neel felt that the natural edifices like mountains and valleys in the Himalayan region conveyed a mysterious message to her and wrote in her account, originally published in 1921: "What I heard was the thousand-year old echo of thoughts which are re-thought over and over again in the East, and which, nowadays, appear to have fixed their stronghold in the majestic heights of Thibet" (1991, 24). Describing his escape from the Spanish prison camp to Tibet, Riencourt equated it "as an escape from the inferno of wars and concentration camps, searching for this forbidden land of mystery, the only place of earth where wisdom and happiness seemed to be a reality" (1950, 4). Many well-intentioned liberals in the West today are likely to agree with Thurman's extolling of the virtues of Tibet as a uniquely spiritual civilization:

> While Western and Tibetan personalities share the complex of modernity of consciousness, they are diametrically opposed in outlook, one focused on matter and the other on mind. . . . While the American national purpose is ever greater material productivity, the Tibetan national purpose is ever greater spiritual productivity. (1998, 10–11)

Self-Affirmation—Self-Criticism

The various strategies identified so far have been characterized by a sense of affirmation: affirmation of narcissism in the name of moral superiority. Landon, in the aftermath of the massacre of Tibetan at Guru during the British Tibet mission of 1903–4, said,

The resistance of the Tibetans had been blown away before us like leaves in autumn, and there was not a man in the country who did not realise that our care of the wounded afterwards, was as thorough as the punishment we inflicted at the moment. Trade and credit are proverbially plants of slow growth, and slower in the East than anywhere else. (in Sharma and Sharma 1996, 35)

The Orient is seen by the Europeans as "a pretext for self-dramatisation and differentness," a "malleable theatrical space in which can be played out the egocentric fantasies" thus affording "endless material for the imagination, and endless potential for the Occidental self" (Kabbani 1986, 11). Authority and control were justified by affirming inherently racist and self-serving ideas like the "white man's burden" and "manifest destiny" in the colonial period. Representation of the Other as irrational, immoral, inefficient, and duplicitous affirms self-representation as rational, moral, efficient, and honest. The sense of affirmation can be seen not only in overtly aggressive imperialist writings but also in those with more humanitarian and liberal content. The significance of essentialist and stereotypical representations of the Other lay not in the intentions of the representer but in the effects on the represented. In their own different ways, aggressive as well as liberal imperialist impulses established and institutionalized control through mobilization of similar yet contradictory representations, production of knowledge, bureaucratic modes of governance, and use of coercive force.

Though affirmation of the Western Self was the ultimate force behind most representations, some also used specific representations to question the Self. That is, representations of the non-Western Other have sometimes been deployed in the service of self-criticism. This can be seen in the case of Western representations of Tibet, especially after the turn of the nineteenth century. "I delightedly forgot Western lands, that I belonged to them, and that they would probably take me again in the clutches of their sorrowful civilization," said David-Neel in 1921 (1991, 61). However, the use of the Other to offer criticism of the Self is not necessarily emancipatory for the represented Other. The differing and even noble intentions of some of those who practiced positive stereotyping of the Other do not preclude the fact that their impact on the exoticized represented was often predictably the same—a prelude to control, dominance, and exploitation. They function in a variety of imperial contexts as a mechanism of aesthetic substitution that "replaces the impress of power with the blandishments of curiosity" (Said 1993, 159). Thus, Tibet remains a service society for the West, offering resources by which the West can criticize itself, question its values. As Harrer reminds us, Tibetans have "a heritage superior to ours . . . [they] might bring succour to the pessimism of the West" (1985, 52). More recently, the actor Richard Gere, known for his advocacy of the cause of Tibetans, lamented: "I would say that the West is very young, it's very corrupt. We're not very wise. And I think we're hopeful that there is a place that is ancient and wise and open and filled with light" (*Frontline* 1998b).

CONCLUSION

Several strategies of representing the West's Other during the period of European imperialism remain integral to Western representations of the Other even in this postcolonial world, sometimes in more subtle ways. Blatant racism is couched in more acceptable liberal marketable terms. An approach that sees representation as a process is better placed to examine the ways in which the Western discovery and consciousness of the East went hand in hand with Western imperial rule over it. Today, the close link between knowledge production and "national interest" (Weldes 1999), between knowledge and power, remains as close as ever and requires more research and analysis from progressive intellectuals and academics. An understanding of the way non-Western people were represented within the colonial discourse can assist in identifying similar processes that continue in the contemporary world. It will highlight the essentially politicized nature of representations of the Other and representational practices within the political.

The representations of the non-West within Western discourses—both academic and popular—remain enmeshed in asymmetrical power relations. How the West represents its Other continues to be intertwined with its perceived interests and its sense of identity and has a productive impact on the represented. In the case of Tibetans, Western representation has been a crucial factor in shaping the identity of Tibet as a geopolitical entity as well as shaping the identity of the Tibetans. Before going into the significance of Western representations in chapters 4–6, the next chapter highlights some of the contours of Exotica Tibet by focusing on a selection of cultural sites.

3

Poetics of Exotica Tibet

The poetics of Exotica Tibet requires a critical postcolonial analysis of Western representations of Tibet, and this can be performed effectively by focusing on a few cultural sites commonly associated with Tibet and Tibetans. This is a (partial) story of Western interactions with Tibet during various historical periods—it is about the production of images of Tibet within these interactions as well as about how the interactions were in turn framed under specific imaginative regimes. The constitutive relation between Western interactions and imaginations of Tibet is the subject of this chapter. Following Doty, these Western interactions can be seen in terms of *imperial encounters*, which convey the idea of asymmetrical encounters in which "one entity has been able to construct 'realities' that were taken seriously and acted upon and the other entity has been denied equal degrees or kinds of agency" (1996b, 3).

Until the beginning of the twentieth century Tibet was seen as an absence on the map, as Landon puts it, the "last country to be discovered by the civilized world" (1905, xi). This was also because it "was never the actual place [of Tibet] that fired the imagination of romantic seekers: it was the idea of Tibet, far away, impenetrable, isolated in the higher spheres of the earth" (Buruma 2000). Preconceived facts about Tibetans were often of the proverbial kind. Tibet was seen as the quintessential Asia of the Western imagination, the poor oppressed land with an ancient culture and spirit (Feigon 1996, 22). Exotica Tibet has been full of contrasts and superlatives.

A significant characteristic of Exotica Tibet is its richness in terms of imageries and imaginaries (for a detailed treatment, see Bishop 1989, 1993; Lopez 1998).[1] "Tibet is, in Foucault's terms, a heterotopia, a plurality of often contradictory, competing, and mutually exclusive places simultaneously positioned on a single geographical location" (Bishop 2001, 204). Representations of Tibet range from extremely pejorative ("feudal hell") to unmitigatedly idealistic ("Shangri-la"). Tibet for some is a blankness[2] upon which they can write their desire; for others, it is an overcoded space mingling the fantastic with utter simplicity. Forman wrote, "In the heart of ageless Asia, brooding darkly in the shadow of the unknown, is to be found a veritable explorer's paradise—Tibet, the strange and fascinating, forbidden land of magic and mystery . . . where the opposites are kin and the extremes go hand in hand" (1936, vii).

In this chapter, I expand my analysis of the poetics of Exotica Tibet by focusing on a selection of cultural sites most commonly associated with Tibet during the twentieth century. I examine the sites in the context of images they portray.

THE IMAGINAL ARCHIVE

An archive of preexisting images and imaginaries as well as the archiving of new ones were central to the way initial encounters between the Westerners and Tibet were made sense of. "Archive" is commonly understood as a place or collection containing records, documents, photographs, film, or other materials of historical interest. But "archive" can also be taken to refer to a repository of stored memories or information, often outside the purview of statist discourses. As Bradley writes, the "archive is the repository of memories: individual and collective, official and unofficial, licit and illicit, legitimating and subversive" (1999, 108). These memories and information can be based on "real" encounters or on fictional ones.

In situations where the culture was relatively unknown—like the Tibetan—hearsay, legends, and fantasies performed an ever more important archival function. Representers of Tibet, especially before the twentieth century, drew upon these archives, supplementing the rare missionary and travelers' accounts. The legendary traveler Marco Polo refers to "Tebet" in the late thirteenth century. Apart from other things (such as the cannibalizing of human beings put to death by the authorities, "canes of immense size and girth," natives as idolators and "out-and-out bad"), Marco Polo fetishizes Asian promiscuity. He highlights a marriage custom where "no man would ever on any account take a virgin to wife" for "a woman is worthless unless she has had knowledge of many men," and therefore Tibetans offer their women to travelers to "lie with them" and thus make them fit for marriage (but once marriage takes place, it is a "grave offence for any man to touch another's wife"). He jokes: "Obviously the country is a fine one to visit for a lad from sixteen to twenty-four" (1958, 79–80, 142, 144, 142–43). A similar, though less fantastical, characterization of Tibet as the strange, tantalizing, available East inviting (by forbidding) Western men persisted during the colonial era. During most of the nineteenth and early twentieth centuries Tibet was off-limits for the Europeans. This led to a "race for Lhasa,"[3] competition among explorers and adventurers to be the first into the "Forbidden City." *The Queen, The Lady's Newspaper* on 12 December 1903 published a brief account of a visit to the "Forbidden Lands" by "a Lady" (just before an article on "fashionable marriages"). When stopped by monks from entering a religious establishment, she fumed: "It was very tantalising and not a little galling to the independent Briton to be stopped in the fair way by a few dirty old lamas" (in IOR: MSS EUR/F197/523).

Richardson argued that the early allusions of Westerners reveal little more than that the Tibetans had a reputation in neighboring countries for "strange ways and rare magical powers" (1962, 61). This reputation persisted during the twentieth century as the production of knowledge about Tibet continued to be inspired by Tibetophilia, fascination with religious and social practices of Tibetans, the spread of Buddhism in the West, countercultural movements in the West, and so on. The fantastic has always been a part of image/knowledge about Tibet, and works have drawn upon an archive of preexisting representations (see Bishop 1989; Klieger 1997; Lopez 1998). The fact that Tibet was never colonized by Europeans facilitated creation of a utopian archive best evident in James Hilton's novel *Lost Horizon* (1933).

Shangri-La: The Utopian Archive

Hilton's *Lost Horizon*, which introduced the term "Shangri-la," was first published in 1933 and made into a film by Frank Capra in 1937. "Shangri" has no meaning in Tibetan; "la" means "mountain pass." The name is apparently inspired by "Shambhala," a mythical Buddhist kingdom in the Himalayas according to Tibetan legend (see Allen 1999; Bernbaum 2001; LePage 1996; Trungpa 1995).[4] The main character in the novel is a British Indian official, Robert Conway, who, along with the younger official Charles Mallinson, a missionary, Miss Roberta Brinklow, and an American businessman, Henry Barnard, is hijacked and taken to an unknown mountainous region somewhere in Tibet. They are transported to a hidden valley of the blue moon. The valley has a lamasery named Shangri-la that combines the best of Western technology with Eastern luxury. The head priest, who is several hundred years old, wants Conway to take over his position. Conway is told that the valley affords a very long life to selected people and the main purpose of the establishment is to act as a sanctuary when the outside world is in chaos. Conway falls in love with a quiet Chinese woman, Lo-Tsen, not knowing that she and Mallinson are becoming lovers. While Barnard and Miss Brinklow agree to stay in the valley (the former to help in gold mining and the latter to convert Tibetans to Christianity), the impatient Mallinson persuades Conway to accompany him and Lo-Tsen to safety outside the valley. Conway departs in despair, all his hope lost as he realizes that he is forever a wanderer between two worlds: "he was doomed, like millions, to flee from wisdom and be a hero" (Hilton 1933, 264).

Though Hilton's Shangri-la has come to be associated with Tibet, in the book itself (unlike a later movie adaptation), apart from its probable geographical location, there is little that is Tibetan about the place. According to Conway, the atmosphere is Chinese, rather than specifically Tibetan (Hilton 1967, 52). Tibetans are the inhabitants of the lower valley who sing in "lilting barbaric tunes" (46), work in the fields, provide entertainment, and live a subaltern life. The inhabitants of the valley are a blend of Chinese and Tibetan and are cleaner and handsomer than the average of either race (Hilton 1933, 129). The high lama is from Luxembourg and most inhabitants of the lamasery are Europeans. In order to keep the lamasery populated, outsiders have been brought in. Father Perrault, the High Lama, explains that they once had a Japanese who was not a fine acquisition; "Tibetans are much less sensitive than outside races and die sooner, even though they are charming"; Chinese are slightly better; the "best subjects, undoubtedly, are the Nordic and Latin races of Europe" (1967, 110).

Hilton's Shangri-la has central heating and combines the mechanics of Western hygiene with much else that is "Eastern" and "traditional." For instance, after his arrival Conway enjoys a bath in a porcelain tub from Ohio, while a native attends to him in a Chinese fashion (1967, 51). Shangri-la is always tranquil yet always a hive of "unpursuing occupations"; the lamas lived "as if indeed they had time on their hands, but time that was scarcely a featherweight" (1967, 139). Inhabitants of the lamasery indulge in various intellectual pursuits—writing, doing pure mathematics, coordinating Gibbon and Spengler into a vast thesis on the history of European civilization, formulating new theories on *Wuthering Heights,* and so on. This is in line with the principal rationale for the existence of Shangri-la: to act as a sanctuary, to be a "war refuge" for preserving the best of modern civilizations (1933, 191–92).

Thus, *Lost Horizon* creates a utopia placed somewhere in Tibet. The utopia is an archive that seeks to preserve the best of the world from the world itself. As the High Lama says to Conway in the film version: "Once the world has spent itself, we shall be here with their books, their music, their way of life" (1937). Shangri-la for Hilton is a secret "archive state" hidden somewhere in the mountains of Central Asia. The High Lama here has a strategic conception of a utopian archive (with the best of Western and Eastern worlds), a fortress as well as a museum, a survivalist archive (Richards 1992, 124–25).

"The archive is also a place of dreams" (Steedman 1998, 67). It reflects not only the achieved but also the achievable and dreams of achieving the nonachievable. Thus, Shangri-la is a repository— of mental peace, spiritual wisdom, "high" culture, and physical wealth. It is a storehouse of desires—Western desires that leave little room for the cultural and historical specificity of Tibet. Western travelers' search for the "real Tibet" often takes them beyond actual Tibetans:

> The real Tibet I was searching for was not out in the open. It was not in the magnificent temples and palaces, in the colorful bazaars, in the happy and carefree life of its farmers or in the entrancing charm of Lhasa's social life. Real Tibet transcends politics and economics; it is invisible, beyond sense-perception, beyond intellect. It is the mysterious land of the psyche, of what lies beyond death, a universe to which some Tibetans have the key and which their subtle soul seems to have explored as thoroughly as Western scientists have explored our physical universe. (Riencourt 1950, 262)

Thus, integral to the Western imagination of Tibet has been a notion of utopia, beginning in the late nineteenth century with theosophists and taken to its extreme in *Lost Horizon* (see Bishop 1989; Dodin and Rather 2001b; Klieger 1997)—Tibet as a sanctuary from the materialism and violence of modern times, a sanctuary for those disaffected with modernity and seeking peace and wisdom. The twining of wisdom/archive/library with contemporary Tibet is seen in the sentiments of many Western[5] supporters of Tibet. Interestingly, the vice-chancellor of Oxford, in his welcome note to the first International Seminar on Tibetan Studies in 1979, quoted from Hilton's novel: "When the High Lama asked him [Conway] whether Shangri-La was not unique in his experience, and if the Western world could offer anything in the least like it, he answered with a smile: 'Well, yes—to be quite frank, it reminds me very slightly of Oxford'" (BOD MS Or. Aris 15 n.d., 99).

"Tibet" in the contemporary period emerged out of a colonial representational regime (discussed in chapter 2) and the archive has played a crucial role in producing and circumscribing this regime. The archive of imaginaries of Tibet shaped the ways in which Tibet was encountered and in turn (re)produced new imageries to be added on to the archive. An important force that constrained and shaped this encounter was European imperialism, particularly its British variant in India.

THE IMPERIAL SCRIPTING OF EXOTICA TIBET

Contemporary journalistic reports about Tibet usually start off with the history of the "drastic opening" of Tibet in 1950 with the Chinese invasion. This reveals a practice of historical amnesia, for they rarely mention the destabilizing influence of Western imperialism in pre-1950s Tibet.[6] As the next chapter will argue in greater detail, the imagination of Tibet as a place and its historical status vis-à-vis China are linked through Western imaginative and *imperial* practices. Here, the focus is on analyzing the poetics of representation within a historical account written by a British colonial official—Colonel Francis Younghusband, who played an important role in one of the most crucial historical moments of the modern imperial scripting of Tibet in the international imaginary—the 1903–4 Tibet mission, more commonly known as the Younghusband mission. The analysis shows the intermeshing of knowledge, power, representations, and encounters within an imperial ethos.

The beginning of the twentieth century saw British imperialism in its heyday, firmly established on the Indian subcontinent. However, Tibet remained tantalizingly outside the arena of European scrutiny, for it was closed to foreigners. The Younghusband mission was designed to force the Tibetans to come into the modern international (read *imperial*) world. In terms of attitude toward Tibet, it was preceded and accompanied by a mix of abhorrence (with the "priest-ridden" system) and fascination (with the nature and simplicity of common people). This ambivalence remained integral to Exotica Tibet during the duration of British imperial rule on the Indian subcontinent. The image of Tibet one can glean from Younghusband's account is that of a backward, quaint people deserving the guiding hand of an enlightened British imperialism. This image is quite different from the idealization of Tibet (though *not* of Tibetans) as seen in Hilton's utopian archive.

An Imperial Adventurer

Younghusband's *India and Tibet* (1910) purports to provide a history of the relations that have existed between India and Tibet from the time of Warren Hastings (late eighteenth century) to 1910, with a particular account of the 1903–4 mission to Lhasa. This story of the British aims toward "the establishment of ordinary neighbourly intercourse with Tibet" (vii) and Tibetans' refusal to oblige.

Reflecting the attitude of a "pioneer" and "frontiersman," the account is full of resentment against bureaucratic and political control exercised by the imperial government over its agents. Younghusband expresses nostalgia for a golden era when the agents of imperialism were left free to pursue their "destiny" without interference. Sarcastic about the centralization of power in London, he says that "the next mission to Lhasa will in all probability be led by a clerk from the Foreign Office in London" (103). Reflecting an aristocratic disdain for "democracy," he says that "as long as what an officer in the heart of Asia may do is contingent on the 'will' of 'men in the street' of grimy manufacturing towns in the heart of England, so long as our action be slow, clumsy, and hesitating, when it ought to be sharp and decisive" (133).

Younghusband is very conscious of the importance of credibility in maintaining imperial rule. For him, it was important to combat Russian intrigue in Tibet, as its loss would have been perceived by bordering Asiatic powers as a sign of British weakness and Russian supremacy. When signing the treaty in Potala Palace, Younghusband ordered everyone to dress in full regalia in order to impress the Tibetans: "Those who have lived among Asiatics know that the fact of signing the treaty in the Potala was of as much value as the Treaty itself" (302). Troops lined the road to the Potala and "a battery to fire a salute or to bombard the Palace, as occasion might require, was stationed in a suitable position" (303).

The invasion was seen as an adventure: when Younghusband received the news that he was to go on the mission, he was elated— "Here, indeed, I felt was the chance of my life. I was once more alive. The thrill of adventure again ran through my veins" (96). About leaving Darjeeling for Chumbi, he writes, "To me there was nothing but the stir and thrill of an enterprise, which would ever live in history" (152). Reflecting a close relation between imperial adventures and scientific pursuits, he describes how at Khamba Jong, while some went out to shoot antelopes and *Ovis ammon,* others indulged in "botanizing or geologizing"; he himself went with "Mr Hayden to hunt for fossils, with Captain Walton to collect birds, and Colonel Prain to collect plants" (123).[7]

Imperialists were flexible (opportunist?) in their perception of natives. The latter were perceived as inherently divided or inherently united depending on the needs of the former. The deputation from Tashi Lama (with his seat of authority in Tashilunpo monastery in Shigatse, the second city of Tibet; he is usually seen as secondary to the Dalai Lama in temporal matters) pleaded innocence, and citing their fear of the wrath of the Lhasa government, requested Younghusband to withdraw to Yatung or across the frontier. Younghusband made it clear that "we must regard Tibetans as all one people, and hold them responsible for the actions of each" (124). Contrary to the self-perception of Tibetans, the British imposed a pan-Tibetan identity.

The mode of trivializing and infantilizing natives is evident as Younghusband writes that the impression left on him was that the Tibetans, "though excessively childish, were very pleasant, cheery people, and individually, probably quite well disposed towards us" (124). He records how he tried again and again to reason with the obstinate Tibetans who refused to recognize British supremacy: "When I saw these people so steeped in ignorance of what opposing the might of the British Empire really meant, I felt it my duty to reason with them . . . to save them from the results of their ignorance" (163). In retrospect, one could argue that the Tibetan delegates, who came to negotiate before the mission finally entered Lhasa, had a better understanding of imperialism. The delegates stressed that it was Tibetan custom to keep all strangers out, otherwise, following the British, other nations too would want to go to Lhasa and establish their agents (as they did in China). In contrast, speaking from the lofty heights of an "internationalism" that was actually based on imperial arrogance, Younghusband "reminded them that they lived apart from the rest of the world, and did not understand the customs of international discourse. To us the fact of their having kept the representative of a great Power waiting for a year to negotiate was a deep insult, which most Powers would resent by making war without giving any further chance for negotiation. But the British Government disliked making war if they could possibly help it" (229).

Distinct from the latter-day idealizations of Tibetan Buddhism for its pacifist character, Younghusband agrees that "Lamaism" had a pacifying effect, but he has a different evaluation of this peace: "But the peace that has been nurtured has been the quiescence of sloth and decadence. . . . Peace, instead of harmony, has been their ideal—peace for the emasculated individual instead of harmony for the united and full-blooded whole" (314–15). The pacifism of Tibetans is contrasted unfavorably with the masculine, energetic, and outward-looking character of the British imperial project.

Carrying on and reinforcing the tradition of Western travelers to Tibet, Younghusband experienced an epiphany there. For a moment, a mystic Younghusband subsumed the imperialist Younghusband. At a camp outside Lhasa, he went off alone to the mountains and, in his own words, "gave myself up to all the emotions of this eventful time." As he writes, from the city came the Lama's words of peace and not hatred and

> I was insensibly suffused with an almost intoxicating sense of elation and good-will. This exhilaration of the moment grew and grew till it thrilled through me with overpowering intensity. Never again could I think of evil, or ever again be enemy with any man. All nature and all humanity were bathed in a rosy glowing radiancy; and life for the future seemed nought but buoyancy and light . . .

and that single hour on leaving Lhasa was worth all the rest of a lifetime. (326–27)

Tibet seems to have had a transformative effect on the hardened imperialist.[8]

Thus *India and Tibet* reflects many characteristics that were typical of imperial literature on Tibet during the time. It shows Tibet as a land of contrasts (between the lamas and the common people) and a land of religion (if a degraded one). It indulges in essentialism and stereotyping and deploys various representational strategies including gaze, debasement, moralization, infantilization, and self-affirmation. In contrast to the image of Tibet as a utopian archive, Younghusband's account is mainly about self-affirmation, a defense of the British imperial project as ennobling for the British and as civilizing for others. An incomplete passage from the discarded notes used for the book reflects Younghusband's confidence in his invasion:"To wantonly invade Tibet in sheer lust of conquest and merely for the sake of painting the map red would of course have been wrong. But" (IOR: MSS EUR/F197/358 n.d.).

He wrote further, "I favour forward policy, which simply recognises that *great civilized* Powers cannot by any possibility permanently ignore and disregard *semi-civilized* peoples on their borders, but must inevitably establish, and in time regularize, intercourse with them, and should therefore seize opportunities of *humanizing* that intercourse "(Younghusband 1910, 428; emphases added).

Youngblood justified the mission, asserting that the Tibetans had "asked me to take them under British protection—having come to the conclusion from what they had seen of us, that we were preferable to the Chinese" (IOR: MSS EUR/F197/108 n.d., 3). While Younghusband was criticized by his own government as well as a large section of the press (see Mehra 2005), he had his defenders. At a lecture delivered in London by a member of the Tibet mission, Douglas Freshfield, the chairman of session assured the audience that the natives whose sensitivities had been hurt by the invasion "would eventually come to see the English were right" and quoted a poem:

The East bow'd low before the blast,
In patient, deep disdain;
She let the legions thunder past,
And plunged in thought again (Freshfield 1905, 273)

TIBET: A LAND OF RELIGION

Tibet's association with religion can be traced back to the early modern age when the first Western travelers were mostly Christian missionaries.[9] The Western assessment of religion as the main, if not the sole, defining feature of Tibetan life and culture has differed over time. Western missionaries as well as many travelers, especially in the beginning of the twentieth century, considered Tibetan culture barbaric and degenerate. However, as the century progressed and the merits of Christianity as well as secularism came under scrutiny in the West, Tibetan Buddhism[10] came to be idealized.

For most Western commentators until the beginning of the twentieth century, the Tibetan "preoccupation" with religion was irrational, superstitious, and downright degenerate, at least when compared to classical Buddhism. This unfavorable comparison between Tibetan and classical Buddhism is not surprising: the latter is a hypostatized phenomenon, created by Europe and controlled by it. It was against this classical Buddhism that all Buddhisms of the modern Orient were to be judged and found lacking (Lopez 1998, 7; see also Lopez 1995). Lamaism was the most degenerate and inauthentic of all. This sentiment is clearly reflected in Waddell's work, which is characterized by modes of stereotyping and essentialism and representational strategies of gaze, classification, debasement, negation, moralization, and self-affirmation. In contrast, the *Tibetan Book of the Dead* is marked by modes of stereotyping, essentialism, and exoticism along with the strategies of differentiation, idealization, affirmation, gerontification, and self-criticism.

Waddell and the Study of Degenerate Lamaism

Waddell, the foremost expert on Tibetan Buddhism at the turn of the twentieth century, bolstered widespread negative images of Tibet ostensibly based on scientific and ethnographic foundations. He had the right credentials to be an expert: he had learned the Tibetan language, he sought to study the religion systematically[11] and scientifically, and most important, he was a white European male.

Waddell's accounts of his journey into Tibetan religion (*The Buddhism of Tibet or Lamaism,* 1895/1972) as well as into the Tibetan landscape (*Lhasa and Its Mysteries,* 1905) are filled with references to a degenerate form of Buddhism, an exploitative priesthood, and a superstitious peasantry. He writes, "The bulk of the

Lamaist cults comprise much deep-rooted devil-worship and sor-
cery . . . for Lamaism is only thinly and imperfectly varnished over
with Buddhist symbolism, beneath which the sinister growth of
poly-demonist superstition darkly appears" (1972, xi). In Tibet, the
impure form of Buddhism became "a disastrous parasitic disease
which fastened on to the vitals of the land . . . a cloak to the worst
form of oppressive devil-worship" (1905, 25). At the same time,
"lamaism" is not all bad as "it preserves for us much of the old-
world lore and petrified beliefs of our Aryan ancestors" (1972, 4).
In a typical blind imperialist un-self-reflexivity, Waddell finds the
Tibetan Regent "hopelessly biased" about the religion of the British
(1905, 408), while viewing his own biases about the religion of the
Tibetans as objective.

The account of the visit to Lhasa is filled with contradictions.
While the text is replete with criticism of the "vampire priests,"
"parasitic priesthood," and "sheer barbarians," it also expresses
nostalgia for the enigma supposedly lost with the invasion and considers Tibet's "charming land and interesting people" (1905, 448).
When visiting Yamdok Lake, Waddell mentions his pleasure at leaving warlike surroundings and entering "again the world of dreams
and magic which may be said to be ever with us in the mystic Land
of the Lamas" (292–93). Upon approaching Lhasa, he compares his
excitement and anticipation to "the emotions felt by the Crusaders
of old on arriving within sight of Jerusalem, after their long march
through Europe" (326) and exclaims: "Here at last was the object of
our dreams!—the long-sought, mysterious Hermit City, the Rome
of Central Asia, with the residence of its famous priest-god—and it
didn't disappoint us!" (330).

Taking a dig at the theosophist imagination of Tibet as the land
of the mahatmas, he writes, "Thus we are told that, amidst the soli-
tude of this 'Land of the Supernatural' repose the spirits of 'The
Masters,' the *Mahatmas,* whose astral bodies slumber in unbroken
peace, save when they condescend to work some petty miracle in
the world below" (1972, 3). In fact, he writes, the Tibetans were entirely ignorant of any mahatmas living in Tibet, nor had they heard
of any secrets of the ancient world being preserved in their country
(1905, 409–10). Many commentators disclaimed the theosophist
idealization of Tibet and deployed the trope of debasement and negation along the lines of Waddell's assertions, but the idealization of

Tibetan religion gained wider currency during the middle and later half of the twentieth century.

Tibetan Religion as an Answer to the West's Malaise

The Tibetan Book of the Dead has significantly contributed to the valorization of Tibetan religion and to the Western imagination of Tibet as a land of spirituality. It was allegedly written in the eighth or the ninth century and discovered in the fourteenth. It organizes the experiences of the *bar-do*, the "in-between"—usually referring to the state between death and rebirth. It was introduced to the West by Evans-Wentz (1949) for the first time in 1927 (and since then it "has taken on a life of its own as something of a timeless world spiritual classic"; Lopez 1998, 47).

The most idealized version can be found in Thurman's translation that seeks to represent Tibetan Buddhism as scientific rather than religious. Thurman dedicates the book

> to the brave and gentle people of Tibet, who have suffered and are suffering one of the great tragedies of our time . . . [and prays] May the Tibetan people soon regain the sovereign freedom they have enjoyed since the dawn of history! And *may the sunlight of Tibetan Spiritual Science once again shine brightly upon a freshened world*! (1998; emphasis added).

In discussing the virtue of pacifism, Thurman argues that during the reign of the fifth Dalai Lama (1617–82), a unique form of government was created that was almost completely demilitarized and gave priority to nonviolence (1998, 9). Representing Tibet as a spiritual civilization, Thurman writes, "In Western culture, the last frontier of our material conquest is the universe of outer space. Our astronauts are our ultimate heroes and heroines. Tibetans, however, are more concerned about the spiritual conquest of the inner universe. . . . So, the Tibetan lamas . . . [who are spiritually adept, the] 'psychonauts' are the Tibetans' ultimate heroes and heroines" (10).

Drawing upon the themes of Western materialism and Eastern spirituality, Thurman contrasts Tibetan "inner modernity" with Western "outer modernity." This difference of personality underlies the difference between the Western (American for Thurman) and Tibetan civilizations: "While the American national purpose is ever greater material productivity, the Tibetan national purpose is ever greater spiritual productivity" (11).

Thus, the idealization of Tibetan spirituality often goes beyond everyday religious practice, concerning itself with realms above religion. As the Tibetophile Hollywood actor Steven Seagal says, "My agenda has no politics. It has no economy. You see. It goes even beyond religion which is also big business and goes into simple human kindness and the way we're supposed to treat each other as human beings" (*Frontline* 1998c). A figure that has been integral to the Western imagination of Tibet as an abode of spirituality is the lama.

THE LAMA

At the end of his time in Lhasa, Younghusband wrote about the Ti Rimpoche, the abbot of the powerful Ganden monastery (who was acting as the chief Tibetan negotiator since the Dalai Lama had fled Lhasa before the arrival of the British in 1904): he was a "benevolent, kindly old gentleman, who would not hurt a fly if he could have avoided it" and he "more *nearly approached Kipling's Lama in 'Kim'* than any other Tibetan" Younghusband had met (Younghusband 1910, 310, 325; emphasis added). Here we see how preexisting images shaped the West's encounter with Tibet. Kipling's fictional lama provided an image of the Tibetan lama against which the British during the early twentieth century measured the actual lamas. With Younghusband begins the tradition of looking for the "Teshoo Lama" figure—elderly yet childlike, respected yet loved, spiritually wise yet with little knowledge of, or interest in, the secular world.

Kim and the Teshoo Lama

Kipling's *Kim*, first published in 1901, presents the Orient for the visual consumption of the West. The novel is about the adventures of Kim in India—a white orphan boy who has grown up among Indians, easily passing himself off as one of them. He takes to the road as a *chela* (disciple, companion) of a Tibetan lama and discovers the diversity of north Indian life while "becoming a man." Initially accompanying the lama on his search for the "fountain of wisdom," Kim is picked up by the British and groomed for working in the British secret service.

Though the depiction of individual Oriental characters such as the Teshoo Lama is positive, it in no way disrupts the cumulative picture and the certainties of Orientalism for "no matter how much a single Oriental can escape the fences around him, he is *first* an Oriental, *second* a human being, and *last* again an Oriental" (Said 1993, 112; emphases in original). In *Kim*, it is the Europeans who provide the Orientals with the first accurate descriptions and proper explanations of their history, religion, and culture. This is evident in the confrontation of the lama with the British curator of Lahore museum. The curator, a "white-bearded Englishman," speaks to the lama, who is trembling with excitement at the sight of Buddhist images: "Welcome, then, O lama from Tibet. Here be the images, and I am here . . . to gather knowledge" (1976, 13). The lama tells the curator that he was an abbot at a monastery in Tibet. In reply, the curator brings out a huge book of photos and shows him that very place, suitably impressing the lama, who exclaims, "And thou—the English know of these things?" (14).[12] Throughout the novel, Tibet figures as a place far removed from the lives of those in India. When the lama enters the story he says to the boys playing in front of the Lahore museum that he is "a hillman from hills thou'lt never see" (12). On his journey in north India with Kim, the lama tells stories of "enduring snows, landslips, blocked passes, the remote cliffs where men find sapphires and turquoise, and the wonderful upland road that leads at last into Great China itself" (48). Later, on the second leg of their journey,

> he told stories, tracing with a finger in the dust, of the immense and sumptuous ritual of avalanche-guarded cathedrals; of processions and devil-dances; of the changing of monks and nuns into swine; of holy cities fifteen thousand feet in the air; of intrigue between monastery and monastery; of voices among the hills, and of that mysterious mirage that dances on dry snow. He spoke even of Lhassa and of the Dalai Lama, whom he had seen and adored. (232)

One dominant representational strategy operating within the text is infantilization. On the one hand, young Kim is contrasted to the old lama. But a closer reading shows Kim to be the real guardian and caretaker as he is practically wise and the lama is childlike in worldly matters. The lama writes in "clumsy, childish print" (13) and follows Kim's instructions obediently and "simply as a child"

(20). Kim asserts his own importance for the lama when he says to him: "Was there ever such a disciple as I? . . . All earth would have picked thy bones within ten miles of Lahore city if I had not guarded thee" (71). Yet in times of crisis, such as when Kim is caught by two British regimental priests and is forcibly enrolled for formal schooling, the lama shows awareness of worldly matters and volunteers to act as Kim's guardian and insists on paying for the cost of his education.

The lama's wisdom in spiritual matters is of course unparalleled and compared favorably with Indian priests of all sorts. He speaks like a "scholar removed from vanity, as a Seeker walking in humility, as an old man, wise and temperate, illuminating knowledge with brilliant insight" (232). Ultimately, the lama finds his "fountain of wisdom" (the "river of the arrow") in his affection for Kim and 'saves' Kim from his illness through his meditation even though Kim has now been trained to be a British spy. He says, "Son of my Soul, I have wrenched my Soul back from the Threshold of Freedom to free thee from all sin—as I am free, and sinless!" (313). Tibet comes to the aid of the West to rejuvenate it spiritually, even as the West retains its secular dominance.

The benign figure of the lama, the one with a "loving old soul" (207), does not preclude Kipling from expressing the general disagreement with Tibetan religion that was prevalent among Europeans at the turn of the twentieth century. For instance, Kipling's lama figure anguishes that the "Old law"—primitive Buddhism— "was not well followed; being overlaid . . . with devildom, charms, and idolatry" (15).

Even though some might find in the figure of Teshoo Lama a charitable depiction of an "Oriental" (see Hopkirk 1997), he is seen as childish, unthinking, and incapable—to the point of self-destruction—of existence in the real world. This portrayal of the lama results from simplistic idealization and ambivalence. From his early function as a father figure for Kim, he gradually reveals his practical inadequacies, as his childlike dependence on Kim grows more explicit. Later in the novel, as compared to the Western patriarchal figures of Colonel Creighton and Father Victor—the European men combining power and "worldly" knowledge—the lama's virtue and behavior increasingly appear gendered as feminine and thus ineffectual (see Sullivan 1993). Kim's search for identity and his love for the lama are both mediated by the ruling structures of power.[13]

The Dalai Lama

Over the past century, the Tibetan lama figure has come to be crystalized in the figure of the Grand Lama, the Dalai Lama.[14] The person of the present fourteenth Dalai Lama, Tenzin Gyatso, has been instrumental in this. The Dalai Lama's contemporary image has moved beyond the confines of images such as Kipling's fictitious "Teshoo Lama." He is not only a figure of unalloyed admiration in the West; he symbolizes Tibet itself.

Pre-twentieth-century accounts of the Dalai Lama were unflattering. Jesuit missionaries Grueber and D'Orville, the first Europeans to visit Lhasa (1661), declined to meet the Dalai Lama, describing him as "that devilish god the father who puts to death those who refuse to adore him" (in Richardson 1988, 23). In the eighteenth century, Ippolito Desideri reasoned that the "alleged incarnation of the Grand Lama must be a work of the Devil (in De Filippi 1932, 204). Du Halde, in his brief description of Tibet, was clear: "The multitude of Lamas in Tibet is incredible . . . So long as he [Grand Lama] continues [to be the] Master of Tibet, Christianity will make little or no progress there" (1738, 388). Interestingly, the earliest reference to Tibet in a novel was in Balzac's *Old Goriot,* where the "Grand Lama" is used as a metaphor for absolute power (Bishop 2001). Positive portrayal of the Dalai Lama is relatively rare, such as in Manning's description of his meeting in 1811 with the ninth Dalai Lama (seven years old): "I was extremely affected by this interview with the lama. I could have wept through strangeness of sensation" (in Richardson 1998, 395).

At the beginning of the twentieth century, the Dalai Lama was an enigma. The Younghusband expedition presented the British public with the idea of the Dalai Lama as the "mysterious god-king of Tibet, embodying a line of spiritual predecessors vaguely envisaged as stretching back into the mists of history" (in Richardson 1998, 382). The fact that during the Lhasa invasion the Dalai Lama fled Tibet and was therefore beyond the control of the British added to the mystery. Yet this mystification did not necessarily translate into admiration. For instance, when the thirteenth Dalai Lama was interviewed in 1911 by William Ellis for *The Continent,* a Presbyterian paper, the interviewer was not deeply impressed. "His face is thoroughly pock-marked . . . his ears, which are large and pointed at the top, are his most noticeable feature. His moustache is waxed horizontally, while his head, in a lesser personage, would be called bullet-shaped" (*New York Times* 1911). Of the things the Lama had to talk about, what most pleased his interviewer was his assertion that, upon returning to Tibet at the end of his long exile following the Younghusband expedition, he intended to send young Tibetan men to America for a Western education. There is not much hint of mysticism here but there is a reference to the "strategic" location of Tibet.

In the early years of the twenty-first century, the Western version of the Dalai Lama as a personification of Tibet has taken a literal form. His exile from Tibet has meant that Tibet has been emptied of its real content (see Barber 1969). "Real Tibet dream comes when you meet his Holiness because then—it's actualized" (Gere, in *Frontline* 1998b). He is seen as embodying Tibet and Tibetan culture: "He creates images of Tibet, builds community through alliances among resident and exiled Tibetan populations, sustains non-Tibetan and Tibetan Buddhist believers, works toward Tibetan self-determination and functions as the central focus of power and identity within the Tibetan diaspora" (Houston and Wright 2003, 218).

Journalistic accounts of meeting with him tend to emphasize elements of Tibetanness in his body or attire or laugh. "The Dalai Lama embodies Tibetan culture and Tibetan cause; he provides the refugees with a concrete example of how to live by the abstract values of their culture" (Forbes 1989, 160; see also Rose and Warren 1995, which calls him the "Living Tibet"). His books are instant best sellers. And yet at the same time, the main reason for his international profile is his *internationalism*, his status as a global spiritual and moral leader. He "is a symbol of continuity with the spiritual traditions of Tibet . . . and, for western admirers, a consistent voice of sanity in an age of violence" (Hilton 2006, 29). The Dalai Lama manages to combine nationalism (always already based on particularistic identity) with universal ideas of compassion and peace (see Gyatso 1998) and this is where his appeal lies.

The Dalai Lama acts as a unifying symbol for matters of religion and politics. We may take the celebration of anniversaries in Dharamsala, the seat of the Tibetan government-in-exile in India, particularly the March 10 Uprising Day and Monlam festival, as illustrating this. Taken together these two represent the paradigm of *chos srid gnyis ldan* (religion and politics combined) with the Dalai Lama on the top. On Uprising Day the secular Tibetan government renews its worldly claims for national independence, using metaphors in currency in the international community. Monlam, on the other hand, attempts to ground the refugee society in the changelessness of the Buddhist doctrine and the priesthood that embodies it. Both represent the dynamic of change and continuity, the nation and religion. The unifying symbol bridging both events is the Dalai Lama, the king and the god, the active agent between this world and the next. He presents contradictory images: a "simple Buddhist monk" and the head of Tibetan Buddhism; human and god; world-renouncing as well as world-encompassing (Klieger 1994, 67). Personal loyalty to the Dalai Lama plays a key role in the government-in-exile's efforts to strengthen the sense of a unified Tibetan identity. In Korom's words, "Faith in Buddhism and in Dalai Lama's office has provided cohesion necessary for maintaining a form of 'proto-nationalism' within a broadly dispersed world society" (1997b, 3). The Dalai Lama is also the chief symbol of the Tibetan cause in the international arena.

> The unique role of the Dalai Lama, who won the Nobel Peace Prize in 1989, is perhaps the major reason for Tibet's international exposure. His spiritual, nonviolent approach and frequent travels around the world not only generate much interest in Tibetan Buddhism but also serve to maintain attention to the status of Tibetans and Chinese practices in the region. (Gurr and Khosla 2001, 280–81)

That Sino-Tibetan conflict has come to revolve around the interpretation of the Dalai Lama as an individual is also evident from Bill Clinton's statement in Beijing: "I have spent time with the Dalai Lama, I believe him to be an honest man, and I believe that if he had a conversation with President Jiang Zemin, they would like each other very much" (*World Tibet News* 1998). On the other hand, critics like Rupert Murdoch support the Chinese occupation by attacking him: "I have heard cynics who say he's a very *political old monk shuffling around in Gucci shoes.* . . . It [old Tibetan society] was a pretty terrible old autocratic society out of the Middle Ages" (*World Tibet News* 1999; emphasis added). These representations fail to convey through their imagery a sense of the process by which the Dalai Lama has come to represent his constituency or that the Tibet he represents is a "political Tibet with a defined territory and customs, or a highly complex society in transition with a wide range of sectors and interests, and a rapidly changing social environment" (Barnett 2001, 300–301). Without denying the centrality of the figure of the Dalai Lama to the Tibetan civilization, it can be argued that the current literalization of the Dalai Lama as Tibet is intimately linked to the Western imagination and Western desires. Another facet of this imagination is Tibet as the "rooftop of the world," allowing for a once-in-a-lifetime temporal and spiritual journey by Westerners.

TEMPORAL AND SPIRITUAL JOURNEYING TO THE "ROOFTOP OF THE WORLD"

Adventure (see Fergusson 1911) and spirituality are integral parts of journeys into Tibet. Lhasa, "a centre where barbaric practices mingle with the most sublime and philosophic studies," attracted Western travelers for "nothing is too strange for anyone to expect in this hidden metropolis of nirvana" (unidentifiable newspaper article by Edward Arnold, in IOR: MSS EUR/F197/523 n.d.). Western travelogues highlight a sense of adventure, surprise, and an encounter with spirituality in travels into Tibet, particularly in journeys to Lhasa (see Hovell 1993). After examining the enchantment with Tibet in terms of its geographically and politically challenging location, I look at two works of travel writing and pick out elements of temporal and spiritual adventure (see Cocker 1992). Apart from stereotyping, the main representational strategies at work include gaze, naturalization,[15] spiritualization, self-affirmation, and self-criticism.

One factor that explains the magnetic power of Tibet is its extreme remoteness from the West, conjuring images of a land of cherished ideals or a wasteland. Tibet's geographical features constitute a uniquely "fantastic" landscape. "It has all the physical features of a true wonderland. . . . No description can convey the least idea of the solemn majesty, the serene beauty, the awe-inspiring wildness, the entrancing charm of the finest Tibetan scenes" (David-Neel 1936, 262).

Throughout the nineteenth and twentieth centuries, the fact that they were "closed" to Europeans added to the mystery of Lhasa and

Tibet. The epithets "the Forbidden City" and the "forbidden land" merely served to enhance the desire of individual Western travelers to defy the authorities. Wellby, who wanted to go to Tibet to find out "what mysteries lay beneath the word UNEXPLORED with which alone our latest maps were enlightened" (1898, 72; emphasis in original) finally gave up when he realized that the only way to succeed "would have been to shoot the most determined of our obstructionists. . . . *Even if supposing we had shot some of them,* it would have been a very hazardous step to have risked a serious scrimmage almost on our very frontier" (72; emphasis added).

The desire to explore the unknown as the main reason to travel to Tibet is nicely expressed in Deasy:

> I had long entertained the desire to travel in some unknown country, and in the spring of 1896, when circumstances were favourable, the wish was transformed into a settled purpose. The vast extent of the territory marked "unexplored" on the map of Tibet, then recently published, at once attracted me, and it was to this inhospitable and almost inaccessible land that I resolved to proceed. (1901, 2)

The opening of Tibet did not follow the British invasion: travel to Lhasa was severely restricted both by the Lhasa authority and the British Indian government. The "forbidden" character of Tibet was etched even deeper in Western imagination when China occupied Tibet and long periods of effective and coercive isolation began. Though Tibet has been opened to travelers in limited numbers since the 1980s, severe travel restrictions remain. Dodging Chinese authorities and encounters with "real" Tibetans (as opposed to "Sinicized" Tibetans) have become a staple of much contemporary travel writing (see, for example, Abbots 1997; Berkin 2000; Kewley 1990; McCue 1999; Morpurgo 1998; Patterson 1990; Scholberg 1995; Wilby 1988).

David-Neel's *My Journey to Lhasa*

Alexandra David-Neel was the first Western woman to be granted an audience with the Dalai Lama in Kalimpong.[16] She was the first to enter Lhasa when she went with a Sikkimese lama (Yongden) whom she adopted as her son and later brought to live in France. She set off in the winter of 1923 disguised as a Tibetan pilgrim, maps hidden in her boots, revolver in her peasant dress; she outwitted officials and bandits, enduring days without food and nights without shelter. Her account of her journey to Lhasa is replete with various themes common to Exotica Tibet. Though it is a travel account, it is also a journey into spiritual realms. As Hopkirk writes in the introduction to a later edition of her book, "her explorations were of the Tibetan mind rather than of the terrain" (David-Neel 1991, xv).

The book, originally published in 1927, starts with her rationale for taking the adventurous but dangerous trip. The British prohibited her from traveling in the Himalayan region,[17] which increased her determination. Once, when she was stopped from proceeding into Tibet,

> I took an oath that in spite of all obstacles I would reach Lhasa and show what the will of a woman could achieve! But I did not think only of avenging my own defeats. I wanted the right to exhort others to pull down the antiquated barriers which surround, in the center of Asia . . . if "heaven is the Lord's," the earth is the inheritance of man, and . . . consequently any honest traveller has the right to walk as he chooses, all over the globe which is his. (xxv)

Her criticisms are also directed against the central Tibetan authority based in Lhasa. It was a period when Tibetans had been successful in pushing out the Chinese army and controlled large parts of the ethnically Tibetan area. According to her, the Tibetans lost much in parting with China, for their "sham independence profits only a clique of court officials" (256).

David-Neel's exoticization is more about the Tibetan landscape and less about the Tibetan people. While she finds most Tibetans very superstitious, she admires the physical landscape: "But is not everything a fairy tale in this extraordinary country, even to the name it gives itself, that of *Khang Yul,* 'the land of snows'?" (277). She derives spirituality not from Tibetan religion but from the geographical and natural landscape. After living the life of a Tibetan mystic, she felt that natural edifices like mountains and valleys conveyed a mysterious message: "What I heard was the thousand-year old echo of thoughts which are re-thought over and over again in the East, and which, nowadays, appear to have fixed their stronghold in the majestic heights of Thibet" (24). She considered the fantastic to be an everyday occurrence in Tibet. Mystics and mysticism are ever present in her pages. Speaking of the mystics' retreat in parts of Tibet, she writes, "This world of the Thibetan mystics is a mystery in the mystery of Thibet, a strange wonder in a wonderful country" (198).

David-Neel is conscious of her gender and the extra significance it has for her trip. When she finally succeeds in her goal, she writes, "All sights, all things which are Lhasa's own beauty and peculiarity, would have to be seen by the lone woman explorer who had had the nerve to come to them from afar, the first of her sex" (259). She concludes, "The first white woman had entered forbidden Lhasa and shown the way. May others follow and open with loving hearts the gates of the wonderland" (310).

Although David-Neel's journey into the wonderland of Tibet was a spiritual adventure, the dominant impression it conveys is that of a travel adventure. In contrast, accounts such as Peter Mattheissen's *The Snow Leopard* are primarily about spiritual journey. Physical adventure comes to symbolize a spiritual quest.

A SEARCH FOR THE SNOW LEOPARD

The Snow Leopard, first published in 1978, is about the search in the Himalayas for the elusive eponymous cat. It is also a celebrated account of the bond between human beings and nature. Written out of Peter Matthiessen's interest in Zen, *The Snow Leopard* (1995) recounts his trip to the remotest parts of Nepal with the naturalist George Schaller in search of the Himalayan blue sheep and the rarely seen snow leopard. Matthiessen confronts the beauty, mysteries, and often violent world of the Himalayas as well as his own equally strange and difficult feelings about life and death. Not surprisingly, the one book he carries with him is the *Tibetan Book of the Dead*.

The author exoticizes natives throughout the book. Praising Sherpas for their primitivism, he writes, "The generous and open outlook of the sherpas, a kind of merry defencelessness, is by no means common, even among sophisticated peoples; I have never encountered it before except among the Eskimos" (1995, 40). His companion calls Sherpas "childish people" (109). Matthiessen is ashamed of himself when he witnesses the "happy go lucky spirit," the "acceptance which is not fatalism but a deep trust in life" exhibited by Sherpa companions (149).

Unlike David-Neel, whose specific goal was to reach Lhasa, Matthiessen has no aim. "I would like to reach the Crystal Monastery,

I would like to see a snow leopard, but if I do not, that is all right too" (93). When all he gets to see are the marks of the snow leopard, he writes, "I am disappointed, and also, I am not disappointed. That the snow leopard *is*, that it is here, that its frosty eyes watch us from the mountain—that is enough" (221). In response to a question— "Have you seen the snow leopard?"—he replies, "No! Isn't that wonderful?" (225). When asked why he took the journey, he replies: "I wished to *penetrate* the secrets of the mountains in search of something still unknown that, like the yeti, might well be missed for the very fact of searching" (121–22; emphasis added).

The Snow Leopard in its spiritual quest also becomes a means through which the Western Self is critiqued. The author writes, "My head has cleared in these weeks free of intrusions—mail, telephones, people and their needs—and I respond to things spontaneously, without defensive or self-conscious screens" (112). The account ends with despair as "I am still beset with the same old lusts and ego and emotions. . . . I look forward to nothing" (272). The elusive snow leopard stands here for the mystical elusiveness of Tibetan culture, for the impossibility of renouncing Western desires.

TIBET: A MYSTICAL AND FANTASY LAND

An integral theme of Exotica Tibet has been the imagination of Tibet as a land of mysticism and fantasy where most events are romantic, extraordinary, and absolutely different from anything in the West. Contrasting this image with the West's self-portrait, Norbu writes, "The West, whatever its failings, is real; Tibet, however wonderful, is a dream; whether of a long-lost golden age or millenarian fantasy, it is still merely a dream" (2001, 375).

In her account of life in the border region of Tibet in *With Mystics and Magicians in Tibet,* David-Neel (1936) mentions having met three *lung-gom-pas* runners—those who take extraordinarily long tramps with amazing rapidity by combining mental concentration with breathing gymnastics. She also refers to her own ability to practice the art of warming oneself without fire in the snows and the capacity to send messages "on the wind" (telepathy) that was a privilege of a small minority of adepts (1936, 210–20).

A prominent mixture of fantasy and mysticism is found in fictional/fantasy literature. The most (in)famous example is the trilogy written by Lobsang Rampa (1956, 1959, 1960), who, although an ordinary Englishman, claimed the trilogy to be the autobiography of a Tibetan lama. His works reflect the centrality of stereotyping, essentialism, idealization, affirmation, gerontification, and self-criticism as some of the dominant tropes in Exotica Tibet.

The Third Eye of Rampa the Mystifier

Tuesday Lobsang Rampa (alias Cyril Hoskin) was a mystifier, in two senses of the term. First, he mystified Tibet, embellishing its various realities with his own fancies, and second, he mystified his readers, playing on the credulity of the reading public (Lopez 1998, 86). Initially he did not disclose his identity; later, when detective investigation revealed that he was an English plumber who had never been to Tibet, he claimed to have been possessed by a Tibetan lama and over the course of seven years to have become a Tibetan not just in his dress but in his molecules. His trilogy consists of *The Third Eye: The Autobiography of a Tibetan Lama* (1956), *Doctor from Lhasa* (1959), and *The Rampa Story* (1960). The most prominent of these is *The Third Eye*, published in 1956 by Secker and Warburg despite opposition from experts on Tibet. The publishers defend their decision by asserting in the preface that it is "in its essence an authentic account of the upbringing and training of a Tibetan boy in his family and in a lamasery. Anyone who differs from us will, we believe, at least agree that the author is endowed to an exceptional degree with narrative skills and the power to evoke scenes and characters of absorbing and unique interest" (in Rampa 1956, 6). It became an immediate best seller. Though the community of European experts on Tibet was outraged, most reviews were positive,[18] and despite the disclosure of Rampa's identity in 1958, the book continued to sell.

Rampa opens *The Third Eye* with statements that are unlikely to have come from a Tibetan: "I am a Tibetan. One of the few who have reached this strange Western world" (9). This supposed autobiography of a young Tibetan lama, his life in Tibet, his training as priest-surgeon, his spiritual and fantastic adventures, and finally his departure from Tibet, is replete with stereotypes and clichés about Tibet that were prevalent in the mid-twentieth century.

Rampa defends Tibetan society's exclusiveness and resistance to progress. He writes, "Tibet was a theocratic country. We had no desire for the 'progress' of the outside world. We only wanted to be able to meditate and to overcome the limitations of the flesh" (14). Tibet is not only gilded with mysticism but also rich in material wealth. Rampa invokes the gold that was a crucial part of the imagination of Tibet in the early twentieth century.[19] "There are hundreds of tons of gold in Tibet, we regard it as sacred metal. . . . Tibet could be one of the greatest storehouses of the world if mankind would work together in peace instead of so much useless striving for power" (206).

The fantastic never leaves the description. After Rampa spends some time in the medical-school-cum monastery, his "third eye" is opened through surgery, allowing him to ascertain people's health and moods from their emanation (101–2). He is also given a crystal used as an instrument to penetrate the subconscious. Later, Rampa sees records of "the Chariots of the Gods" (UFOs?) and argues that some lamas had established telepathic communication with these "aliens" (140). He mentions that levitation is possible but astral traveling is easier and surer. He describes his trip to a secret volcanic territory in the north with tropical vegetation where he sees a few yetis and offers:

> I am prepared, when the Communists are chased out of Tibet, to accompany an expedition of sceptics and *show* them the yetis in the Highlands. They can use oxygen and bearers, I will use my old monk's robe. Cameras will prove the truth. We had no photographic equipment in Tibet in those days. (220; emphasis in original)

Nor is the audience (the West) ever absent from the narrative. The "autobiography" indulges in the representational strategy of (self-)criticism when Tibet is compared favorably to the West. The Dalai Lama warns Rampa that, while one could discuss the "Greater Realities" in Tibet and China, in the West one had to be extra careful because Westerners "worship commerce and gold"—"they ask for 'proof' while uncaring that their negative attitude of suspicion kills any chance of their obtaining that proof" (112).

Yeti, time travel, hypnotism, telepathy, levitation, astral travel, clairvoyance, invisibility—Tibet is a land of possibilities! It combines mysticism and fantasy, being both a lost horizon and a future utopia.

THE WEST'S PLAYGROUND

Exotica Tibet is a product of the Western imagination. It therefore comes as no surprise to see Tibet operating as a physical and imaginative playground for Westerners and their desires. Representational strategies of self-affirmation and self-criticism are as integral to the Western imagination of Tibet today as they were in the past. Tibet is seen as offering essential spiritual services to humanity. Tibet provides a set for the "drama of white people" (Norbu 1998, 20). The role of Tibet as a colorful[20] and transformative backdrop can be explored in *Seven Years in Tibet*—both the book and the Hollywood movie.

Seven Years in Tibet

Seven Years in Tibet (1956) is an account of the Austrian Heinrich Harrer's time in Tibet. With the outbreak of the Second World War, the British in India interned Harrer. After some unsuccessful attempts, he escaped in 1944 and, along with Peter Aufschnaiter, crossed the Himalayas into Tibet. After dodging officials, they managed to reach Lhasa in early 1946. Instead of being turned back, they were accepted by the authorities in Lhasa. Harrer's account of his stay in Tibet covers a crucial time in Tibetan history, its last years as an independent state. He also became an official paid by the Tibetans and tutored the young Dalai Lama before he was forced to leave Lhasa in 1951 when the Chinese took control.

It is interesting to note that Harrer and his companion set out for Lhasa just after the war was over. So it was not the escape from the British but the "lure of the Forbidden City" that encouraged them (86–87). In the tradition of previous travelers to Lhasa, Harrer describes his first sight of the golden roofs of Potala: "This moment compensated us for much. We felt inclined to go down on our knees like the pilgrims and touch the ground with our forehead" (113).

Though the representational strategies of idealization and self-criticism are dominant, Harrer's attitude is full of ambiguity. He writes of his infuriation with the "fatalistic resignation" (145) with which Tibetans lent themselves to backbreaking toil (they did not use the wheel) and is scathing about the Tibetan government's attitude toward modern medicine, hygiene, and sanitation. He writes disparagingly of the prevalence of venereal disease and homosexuality (186). Yet he "did not miss the appliances of Western civilization. Europe with its life of turmoil seemed far away" (156). While pondering whether progress in the form of a motor road to India would be good, he thinks, "One should not force a people to introduce inventions which are *far ahead of their stage of evolution*. . . . Tibetan culture and way of life more than compensates for the advantages of modern techniques" (185; emphasis added). The admirable aspects of Tibetan culture, for Harrer, include the "perfect courtesy of the people" and "cultivated and elegant" upper-class women. In his more recent *Return to Tibet* (1985), Harrer provides an even more nostalgic account of Tibet as a surrogate society: "Would it not be marvellous if our young people could also possess their land of mystery and magic, their Shangri-La, a goal they would exert their best efforts to attend?" (173). He affirms that this Shangri-la for him was Tibet.

In its film version, *Seven Years in Tibet* (1997) loses almost all its ambiguity. It becomes the story of Harrer, a self-centered and individualistic Westerner, who is transformed in Tibet. Superlatives abound in descriptions of Tibet—"roof of the world," "highest country on earth," "most isolated," "medieval stone fortress towering in the centre of Asia," and so on. In *Seven Years in Tibet* the people of Lhasa "casually offer pearls of wisdom about the harmony of Tibet in comparison to the West" (Hansen 2001, 105): one Tibetan says, "We admire a man who abandons his ego, unlike you, who admire those who reach the top." Yet the movie, along with Martin Scorsese's *Kundun* (also see *Frontline* 1998a), played a crucial role in highlighting Tibet in the Western popular imagination. It brought to the attention of consumers of Hollywood that there is/was a place called Tibet. The film adaptation of *Seven Years in Tibet* follows a certain shift within Exotica Tibet—a conflation of the Dalai Lama with Tibet. While Tibet was clearly a set for an adventure for Harrer in the book, Brad Pitt as Harrer in the film is more humble and self-conscious, and the figure of the young Dalai Lama is particularly prominent.

4

The West and the Identity of "Tibet"

Tibet as it emerged in the modern world as a geopolitical entity has been scripted in a tale combining imperialism, Orientalism, and nationalism. This chapter foregrounds the role of Western representations in the framing of the "identity of Tibet," that is, Tibet as a geopolitical entity. The West is not seen as an outsider in the "Tibet question" but as a constituent part of it. Specific Western conceptualizations of territoriality, practices of imperial diplomacy, and contemporary foreign policies have constructed the "Tibet" within the "Tibet question."[1] Through a historical analysis of the crucial role played by British imperialism in the framing of the Tibet question in terms of sovereignty and independence, this chapter brings into relief the constitutive relation between the discourse of sovereignty and the practice of representation. It argues that Tibet is not some prediscursive geographical entity but a place that is discursively constructed through imaginative practices of the various actors involved.[2] The chapter also briefly explores ways in which popular imaginations of Tibet have impacted the foreign policy of prominent Western states toward Tibet since the Chinese takeover in 1951.

The contemporary Chinese claim over Tibet is based on a version of Chinese history that sees the present-day nation-state as a successor to a longer history of Chinese civilization marked by a number of imperial phases. Tibet was historically linked with various

Chinese empires and therefore the Chinese deem it part of modern China. What the exact nature of Tibet was within different empires in China is not considered a crucial factor, for what is important is that Tibet was subordinate to the Sino-centric empires. It is this historical subservience that underpins the argument asserting Chinese sovereignty over Tibet *forever*. On the other hand, Tibetans have argued that "Tibet was an independent, sovereign nation when the armies of the People's Republic of China ('PRC') entered Tibet in 1950. Tibet at that time presented all the attributes of statehood" (TPPRC 2000, 1). They seek to explain the traditional Sino-Tibetan relations in terms of principles that are not transferable into the modern notion of sovereignty. The personal, religious, and ambiguous nature of Sino-Tibetan relations is ridden roughshod over by the modern concept of sovereignty—China *never* had sovereignty over Tibet. All sides (Tibetans less so than the others) underplay the fact that sovereignty talk itself is alien to the traditional modes of interaction in the Sino-Tibetan world (Sperling 2004; see also Constantinou 1998).

The status of Tibet vis-à-vis China before 1951 has been articulated in terms of various concepts, including sovereignty, suzerainty, independence, indirect rule, autonomy, vassalage, protectorate, overlordship, and colony (for a range of views, see Chiu and Dreyer 1989; Government of Tibet in Exile n.d.; Petech 1950; Norbu 1990; Shakabpa 1984; Smith 1996; Van Praag 1987; Wang Jiawei and Nyima Gyaincain 1997; Wang Lixiong 2002). However, for the most part, it is sovereignty that is asserted and contested. On the one hand, the Chinese state marshals arguments buttressing its historical claim of sovereignty over Tibet; on the other, Tibetan exiles and their supporters make counter claims and assert that Tibet was for all practical purposes independent from China. Though both sides mobilize history to make their claims, the concept of sovereignty is often left unproblematized. This is not surprising as sovereignty is an "essentially uncontested concept" (Walker 1990, 159; for different perspectives on sovereignty, see Bartelson 1995; Biersteker and Weber 1996; Hannum 1990; Hinsley 1986; Hoffman 1998; James 1986; Krasner 1999; Shinoda 2000; Weber 1995).

Crucially, the revolutionary communist regime that took over China in 1949 had no qualms about staking claims in Tibet based on a debatable imperial legacy, which it had denounced in other spheres. There was no radical break from the past in making assertions over the boundary of China. The Chinese, who during the nineteenth century rejected the Western mode of international relations as alien, exerted their control over Tibet after 1950 using the absolutist modern European conception of sovereignty. Importantly, in the process it also ignored the different worldviews within which the Mongol and Manchu emperors interacted with Tibet (see Klieger 1994; Norbu 1990; Shakya 1999). Unlike the British, who used "suzerainty" and "autonomy" to designate Sino-Tibetan relations, since 1905 the Chinese have consistently argued that China's position is that of a sovereign and not a suzerain (see Carlson 2004, 2005). At the beginning of the twenty-first century, even though there is no space for "suzerainty" within international law and politics and all the states recognize the Chinese claim of "sovereignty" over Tibet, the pro-Tibet lobby contests this affirmation of sovereignty by highlighting the difference between suzerainty and sovereignty within international law. As Oppenheim argued: "Suzerainty is by no means sovereignty. It is a kind of international guardianship, since the vassal State is either absolutely or mainly represented internationally by the suzerain State" (in Van Praag 1987, 107).

IMPERIALISM AND THE CONSTRUCTION OF MODERN TIBET

The genealogy of the modern idea of sovereignty as it was transplanted in the non-Western world reveals its close connection with European imperialism. Until the first half of the twentieth century, the international community of states was based on a double standard. While the "civilized" world (read as Europe, and later the United States and Japan) had a right to sovereign statehood, the rest of the world was open to various forms of imperial control. The "[d]egree of civilisation necessary to maintain international relations was considered as one of the conditions for statehood" (Hannum 1990, 16). The Tibetan example is typical of how imperial efforts throughout the non-European world were empowered by Western understandings of the non-Western states. Not only did imperial powers actively delegitimize non-Western modes of political interaction but they refused to recognize the intricacies of non-Western interstate relations (see Strang 1996). Within this context, at the beginning of the twentieth century, the traditional Sino-Tibetan relationship was considered by the British to be "irrational" and lacking legitimacy because it did not conform to the modern European ideas of diplomacy. For a large part of the nineteenth century, to the British in India, Tibet was a "forbidden land" ruled by "strange lamas" under some form of Chinese political control. While some, including Bogle, named this control "sovereignty" (Markham 1876, 195), most used the terms "overlordship" or "suzerainty." In one of the first European accounts, the Christian missionary Ippolito Desideri saw Tibet as part of the "Chinese dominion" (De Filippi 1932, 165). On the other hand, Fathers Huc (1982/1851) and Gabet, the "Lamas of the Western Heaven," in the middle of the nineteenth century described the Chinese rule as "nominal" (in Nish 1995, 294). This recognition of Chinese political dominance was based on the presence of Imperial *amban* (resident) and troops in Lhasa, the role of the Manchu emperors in the recognition of the Dalai Lama and the Panchen Lama, and the Tibetan refusal to articulate Tibet's status in modern terms.

Due to their own familiarity with feudalism and with the Chinese international system of tributary relations (Wiggins 1995), it is not surprising that the British interpreted the Sino-Tibetan relations in terms of suzerainty and a protectorate system. British policy toward Tibet was shaped by conflicting dynamics including the infeasibility of direct colonization, the security of British India's northern frontiers, the conceptualization of Tibet as a buffer state with a strategic location (see McKay 2003), British commercial interests in the Chinese empire, shifting alliances within Europe, and the like (see Norbu 1990). These conflicting interests shifted over time.

Tibet as outside the Modern Geopolitical Imaginary

In the eighteenth century, Tibet was seen as a possible backdoor to China as well as a potential trading partner.[3] There were a few Europeans (mostly Christian missionaries) who had traveled and lived in Tibet and Lhasa before and after the British attempts to establish a relationship in the second half of the eighteenth century. While their accounts fed into the image of Tibet held by the British, their role was merely to arouse curiosity. The main focus of expanding British colonialism was on exploring the possibility of commercial interactions (see Cammann 1951). Even before the first-ever official attempt to establish relations with Tibet through George Bogle, the following observation was made about Tibet (in the Extract of Bengal Secret Consultations of 9 May 1774): "They are represented as a quiet people numerous and *industrious,* living under a well regulated Government, having considerable intercourse with other Nations, particularly with the Chinese & Northern Tartars, and possessing at home the principal means of Commerce, Gold and Silver in great abundance" (IOR: H/219 1768-84, 336; emphasis added).

This view is bolstered by Bogle (in Markham 1876) as well as Turner (1971/1800). Both official travelers to Tibet also made observations about Chinese influence in Tibet. Bogle in a letter in February 1775 mentions that while Teshoo Lama was influential, the real seat of government was Lhasa, and the "Emperor of China is paramount sovereign"; in another letter he further clarifies:

> The Emperor of China is acknowledged the sovereign of the country, the appointment to the first officers in the state is made by his orders, and in all measures of consequences, reference is first made to the court at Pekin, but the internal government of the country is committed entirely to natives, the Chinese in general are confined to the capital, no tribute is extracted, and the people of Thibet except at Lahasa, hardly feel the weight of a *foreign yoke.* (IOR: H/219 1768–84, 354, 397–98; emphasis added)

Turner, in a letter dated 2 March 1784, points out that in Tibet there is an "acknowledgement of the supremacy of the Chinese government" (IOR: H/219 1768–84, 485). But there was no serious attempt to name Sino-Tibetan relations in precise terms. Representations of Tibet did not feed into political actions. There could be various explanations for why British imperialists did not seek to define Tibet at this moment. The empire in India itself was in the process of initial expansion and consolidation. Large parts of Asia and Africa remained outside European control and hence were seen as open space for inquiry. Tibet did not hold any special value. For the British, India and China did.

The nineteenth century witnessed a closure of Tibet to the Europeans. Some travelers did manage to get in (see Woodcock 1971), but there was no official interaction between Tibet and the rising and consolidating British empire in India. By the end of nineteenth century, British India had within itself the cis-Himalayan regions of Ladakh, Bhutan, Sikkim, and Assam, some of which in turn had politico-religious relations with Tibet. Tibet saw these regions as under its influence. For British India this had a dangerous implication for the security of its northern frontiers and hence required clarity. But within the traditional Tibetan worldview, there was no imperative to define boundaries. McGranahan identifies five key features that made traditional Tibetan systems of statehood differ-ent from modern European systems: local determination and sanc-tioning of boundaries; sovereignty and boundary not coterminous; overlapping zones between polities; no imperative for an external ratification of rules; and privileging of power relationships between territory and center over territorial integrity (2003, 268).

Observations by Indian spies who had been active in the second half of the century pointed to continuing Chinese dominance. For instance, Sarat Chandra Das, who managed to reach Lhasa in dis-guise in the 1880s, argued that the "political relations between Tibet and China are now so intimate that the Imperial Residency estab-lished at Lhasa in the first quarter of the last century has converted Tibet from a protected state into a dependency of China" (1902, 178). But Tibetans refused to honor any Anglo-Chinese agreement concerning them without justifying their action by using a modern vocabulary of sovereignty or independence.

The British blamed this on the backwardness of Tibetan reli-gion, narrow priestly interests, Chinese jealousy, and a lack of under-standing of genuine friendly motives of the British (see Engelhardt 2002). The *Times* reported in 1885, "We hear complaints every-where of the stagnation of trade. Here is a large market if we only insist on admission . . . Tibetans . . . are debarred from intercourse with India through sheer ignorance and the tenacity of tradition" (in Walker 1885, 27). Macaulay in his 1884 report blamed Cornwallis, who had succeeded Hastings as the governor-general of the East India Company, for not helping Tibetans in the Gorkha war in 1792 and thus contributing to their "closed" nature; he laments that had Hastings been in charge, he "would have required no pretext [for military action] beyond the fact that an unprovoked act of brigand-age had been committed on *a helpless child*" (1972, 71; emphasis added). Paternal imperialism prevented the actors of the time to comprehend Tibetan actions in terms of fear deriving from an under-standing of the violence of modern imperialism. Aris, on the basis of his study of a late-eighteenth-century Tibetan text, argues that a positive sympathy can be detected for the undefeated Marathas and their long oppositional stand against both the Mughals and the British (1994, 12)—this surely indicates some awareness among Tibetans of the nature of imperialism in India.

By the start of the twentieth century, the undefined Tibet was no longer an unmapped land to the north of the Himalayas but had come to be perceived as a buffer state, a state that could act as a buffer against the new threat on the horizon—Russian imperial expansion in Central Asia.[4] Tibet acquired new importance within the "Great Game," and the British sought to have a friendly state to buffer British India from hostile forces in the north. Chinese imperial power was in decline and seen more as a nuisance.

Filling in the Blank Space

At the start of the twentieth century, there were two phases in British India's policy toward Tibet, the watershed being Curzon's telegram of 8 January 1903. In the first phase, Curzon unsuccessfully tried a policy of direct approach, that is, of communicating with the Dalai Lama. That "the Dalai Lama had the temerity, one had almost say the cheek, to return the Indian Grand Mughal's letters unopened was sufficient cause, in Curzon's eyes, for a march to Lhasa, if only to show the Tibetan barbarians some elementary rules of human behaviour, of a code of (international) conduct!" (Mehra 1968, 360). Curzon pushed for a more active, confrontational policy.

The British Indian government informed the Home government, in a letter dated 13 February 1902,

> The policy of isolation followed by the Tibetans is not compatible either with proximity to the territories of *a great civilised power* at whose hands the Tibetan Government enjoys the fullest opportunities both for intercourse and trade, or with due respect for the treaty stipulations into which the Chinese Government has entered on its behalf (IOR: V Cd.1920 [1904], 153; emphasis added)

The result of this new forward policy was the mission led by Francis Younghusband in 1903–4. In fact, this mission not only showed Tibetans their place in the imperial scheme of things but also emplaced Tibet in the modern geopolitical imaginary.

In his famous dispatch of 8 January 1903, Curzon mentions his two failed attempts (the third attempt was being made) to get in personal touch with the Dalai Lama; the failure of measures to "materially" improve British position on the border; persistent rumors about the Russo-Chinese deal; and his own conviction that "some sort of relations" existed between Russia and Tibet, changing the scenario:

We regard the so-called suzerainty of China over Tibet as a consti-
tutional fiction—a political affectation which has only been maintained because of its convenience to both parties. China is always
ready to break down the barriers of ignorance and obstruction, to
open Tibet to the civilizing influence of trade, but her pious wishes
are defeated by the short-sighted stupidity of the Lamas. In the same
way, Tibet is only too anxious to meet our advances, but she is prevented from doing so by the despotic veto of the suzerain. This solemn farce has been re-enacted with the frequency that seems never to
deprive it of its attractions or its power to impose. (IOR: V Cd.1920
[1904], 154–55)

Many other British Indian officials agreed with Curzon's view
of Chinese control as mere "tutelage" (Sandberg 1904, 13). Charles
Cock's memorandum in 1903 pointed out that "China is a hopeless
factor" that had "no real hold over Tibet, and was only made use of
by the Tibetans as an excuse for not communicating directly" with
the British (IOR: L/P&S/18/B144 1903, 41). But there were dissenting voices too. For instance, Curzon's position went against the
observations made about de jure Chinese authority in a memorandum written by William Lee-Warner in 1902, arguing that the 1890
Convention "practically recognises Chinese sovereignty over Tibet,"
and after the rumors of a Russian protectorate over Tibet, "We have
warned China, thus again recognising Chinese sovereignty" (IOR:
L/P&S/18/B138 1902, 23).

Dissenting voices were ignored, the mission was sent, and as
Tibetans continued to resist British demands for opening up negotiations, the mission forced its way to Lhasa. The Dalai Lama fled but
the Tibetan government was forced to sign the Lhasa Convention,
a treaty that was described by Candler as "the result of an impression, upon the least impressionable People in the world" (in IOR:
MSS EUR/F197/108 n.d., 3). Even though Curzon rejected Chinese
control as a fiction unhelpful to a modern civilized power such as
British India, the Lhasa treaty signed at the end of the invasion did
not indicate a defining of Tibet in terms of independence.[5] This
is understandable, for the British government was by now clearly
averse to "any policy in Tibet which would tend to throw on the
British Empire an additional burden" (IOR: MSS EUR/F197/106,
46). In a speech delivered on the signing of the Lhasa Convention on
7 September 1904, Younghusband mentioned "Chinese suzerainty"
even though it was not included in any written text:

The Convention has been signed. . . . In the Convention the British Government have been careful to avoid interfering in the smallest degree with your religion. They have annexed no part of your country. They have made no attempt to interfere in your internal affairs. They fully recognise the continued suzerainty of the Chinese Government. . . . You have found us bad enemies when you have not observed treaty obligations and shown disrespect to the British Representative. You will find us equally good friends if you keep the present treaty and show civility. (Ibid., 271)

Tibet was forcefully brought into the international arena. Campbell points out in a memorandum dated 5 April 1906 that the *Amban* representing the Qing imperial authority refused to sign the Anglo-Tibetan Convention in 1904 on the ground that it "robbed China of her suzerainty" and because the Chinese objected to the British "making any Convention with Tibet" (IOR: L/P&S/18/B157 1906, 178). In fact, Britain signed an Adhesion Agreement with China in 1906 as a follow-up to the Lhasa Convention.

This forced opening of Tibet had significant geopolitical impact as it led to an increased Chinese awareness of vulnerability at its "backdoor" (see Liming 1994; Tuttle 2005). Ironically, the Chinese central government sought to establish firm control over Tibet (first during the immediate aftermath of British invasion, and then from 1949 onward), ignoring its own history of a more loosely defined relationship with Tibet. In an official memorandum titled "Events in China, Korea and Siam, 1908," the change in Chinese stance is recognized unambiguously: "One clear result of her recent policy respecting the Dalai Lama is that China has officially proclaimed herself the Sovereign Power of Thibet, and can no longer evade the full responsibilities of its government" (in Nish 1995, 291). One can therefore see the Sino-Tibetan 1951 Seventeen Point Agreement and the events since then as completing what had been implemented initially in 1908 but was interrupted due to a civil war within China. The Dalai Lama's pleas for help from the British against new aggressive Chinese invasion were not accommodated, even though he appealed to the paternal aspect of British imperialism:

At such a time, when a big and powerful nation is trying to swallow up a smaller and weaker nation, we cannot help appealing to other powerful nations for aid and assistance, which the law of nations should make you feel bound to grant us, being impelled by regard for the duty imposed by the dignity, power and justice of your Mighty Empire. (IOR: L/P&S/10/150 2750 5-7 1908, 24)

However, the collapse of the Qing Imperial dynasty and internal crisis in China offered Tibet the opportunity to remove Chinese troops and establish a state free of Chinese political dominance. Even though the Lamaist state (1913–51) enjoyed de facto independence, there was no serious attempt to recognize it as independent.

Writing the "Chinese Suzerainty–Tibetan Autonomy" Formula

The British throughout the first part of the twentieth century stuck to the formula—Chinese suzerainty–Tibetan autonomy. In a memorandum of 17 August 1912, the British government clarified its stance: "While recognising the Chinese suzerainty, they were not prepared to admit the right of China to interfere in the internal administration of Tibet" (Foreign Office 1920, 41). Thus, "Outer Tibet would become an autonomous state under Chinese suzerainty and British protectorate" (ibid., 43).

The desire not to let support for Tibetan autonomy be interpreted as support for Tibetan independence is reflected in a letter of the India Office dated 11 July 1912 clarifying the British position on Tibet. It was modified internally before being presented to the outside world and stated:

> (1) His Majesty's Government, while they have formally recognised the "suzerain rights" of China in Tibet, have never recognised, and are not prepared to recognise, ~~Chinese sovereignty over that country.~~
> ~~(2) H. M.'s Govt. does not admit~~ the right of China to intervene actively in the internal administration of Tibet. (IOR: L/P&S/10/265 1912, 47)[6]

Even when Morley was projecting the British as an "honest broker" in the Simla Talks (BOD MS Asquith 93 1913, 235), the British did not really care about the suzerainty-sovereignty issue so long as their interests were being met. In a secret memorandum dated 3 December 1924, J. P. Gibson made it clear:

> The Tibetan desire to come to a permanent settlement with China is reasonable; but I doubt whether the Govt of India will allow Major Bailey to say that they will approach the Chinese Govt at the first favourable opportunity . . . so long as no Chinese attack is made on

the Tibetan frontier, *we would much prefer to let sleeping dogs lie.*
(IOR: L/P&S/10/718 1917, 74; emphasis added).

As Willoughby pointed out, Chinese "suzerainty (however shadowy)
has been constantly admitted by us" (1924, 199). Colonel Weir's
recommendation to make "friendly overtures" to China to secure
at least "semi-independence" for Tibet was rejected because, as a
British Indian bureaucrat cautioned in 1929, there was the "danger
of China being baited into action" if "we flaunt our connection with
Tibet in her eyes" (IOR: L/P&S/10/1113 1924, 15, 151). Of course,
this simple British policy formula was a contested one. There were
tensions between British India emphasizing Tibetan autonomy and
British Home government in London exercising caution under the
influence of Foreign Office (see McGranahan 2003; McKay 1997;
Palace 2005). But even pro-Tibetan British officials, who tried to
create a sense of nationalism among Tibetans (see McKay 2001),
were careful in not encouraging Tibetan assertion of de jure independence. Chapman wrote in 1940, "We do not want to encourage
the Tibetans to become once more a warlike nation; but in these
days a country must be able to defend itself, and it has always been
our policy to assist Tibet to maintain her position as an independent
autonomous State under the nominal suzerainty of China" (1992,
110). In a letter dated 23 March 1912, the Viceroy had argued that
for the security of British India the "geographical position of Tibet
renders it absolutely necessary [that the] country should continue [to
be] *kept in state of political isolation*" (IOR: L/P&S/10/265 1912;
emphasis added). Here, Exotica Tibet was a good ally for the British
imperial policy. A "forbidden kingdom," the "mysterious Tibet,"
and "closed Tibet"—these representations suited British interests for
they effectively depoliticized the British imperial writing of Tibet's
geopolitical identity in ambiguous terms. Ambiguity of geopolitical
Tibet, nurtured by Exotica Tibet, was an asset for the British imperial policy.

Britain found the scenario of effectively independent Tibet coupled with British international rhetorical commitment to Chinese
suzerainty convenient and avoided any change to this status quo so
as not to offend China. For instance, in February 1917 in response
to the India Office's letter demanding a vigorous protest at the inclu-
sion of Tibet in the Chinese parliament, the Foreign Office wrote on
behalf of Balfour:

The Chinese Government are extremely sensitive on the subject of the Tripartite Convention of 1914. That they have any intention of signing that instrument there is no reason to believe nor do His Majesty's Government possess at the present moment any means of forcing them to do so. It would therefore appear that a protest so strongly worded as that suggested would serve no purpose *but would, on the other hand, produce extreme irritation in the Chinese Government and Parliament* at a moment when China is particularly well disposed towards this country and is even contemplating throwing in her lot with the Allied cause. (IOR: L/P&S/11/68 1913; emphasis added)

As a stable government in China emerged with the communist victory and the British withdrew from India, the "Chinese suzerainty–Tibetan autonomy" formula had reached a dead end. As pointed out earlier, China since the start of the twentieth century had always maintained its sovereignty over Tibet, and now it was in a military position to enforce it and "liberate" Tibet. The British, with the end of the empire in India, no longer conceptualized Tibet as strategic. India, with its anti-imperialist nationalism, saw Tibet as a remnant of British imperialism in the region (Norbu 1997). The belated Tibetan attempts to gain international support for a recognition of their independent status in the late 1940s came to nothing (see Shakya 1999; see also Fleck 1995) as "Tibet's" geopolitical identity got translated from *suzerainty*-autonomy to *sovereignty*-autonomy. Sautman argues that there is nothing exceptional about the Tibetan case, for "long suzerainty provides the basis for territorial sovereignty in relation to other states" (2002, 93). Whatever the international rights and wrongs of this translation, it is clear that the use of the modern conception of sovereignty was new and alien to traditional Sino-Tibetan relations (see Sperling 2004).

DELEGITIMIZING TRADITIONAL SINO-TIBETAN "INTERNATIONAL" RELATIONS

The failure of the British to understand the existing complex Sino-Tibetan relations had as much to do with their heady faith in the superiority of European norms as with their conflicting interests in the region. Where does this leave indigenous modes of interaction between China and Tibet? The "intent expressed by both sides through this relationship was not founded on the present-day under standing of sovereignty and interstate relations, influenced for the most part by the West" (Schmitz 2004, 48). The nature of the Tibetan state was interlinked with Sino-Tibetan relations.

Traditionally, political actors interpreted and understood their interstate relations in vocabularies familiar to them. Sino-Tibetan intercourse was no exception. The same relations could have been understood by the Chinese imperial officials in Confucian tributary terms and by the Tibetans as Buddhist *mchod-yon*. This does not validate the primacy of either worldview but reveals the complexity of the issue involved. Grounding the interaction in some universally accepted terms was unnecessary within the Chinese as well as the Tibetan worldview.

Personal, moral, religious, and political overtones were a significant part of the relations. While some have argued that *mchod-yon*, "patron-priest relations," was the main characteristic of the Sino-Tibetan world (see Klieger 1994), others have clarified that this was more about personal relationships between rulers and not about statehood (see Barnett 1999). Shakya points out that the concept indicates that the Tibetans viewed the Chinese emperor only as a secular institution, which is far from the case—Manchu emperors, for instance, were often referred to as Jampeyang Gongma, the incarnation of Manjushri, defining them not as merely secular patrons but as occupying a space within a Buddhist pantheon exercising some measure of secular authority in Tibet (1999, xxiii). The link between China's imperial dynasty and Tibet had a pronounced religious character and

> is an example of the purely Central Asia concept of Patron and Priest in which the temporal support of the lay power is given in return for the spiritual support of the religious power. . . . It is an elastic and flexible idea and not to be rendered in the cut-and-dried terms of modern western politics. There is no precise definition of the supremacy of one or the subordination of the other; and the practical meaning of the relationship can only be interpreted in the light of the facts of the moment. (Richardson, in Addy 1984, 27)

However, it is clear from observations of all nineteenth-century commentators and travelers that there was a definite political dimension to the relation too. Political dominance by the Chinese imperial dynasty was founded on a military supremacy even though

for the most part China did not assert its dominance in politico-
military terms. And throughout modern history, the relationship
evolved depending on the internal and external situation in Tibet.
Sperling argues rightly that it is a fallacy to underplay the political
dominance entailed within the concept of *mchod-yon* (2004). Li
points out that "the patronage relationship between China and
Tibet in a Buddhistic sense is not comparable to any Western system
and no exact equivalent can be found in Western terminology. At
least, the Chinese part as a patron, who is supposed to give and not
to take, should not be construed as a sign of weakness or as a sort of
bribery" (1954, 215–16).

And yet, the patron derived a lot of symbolic resources from its
priest. Tibetan Buddhism, with the support of senior Tibetan lamas,
was seen as a sobering and controlling factor and a useful ally in
the diverse Qing empire. And at the same time, the Qing imperial
dynasty saw the Tibetan religious hierarchy as coreligionists and
hence the senior lamas as integral to its own well-being. Tibet was
a tributary state but it was a special one because of the charismatic
lamas' dominant influence in Buddhist Central Asia (Norbu 1990).

The "confusion" about Sino-Tibetan relations arises partly out
of the nature of the Tibetan state. It was not a state in the modern
European sense simply because it was *not* a modern European state.
The model of sovereign statehood that is the dominant vocabulary
for collective political self-expression today is a product of decades
of violent scripting upon the shifting sands of diverse and ambiguous
political communities. Traditional Tibet could not be cartographi-
cally and geopolitically mapped in modern times without recourse
to epistemic and military coercion. This is what happened through
the activities of European imperialism and then modern Chinese
state making. McGranahan rightly argues that the traditional Tibet
state did not conform to either the "colonial model" or the "united
model" (as claimed by the Tibetan government in exile) but was
a "contested" state that, if mapped, would "have to be a series of
maps demonstrating change over time, and including the 'hard' lines
of modern nation-states, graphical indication of contested territo-
ries, and gradual shading to designate areas of stronger and weaker
connections to Lhasa, as well as the historically expansive borders
of Tibet" (2003, 287).

The strangeness of Tibet as a state was not a result of the odd, irrational, fantastic, mystical, Tibetan way of being. In fact, there was nothing "strange" about Tibet. It was the universalization of specific particularistic European ideas through imperialism and decolonization that rendered the Tibetan state as strange and different and an anomaly by 1950. In his detailed study of the Tibetan state, Samuel reveals that "Tibet was a society that combined the literacy and rationality that we associate with centralized states with the subtle exploitation of shamanic processes more familiar from stateless and tribal peoples" (1993, 577; see also Samuel 1982, 1994).

This does not mean there was no Tibet before British imperialism and then the modern Chinese state constructed it. There certainly was the place of Tibet (even though it was not called as such), which had its own lived, competing, and complex histories and realities. But it could not be easily translatable into modern politico-legalistic terms. Even when China had "the upper hand" (Bataille 1992, 33), Tibet "enjoyed local autonomy over domestic matters" (Grunfeld 1987, 57), and more significantly, on the basis of simple experienced reality, Tibetans considered themselves not to be a part of China (Barnett 1999). The use of "Tibetan" as a category as different from "Chinese" itself may be a commentary on the separate Tibetan identity. While not being clear about the boundaries of Tibet, all foreign travelers seem to find it easy to differentiate between Tibetans and Chinese (for instance, Pratt 1892).

What Ward wrote in 1941 is an indicator of the alienness of the modern European conception of distinct geopolitical identity in the Tibetan context:

> The Tibetans are a realistic people. They do not understand trigonometry. But they have solid understanding of their own culture, and its natural environment. So while the India government talks . . . about a natural frontier based on the position of peaks in relation to one another and to remote astral bodies, the Tibetan walks over the passes and descends the India side of the Assam Himalayas until he reaches a point where trees of a certain kind cease, or crops of a certain kind fail, or where the summer temperature is too high for him, or there are too many flies. That, to him, is the natural frontier of Tibet. It is slightly fluid, and vague, and it bears no relation to the stars; but it is practical. There he stops, and marks the spot by building, not a fort, but a monastery to the greatest glory of his religion. (BOD MS Or. Aris 18 n.d., 232–33)

However, the traditional fuzzy setup of the Tibetan state and Sino-Tibetan relations became problematic when the sociocultural and political environment was altered. This occurred first with the arrival of Western colonial powers in Asia and second with the transformation of the traditional Confucian-dominated Chinese polity toward a more Europeanized political system, which produced Republican China and the growth of Chinese nationalism (Shakya 1999, xxiii). Since the early twentieth century, as the Chinese learned the modern European diplomatic language, they began to assert their relationship in terms of sovereignty. Tibetans, on the other hand, were late in adjusting to the modern world and refused to comply with treaties between British India and China concerning Tibet.

Thus, it was a "forceful interpretation of Sino-Tibetan relations in terms of European international law and *praxis* of (British) imperialism" (Norbu 1990, 67; emphasis in original) that lies at the genesis of the Tibet question, not some intractable nationalist and historical conflict between the Chinese and the Tibetans. The Westernization of international relations made it inevitable that when China gained control over Tibet in 1951 there would no longer exist the traditional symbolic relationship but rather an absolute rule. For the first time in its history, through the Seventeen Point Agreement,[7] Tibet acknowledged Chinese sovereignty in writing, leaving no space for an ambiguous term like "suzerainty." The internationalization of the Westphalian international order based on sovereign statehood had a differential effect on Tibet and China—it allowed the regional hegemon (China) to assert and exercise control over Tibet.

TIBET'S CURRENT STATUS: A WESTERN IMPERIAL LEGACY

Tibet, which as a political entity operated with other external powers (especially Mongols and Hans) on principles such as patron-client relations and *chos srid gnyis ldan* (politics and religion combined; see Burman 1979; Kolas 1996),[8] has become yet another victim of modern ideas such as territorial sovereignty and the separation of religion and the state. This raises the question of the relevance of the European model of the nation-state for many parts of the non-Western world. Present-day international politics ensures that claims to independence are afforded more recognition when stated in terms of the nineteenth-century European ideal of the nation-state under a nationally representative government (Samuel 1993,

143). This makes the task of the Tibetans more difficult as Tibet was never a centralized nation-state. The closest it came to the European model was between 1913 and 1951, but the lamaist state failed to become a modern state (Goldstein 1989) or to be recognized as such (Shakya 1999).

The extrapolation of Western ideas in a situation where people operated by way of a totally different worldview has facilitated the victimization of communities like the Tibetans. Developments during the era of imperialism have serious ramifications in many parts of the contemporary world. Conventional IR that has ignored the history and politics of imperialism (by considering it to be a legitimate area of inquiry primarily for imperial history) is therefore not well suited to provide a contextual understanding of such international problems as the Tibet question. For an effective analysis of the debate over the historical status of Tibet, critical international theories could contribute to the historicization of the concept of sovereignty, while postcolonialism can help bare its linkage with imperialism.

EXOTICA TIBET AND THE DEPOLITICIZATION OF THE TIBET QUESTION

What the above discussion of the historical writing of Tibet in the modern geopolitical imaginary reveals are the mutually constitutive relations between representations and imperialism, knowledge and power. Exotica Tibet was not confined to the cultural sphere. For instance, the accounts of British Indian officials like Charles Bell and Hugh Richardson show that their "more prosaic view did not destroy this exotic representation but tacitly encouraged it" (McKay 1997, 207). Prevalent attitudes toward Tibet often reflected contemporary political preoccupations. As discussed earlier, during the Younghusband invasion most British writings depicted a despicable state of affairs within Tibet. Then came a shift toward a positive exoticization (see Hansen 1996). Bell's writings played an important role in transforming the image of Tibet in the West in the 1920s and 1930s. Tibetan Buddhism (more commonly known as Lamaism) was seen in a new context. For instance, Shuttleworth points out, "After reading Sir Charles' book [The Religion of Tibet], one comes to realize that something of the pure flame of Buddhism still lights up the Tibetan Church, and that Lamaism is more than a museum of dead, grotesque monstrosities, that serves no purpose except to provide a livelihood for its priestly custodians" (IOR: MSS EUR/ D722/18 n.d.).

Romantic paternalism continued to mark the representations of Tibet even after World War II (see Klieger 2006). For instance, the U.S. War Department in 1947 could envisage only two possible uses for Tibet: "as a country offering great waste areas in which rockets could be tested, or as a final retreat (Shangri-la) to which peace-loving people could flee when atomic war breaks, for Tibet is too remote to be of significance in any war" (in Knaus 1999, 26; see also Laird 2002; Margolis 2000; Peissel 1972).[9]

Exotica Tibet, especially in the second half of the twentieth century, has disproportionately emphasized Tibetan religiosity, which has led to the sidetracking of the political question of the status of Tibet. Let us note the shifts in the wordings of the United Nations resolutions passed with regard to Tibet. In November 1950, El Salvador submitted a draft resolution to the UN General Assembly that clearly recognized Tibet as a historically independent state. The draft resolution opened: "Taking note that the peaceful nation of Tibet has been invaded, without any provocation on its part, by foreign forces" (*International Campaign for Tibet* 2006). But no discussion was carried out as Britain, India, and the United States asked for deferment in the hope of a peaceful resolution. This was the only instance of a clear attempt on the part of a state to raise the issue of Tibet in unambiguously political terms. The three resolutions subsequently passed by the General Assembly tended to emphasize Tibet's uniqueness, its cultural and religious life, and the human rights of Tibetans. European countries did not want Tibet to be raised as an issue in the UN for fear that it might set a precedent for their colonies (Shakya 1999, 221). The United States did not want to offend Nationalist China. India saw Tibet mostly as a thorn in the side of Sino-Indian relations. Communist states supported Chinese rights of sovereignty. It therefore comes as no surprise that the resolutions passed regarding Tibet in the UN General Assembly were sponsored by small countries seen as internationally insignificant. And even here, the language was usually tempered. Resolution 1353 (XIV), apart from other UN principles, "*mindful also* of the distinctive cultural and religious heritage of the people of Tibet and of the autonomy which they have traditionally enjoyed" (emphasis in original), affirmed respect in the Charter and called "for the respect for the fundamental human rights of the Tibetan people and for their *distinctive cultural and religious life*" (General Assembly 1959; emphasis added). The sponsors, Ireland and Malaya, clarified in their opening statements that the resolution was based not on the political aspect of Tibet's status but on the violation of human rights only (Shakya 1999, 228–29). The 1961 Resolution 1723 (XVI), in contrast, did mention the "right to self-determination" (General Assembly 1961), but the 1965 Resolution 2079 (XX) focused on violation of human rights. Thereafter, with the changing dynamic of China's relations with Western states as well as other nonaligned states, Tibet as an issue did not evoke interest among states.

With the Sino-American rapprochement in the 1970s, little was heard about the destruction of traditional life within Tibet, which intensified during the Cultural Revolution. But considerable attention was paid to the Tibet question when other communist regimes fell in Eastern Europe and the discourse of human rights emerged on the international plane. The linkage of the Tibet question to the West's political interests may be unsurprising, but if we are to address the Tibet question effectively, we need to move beyond conventional international politics with its emphasis on realpolitik and sovereign statehood. For the existence of a "Tibet question" on the international plane is less political and more cultural fascination for Tibet in many parts of the world, and due to the personal appeal of the Dalai Lama (Sautman and Lo 1995, 1). The recent high international profile for the Tibet question is not a result of states "rediscovering" Tibet but rather of nonstate actors becoming international actors. It is connected with transnational movements that are seen as increasingly challenging the international system that solely privileges nation-states.

CONCLUSION

Contemporary international politics privileges sovereign statehood. Broadly speaking, there are two options available for those who are not already legally recognized members of the international society of sovereign nation-states. First is to present one's own histories and lived realities as a distinct historical reality that is in turn commensurate with the existing notion of the international. The second option is to challenge the given notion of the international as limited, unfair, and unhelpful and to push for alternative ways of being international that recognize the complexity of the world we live in. Diasporic Tibetans led by the Dalai Lama and their non-Tibetan sympathizers have experimented with both the options. They have used the dominant *realist* vocabulary of international relations— arguing for a historically independent quasi-national state of Tibet before the Chinese invasion in 1950. At the same time, they have also made use of more recent *nonrealist* concepts of human rights, trans-nationalism, environmentalism, and identity politics to challenge the Chinese control over Tibet. The nonrealist route has provided the Tibetan diaspora with means to foster a sense of Tibetanness and to acquire international publicity. In fact, the Tibet question as a problem of international politics would hardly have been noticed had it not been for high-profile support from nonstate actors. It is the *uniqueness* of Tibet that is seen as attracting global publicity for the "Free Tibet" or "Save Tibet" movement.

This uniqueness is a direct product of Exotica Tibet. While the strategy of mobilization of a unified Tibetan identity and support from the non-Tibetans has worked in terms of challenging the legitimacy of Chinese sovereignty over Tibet at the nonstate level, it has its own serious limitations. Lopez has put it bluntly: Tibetans are "prisoners of Shangri-la," captured within the Western images of Tibet and Tibetans as unique. Others have also criticized the focus on nonrealist tools such as human rights (Barnett 2001; Norbu 1998) as essentially depoliticizing and distracting from the main issue. The discourse of human rights and the image of Tibetans as uniquely religious allows for Western states to pay lip service to the call for protection of cultural and religious rights of Tibetans without questioning the broader issues of the Tibetan right to self-determination. Western state leaders who meet the Dalai Lama (for instance, the American president George W. Bush in May 2001; see CNN.com 2001), go to great lengths to explain that it is a private meeting with a religious leader. The Dalai Lama, as a political leader, has a smaller audience in the West. In the West, it is common to come across legislative branches of the government passing resolutions condemning Chinese policies in Tibet (see Barnett 1991) but executive branches going out of the way to assure China of their recognition of Chinese sovereignty.

The realist route is seen as the only realistic and effective one by those rightly skeptical of the depoliticizing move of human rights discourse as mobilized by Western states. Yet, as the next chapter argues in greater detail, it is unfair to blame the Tibetan diaspora for making use of the limited and limiting vocabularies of political expression. And to dismiss human rights as idealistic or "to criticize those who engage in the human rights discourse for the unseemly politicization of a set of ideals (two sides of the same realist paradigm), is to deny political agency to people" (Mountcastle 2006, 100). Either Tibetans challenge Chinese claims to sovereignty with their own alternative claims of independence based on historical and international legal sources, or they accept the reality of Chinese sovereignty and work within it to modify it, or they do both. Tibetans in diaspora have no option but to keep making their claims using the dominant realist vocabulary of nationalism, statehood, sovereignty, and independence while at the same time exploring emerging nonrealist norms of human rights to gain an international profile. In either case, the West as a political actor and even more crucially as a source of universalized ideas remains integral to the Tibet question.

5

The Politics of Tibetan
(Trans)National Identity

The epistemological model that offers us a pregiven subject or agent is
one that refuses to acknowledge that agency is always and only a political
prerogative.
—JUDITH BUTLER, *FEMINISTS THEORIZE THE POLITICAL*

Until the last decades of the twentieth century, the preoccupation
with religion and history contributed to a relative neglect of the issues of contemporary Tibetan identity within social and political
studies (see Shakya 1996). The signifier "Tibetan" is usually seen in
terms of an ontological essentialism.[1] This often leads to a papering
over of the socially constructed and politically contested nature of
Tibetan cultural and political identity, or "Tibetanness," as it may
conveniently be called (for different approaches, see Klieger 1994;
Korom 1997a, 1997b; Nowak 1984). This chapter, along with the
next, examines the articulations of Tibetanness in political and cultural spheres, argues for new ways of theorizing these identities, and
interrogates the constitutive role played by Exotica Tibet in these
identity discourses.

While acknowledging that the distinction between the cultural
and the political may be construed as depoliticizing culture and un-
culturing politics, I start by looking at cultural and political identities
separately for analytical purposes. At the same time, I highlight the
interlinkages between them. The study of cultural identity must be

a concern of IR and not relegated to anthropology or cultural studies for at least two reasons. First, the distinction between cultural
and political identity is blurred and at best problematic. Second, for
Tibetans living under occupation and in displacement, every expression of a distinct culture is a political act in itself.

For the purpose of studying the political and cultural facets of
Tibetanness, I experiment with two approaches. In this chapter, I
bring out the various dynamics, including interaction with the West,
that constitute Tibetanness as a national identity mainly, though not
exclusively, in the diaspora. In the next chapter, I examine the cultural expressions of diasporic Tibetans, highlight the role of Exotica
Tibet, and offer a new and innovative way of theorizing Tibetanness
with an emphasis on postcolonial symbolic geography and cultural
identity discourses.

Identity is not an essence but a performance, an articulation, a
discourse. Tibetanness is as much a process as it is a product—it
is a productive process. The performance of Tibetan identity does
not take place in a vacuum but in a power-laden international political and cultural environment. This international context, in turn,
is marked by asymmetries of structural and representational power
in which the West remains dominant. Tibetanness has to be articulated within this asymmetrical context and hence Western representational practices play a crucial role. This role is not merely an
embellishment; rather it is constitutive. At the same time, however,
instead of looking at Tibetanness as merely a product of Western
representations (Exotica Tibet) and Tibetans thus as "prisoners of
Shangri-la" (see Lopez 1998), we ought to acknowledge Tibetan collective agency. This agency is not in opposition to, and autonomous
from, representational discourses but very much a part of them. At
the same time, agency is not exhausted by any one particular representational discourse but is produced out of creative negotiations
with various discourses and interstitial spaces shared by them.

There are creative tensions within Tibetan identity articulations
and between these articulations and Exotica Tibet. How has Exotica
Tibet affected Tibetanness? What is the politics of Western representations of Tibet in terms of its impact on Tibetan cultural and
political identity? I raise these questions in this chapter and the next.
While the emphasis will be on the various facets of contemporary
identity articulations, the poetics of representation—Exotica Tibet

as outlined in previous chapters—will always be present, sometimes lurking in the background, sometimes coming to the forefront.

DIASPORA AND OTHERWISE

Two qualifying and clarifying points need to be made before I move on. First, I do not intend to cover all aspects of Tibetanness as articulated by Tibetans everywhere. In fact, my focus is on identity discourses circulating mainly within the Tibetan diaspora. These constitute a very small percentage of the total Tibetan population, as most Tibetans still live inside Tibet. The rationale for choosing to study the diaspora is primarily practical: there are limitations on researching in Tibet due to the sensitivities of the Chinese state. Within the diaspora, there is a deliberate focus on elite discourses as it is largely the elite that shape how Tibetanness is articulated both within Tibetan communities and for the outside world. This is symptomatic of most "national" groups, but the predominance of the figure of the Dalai Lama as the head of the Tibetan government-in-exile makes it even more so in the Tibetan case. This does not mean that popular articulations are mere copies of the elite discourses or that the Tibetans living within Tibet imitate discourses prevalent in the diaspora. While Tibetanness is a project of creating sameness, it is in fact difference, dynamism, and disjuncture that characterize it most.

Second, a clarification with regard to semantics is necessary. Why use the term "diaspora" when the terms "exile" and "refugee" have wider currency among Tibetans and analysts? Within the international legal regime, most of the Tibetans living in South Asia and Western countries are refugees, and Tibetans often perceive themselves to be political refugees. Within the Tibetan governmental and intellectual community, exile is a more favored term. While these terms continue to be popular, Tibetanists as well as the Tibetan elite themselves are increasingly adopting "diaspora" to make sense of Tibetan identity (see also Baumann 1997).

Within the fields of political and social studies, a diaspora is widely conceived as any segment of a people living outside their homeland. For instance, emphasizing the need to look at the triadic networks of homeland (or trans-state organization), host country, and ethnic diaspora, Sheffer writes, "Modern diasporas are ethnic minority groups of migrant origins residing and acting in host countries but maintaining a strong sentimental and material link with their countries of origin—their homeland" (1986, 3; see also Cohen 1997). The recognition of diasporas as important international actors is a big step forward in the field of international politics (otherwise dominated by studies of nation-states), even though we have to avoid taking basic terms such as "homeland," "identity," and "host land" as unproblematic. This allows us to appreciate the crucial role played by the Tibetan diaspora in highlighting the case of Tibet as a problem of international politics. Though this has had little impact on the conduct of states vis-à-vis China—not surprising, given that the international community is precisely a community of recognized nation-states, a status denied to Tibet—the Dalai Lama–led Tibetan diaspora is considered, rightly or wrongly (see Barnett 2006) as the legitimate speaker for the entire Tibetan population in the international arena. The story of the creation of the Tibetan community-in-exile illustrates the successful strategies of the Dalai Lama–led Tibetan government to foster and maintain a distinctive Tibetan national identity with a mix of religious, cultural, and political elements.

A more nuanced understanding of diaspora (see Brah 1996; Tololyan 1991, 1996; Vertovec 1997) conceptualizes diaspora less as a subcategory of the migrant community and more as a subjective understanding of the experience of migration. The use of the term "diaspora" indicates the adoption of new ways of approaching and understanding questions of identity politics. Diasporic subjects are seen not as some anomaly to the norm but as distinct versions of a modern, transnational, intercultural experience. "The diaspora experience . . . is defined, not by essence or purity, but by the recognition of a necessary heterogeneity and diversity. . . . Diaspora identities are those which are constantly producing and reproducing themselves anew, through transformation and difference" (Hall 1990, 235).

The adoption of the term also reflects the keenness of the Tibetan intellectuals to appropriate any vocabulary that provides them an opportunity to express their identity to the external world. It enables us to theorize Tibetan diasporic identity in terms of contradictions and possibilities (see Anand 2003), a task that is undertaken in this chapter. These contradictions not only constrain and contain the possibilities for self-expression that are available but, more significantly, are productive of the very identities in question (see Venturino 1997). This approach also challenges the "victimisation paradigm"[2] so familiar in analyses of Tibetan identity.

THE POLITICAL DISCOURSE OF TIBETANNESS

Since 1959 the Chinese, the Tibetan elite in exile, and their Western supporters and detractors have competed to legitimize their own representations of Tibetan history and current events. This "confrontation of 'representations'" (Goldstein 1997, 56) is about history and political status; at the same time it is intimately connected to cultural representations and identity. It is not possible to speak of Tibet or Tibetans without taking into account the constitution of these categories within representational practices and identity discourses. As argued in the previous chapter, the Tibet question is as much a political issue as it is connected to cultural politics of the modern world. Rather than take political identity as something given, we should see it as socially and politically constructed. In the words of Malkki: "Identity is always mobile and processual, partly self-construction, partly categorisation by others. . . . [it] is a creolized aggregate composed through bricolage" (1992, 37). "Tibet" in this sense is an "imagining community."[3] A unified Tibetan nation currently exists only through the anticipated (re)construction of its parts: occupied country, dispersed communities, and a globally networked politico-cultural support system of Tibet support groups (Venturino 1997, 103). Thus Tibetan national imagination is a product/process of strategic essentialism oriented toward the goal of reclaiming the Tibetan homeland.

Tibet as an Imagining Nation

The issue of Tibetan national identity inevitably involves the question of whether Tibet is/was a nation. While Tibetans argue that theirs was a historical nation, China denies this. This rhetoric ignores that the need to present one's own community as a nation is a modern phenomenon. Nationalism is on the one hand an ideological movement toward the construction of a nation. On the other hand it is a product of heightened consciousness of national identity among a people. As Mayall (1990) points out, nationalism has become structurally embedded as the basis of the modern state everywhere.

Given this scenario, it is hardly surprising that Tibetans have had to appropriate the language of nationalism in order to deal with both Chinese occupation and modernity. Tibetans claim that they have the right to determine the course of action that Tibet as a body politic, as a nation, should take. While the Tibetan issue is often discussed in terms of the preservation of a culture, the most important question concerns the right of people to self-determination. The Dalai Lama–led government-in-exile claims to speak for this right of all Tibetan people: "The whole of Tibet known as Cholka-Sum (U-Tsang, Kham and Amdo) should become a self-governing democratic political entity founded on law by agreement of the people for the common good and the protection of themselves and their environment, in association with the People's Republic of China" (His Holiness the Dalai Lama 1988).

This statement reflects a desire to project Tibet as "one" political unit, something that did not exist historically, at least during the modern period. The Anglo-Tibetan encounter forced the Tibetans to confront the differing perceptions of nation and state identity held by traditional and modern societies. Conscious though half-hearted attempts by the Tibetan government before 1950 to model itself on a nation-state line (see Goldstein 1989; Shakya 1999) clearly failed. However, the discourse of nationalism has had better luck in the diaspora. The Tibetan government-in-exile in Dharamsala makes claims not only over Central Tibet but also over Amdo and Kham. The claim is based not on the historical evidence of political control but on the existence of certain cultural and religious commonalities. So, should the claim of the Tibetan government-in-exile to represent Tibetans of all three provinces be seen as a case of historical fraud? Certainly this is not necessarily the case.

The distinction between "political" and "ethnographic" Tibet made by commentators including Bell (1924, 1928; see also Goldstein 1997), while intellectually relevant, suffers from ethnocentrism. Concepts and categories used in the West are automatically considered to be transparently transferable and universally applicable. The Tibetan body politic is often read in such terms. While the close connection between politics, religion, and culture in the case of Tibet is recognized, analyses often fail to transcend the belief in the separation of the sacral and the temporal that lies at the base of Enlightenment thinking and informs most scholarly endeavors. In the case of Tibet, however, politics, culture, and religion are intrinsically interconnected. This can be seen in the concept of *chos srid gnyis ldan* (dual religious and secular system of government) that is said to have characterized the Tibetan polity before 1959 (for details, see Kolas 1996; Smith 1996). The Dalai Lama combined both strands at the top of the "religious" and "secular" hierarchies. Despite the existence of local deities, rituals, and practices, Lhasa acted as a nerve center of religious practices. Not only was it the destination of many pilgrimage routes; it also had big monasteries of various prominent sects of Tibetan Buddhism. It was a center for learning and for trade. Thus, the limited temporal authority of the so-called Lamaist state (or the Lhasa government) did not affect the significant influence Lhasa exercised over the entire region inhabited by Tibetans. Since the Dalai Lama–led government-in-exile claims to be a continuation of the Lhasa government from 1959, it is within its right to speak for all Tibetans, especially in the long-drawn situation of crises in which the historical markers of Tibetan identity are under the threat of erasure. This use of "Tibet" as a political device is legitimized by several instances of similar historical practices. Indeed, modern nationhood involves the binding of community into a territory as, in the words of Bennett, "occupants of a territory that has been historicized and subjects of a history that has been territorialized" (1995, 141).

Bell's distinction between "political" and "ethnographic" Tibet, while being problematic, is nevertheless useful. While political Tibet was U-tsang, the boundary of ethnographic Tibet extended to include Amdo and Kham. What bound the people in the regions was not allegiance to one temporal authority but elements of common culture and religion. These elements may be seen as forming the basis of a Tibetan *ethnie* or ethnic community. As Smith argues, ethnie includes a collective proper name; a myth of common ancestry, shared memory of a rich "ethnohistory" (especially of a golden age); differentiating elements of common culture; association with specific homeland; and, last, a sense of solidarity for significant sectors of the population (1991, 21). All these features were present in varying degrees in the history of Tibetans.

More often than not the proponents of nationalism take a primordialist view. Such a view has been rightly contested in the academic discourse on nationalism (see Anderson 1983; Balakrishnan 1996; Bhabha 1990; Billig 1995; Chatterjee 1986, 1993; Eley and

Suny 1996; Gellner 1983; Hobsbawm 1990; Hobsbawm and Ranger 1992; Smith 1991),[4] and it has been argued that "invented traditions" (Hobsbawm and Ranger 1992) are used to create "imagined communities" (Anderson 1983). Nationalism is seen as a theory of legitimacy, "a political principle that holds that the political and national unit should be congruent" (Gellner 1983, 1). According to their critics, instrumentalist scholars of nationalism often overemphasize the capacity of nationalism as an ideology to engender nations. Smith argues how modern nationalism crucially depends on its primordial ethnic past (1991). However, I retain skepticism about the primordiality of the past and, instead of trying to situate myself somewhere "in-between" in the Instrumentalist-Primordialist debate, I adopt a discursive approach (see Balakrishnan 1996; Bhabha 1990; Chatterjee 1986, 1993), striving for a more diversified and inclusive understanding of nationalism that highlights its cross-cultural variants. While the centrality of a process of imagination in constituting a nation is noteworthy, the existence of an archive from which this process draws resources is also undeniable. While this archive shapes the imagining community, the process of imagination not only draws upon an existing archive but in the process re-creates it.

In the case of Tibet, this archive may be seen in terms of what Hobsbawm calls "proto-nationalism": "variants of feeling of collective belonging which already existed and which could operate, as it were, potentially on a macro-political scale which could fit in with modern states and nations" (1990, 46). Dreyfus (1994) has applied this idea of protonationalism to the Tibetan case and argues that a sense of belonging to a unique community that is political, despite the lack of any institutional expression, can be found in various aspects of Tibetan life even before 1959.

Even if we recognize that significant elements of Tibetan "national" identity preceded the twentieth century, it is only the interaction with modernity and colonialism that gave specific meanings to elements of a common identity. Tibetanness is a product of the processes of modernization, colonialism, and displacement. Before moving into a detailed discussion of diasporic Tibetanness, let me make a brief observation on the discourse of Tibetan national identity as circulating within Tibet.

DISCOURSE OF TIBETANNESS AS ARTICULATED IN CHINA'S TIBET

Discussion of Tibetanness as being processed and produced in diaspora should not ignore Tibetan identity as articulated within Tibet, that is, in China's Tibet. After suffering severe repression during the period of Cultural Revolution, Tibet has witnessed "economic liberalization" followed by some relaxation on religious practices. This, in turn, has led to a revival of cultural and religious identity. While there is little doubt that some cultural elements were encouraged by Chinese-Tibetan authorities in a typical modernist pattern of museumizing "exotic"/minority cultures, active support of the local people has been more important in this revival. However, as contributors to Goldstein and Kapstein (1998) point out, "revival" is a problematic term for what is happening in Tibet both because it fails to appreciate changes and because its meaning is often conflated with restoration. Despite attempts to objectify, culture is always in flux. In the case of Tibet, some individual traits are common with the past, some have changed in appearance and some in the importance attached to them, and some are now extinct (see Adams 1996, 1998; Kolas and Thowsen 2005). Moreover, one should realize that what passes as revival is deeply informed by contemporary politics. The key issue affecting the revival is the Tibet question—the conflict over the political status of Tibet vis-à-vis China (Goldstein, in Goldstein and Kapstein 1998, 14).

As the much-studied Lhasa demonstrations that took place more than a decade ago indicate, religion still plays an important role in the assertion of national identity by the Tibetans. Most demonstrations started at the initiative of monks and nuns[5] and most centered on the Jokhang temple in the Barkhor area of Lhasa. However, something fundamental has changed. While earlier revolts broke out for explicitly religious purposes, now a more instrumentalist and activist view of religion is taken (see Schwartz 1996; for a different view on the significance of the political in these protests, see Mills 2001). The official policy of religious tolerance is used to make political demands. The priority of many monks and nuns who participate in the demonstrations, often at high costs (including arrest, torture, expulsion from their institutions, and in extreme cases, execution) seems to be the political struggle for independence (see Barnett and Akiner 1996).[6] They are willing to risk the religious freedom granted to them for their political demands. Even in the name of religion, what is emphasized is not aspects of Buddhism (which is limiting for any nationalist aspiration on account of its universalistic dimensions) but specifically Tibetan elements of the religion.

The religious/cultural revival as well as instances of political protests inside Tibet exemplifies a rich mixture of traditional and innovative strategies in Tibet's struggle for survival against an authoritarian state system. The Chinese official rhetoric of a "multinational" state has offered the opportunity to Tibetans to reclaim, in part, a heterodox vision of history in which separateness and Tibetanness are highlighted and valorized. Often, the target of sporadic protests in Lhasa and elsewhere are the Western tourists who are considered potential supporters for the Tibetan cause. The main factor influencing the political protests and assertion of national identity in Tibet, therefore, is not religion per se or its suppression but Chinese political occupation.

In all these struggles over national identity, the key symbol for Tibetans has been, not surprisingly, the Dalai Lama. The Chinese realized the potential subversiveness of allowing Tibetans the religious freedom to worship his figure. They have thus tried to ban his worship and "encourage" other Tibetan lamas to denounce him as a "splittist" (one who is trying to split Tibet from its motherland, China). The Dalai Lama's traditional dual role as the head of religious and political systems has indeed been important. However, the political side of *chos srid gnyis ldan* is increasingly identified with democracy, and young Tibetans look upon the Dalai Lama as a world leader and as a symbol of democracy and human rights (Schwartz 1996). As happened to former imperial powers, such as the British in India, the nationalists to a large extent have taken the discourses of the dominant power and used it against them. China's claim that it is modernizing Tibet is questioned by those who have developed an alternative vocabulary (and alternative meanings) on the basis of a continuing flow of information and ideas from China as well as the outside world on democracy, human rights, and national struggles (see Sperling 1996). Observers of Tibet are increasingly recognizing this resilience among the Tibetans and the various innovative uses to which traditions have been put in the service of national identity. Such critical endeavors are certainly a way forward as compared to the idea and practice of Exotica Tibet, of a "lost horizon," a Shangri-la lost forever to the world, as espoused in most popular literature in the West.

(DIS)PLACED TIBETANS: NATIONALISM IN EXILE

A repressive state regime is not the only limitation on articulations of national identity within Tibet. Lack of organized opposition to China may also be attributed to the fact that significant numbers of religious and lay elite of traditional Tibet (along with the Dalai Lama) fled across the border to India. Since 1959 more than a hundred thousand Tibetans have become refugees. Most of them live in various settlements in India and Nepal. Others have dispersed to several countries, including Australia, Switzerland, Canada, and the United States. The nerve center of the refugee community, however, is Dharamsala, which is the seat of the Tibetan government-in-exile. The Dalai Lama's government from the outset has sought to project itself as a continuation of the pre-1959 Lhasa government. Though this government is not recognized by any state in the international community, for all practical purposes the Tibetans living in the diaspora, and many inside Tibet, consider it the legitimate authority. Continuity with the traditional Tibetan state (pre-1950) is stressed. The authoritarian state apparatus in Chinese-occupied Tibet, combined with censorship of information, ensures that Tibetan nationalism is far more developed in the diasporic community. The discourses of international human rights, democracy, decolonization, and self-determination have allowed sophisticated articulations of national identity among the Tibetans in exile. The idea in the world media of what constitutes Tibetanness often comes from the words and actions of the exile community.

Tibetanness, as many observers of Tibetan diasporic communities realize, is a highly contested and pluralistic identity. Tibetanness is articulated, in theory and in praxis, at several hierarchical as well as overlapping levels. It is a discursive product of many complementary and contesting dynamics such as the policy pronouncements of Dharamsala, the politics of more radical elements, gendered and generational practices, Exotica Tibet, and so on. Several factors influence and shape it, some of these directly related to the politics of representation. These include refugee status,[7] space-time projections of homeland,[8] the personality of the Dalai Lama, the overriding need for the preservation of culture, Western audiences with preconceived notions about Tibet and Tibetans (Exotica Tibet), self-perception, and most important, the desire to project a sense of continuity in a changing external environment. In order to understand what the category "Tibetan" means, it is important to look at some of these factors. Discussion of Exotica Tibet as a major factor foregrounds the productive role played by representational practices.

Interaction with Western Audiences: Exotica Tibet

A very important dynamic shaping Tibetan political identity has been interaction with Western audiences. The role of the West can be examined as within rather than outside the Tibet question by looking at the theme of Western representations of Tibet and its interface with Tibetan (trans)national identity. Scholars like Lopez (1998) show that Tibetans are "prisoners of Shangri-la"—constrained by their image as a religious, peaceful, exotic, and idyllic community. The dominant representation of Tibetans in the West in the early twenty-first century is as peaceful, nonviolent, religious, spiritual, compassionate, and close to nature. A corollary to this representation is the idea that the inherently good-natured Tibetans are victims of forced modernization brought about by Chinese rule. The emphasis is both on the uniqueness of the Tibetan culture and on its universal relevance.

Exotica Tibet, presenting Tibetans as victims, has helped mobilize many non-Tibetans for the "Save Tibet" cause. The Tibet movement, referring to the transnational efforts made on the part of Tibetans and their non-Tibetan supporters to demand the right of self-determination for the Tibetan people, has gained some high profile support, including Hollywood stars, U.S. Congress members, and members of European parliaments. The worldwide network of Tibet Support Groups (TSG) is unique in this respect (see Venturino 1997). They include organizations focusing on a wide range of themes—Tibetan Buddhism, human rights, spreading awareness about the situation in Tibet, and demand for independence (*rangzen* is the term used for this). The presence of support for Tibet is particularly significant in the virtual world where most of the Internet sites related to Tibet are pro-Tibetan. In fact, there is an increasing realization within the Tibetan diaspora of the possibilities offered by the Internet as a means for disseminating information and mobilizing support. Though the motives of participants in the Tibet movement vary,[9] what seems to unite them is a broadly defined Tibet cause. When the Tibetans went in exile they found that "Tibet" already existed in the Western imagination, and given their limited options, they conformed to that image in order to gain support (see Lopez 1998). Tibetans, Tibetophiles, and Tibetologists all have contributed to the romance of Tibet—to Exotica Tibet—which paradoxically renders problematic the struggle for independence from Chinese occupation. Moran, on the basis of his study of Tibetan diaspora in Nepal, warns against an Orientalist valorization of Tibetans, for "there is also the danger that if Tibetans fail to deliver the uni-dimensional spiritualized goods, there is no basis through which to approach them except through scorn" (2004, 6–7). Even though Western patronage offers an important source of symbolic and economic capital for individual Tibetan refugees, it remains precarious (see Prost 2006).

The support of the "Free Tibet" movement is often based on the supposed cultural uniqueness of Tibetans rather than on the recognition of the political right to self-determination. Richard Gere, the Hollywood actor, uses the analogy of David and Goliath to offer hope to the Tibetans and reminds them, "You must maintain that sense of uniqueness and that genuine cultural commitment to nonviolence. If you pick up arms and become like the Palestinians, you'll lose your special status" (in Schell 2000, 56). As Baird recognizes in the *New Internationalist* (1995) special issue on Tibet, the romantic image has hampered the Tibetan struggle for self-determination: "If Tibetans are presented as a dreamy, unrealistic people, obsessed with religion, their struggle is unlikely to be taken seriously by a world driven by more secular values. Their demand for independence will be seen as pie-in-the-sky and their ability to rule themselves will be open to question" (1995, 1).

However, rather than paint Tibetans as victims, we can view the Shangri-la image in a different light. Exotica Tibet is not only restrictive of options but is also "a soft power resource that can be manipulated to get attention and to get some access to the stages of world politics" (Magnusson 2002, 211). For instance, Klieger (1997) argues that Tibetans have been active in the creation and presentation of their own identity.[10] Not only have they participated in portraying an image of themselves to outsiders but their self-perception too has been a result of this self-reflexivity. Calling this conscious and selective presentation of self "Tibetan hyperreality," he writes: "Tibetan hyperreality is created from a conscious and selective presentation of self to an audience with highly conditioned expectations. Tibetan culture as currently presented in most Tibetan cultural centres in the West is idealized, homogenated and pasteurized. It has . . . remarkably allowed the perpetuation of Tibetan identity despite the vicissitudes of exile" (ibid., 67).

In the process of strategically deploying their culture to the Western audience for mobilizing political support, Tibetans have redefined and reconstructed Tibetan culture and identity. The Dalai Lama–led government-in-exile self-consciously makes representations of reflexive, politicized notions of culture and identity that are dependent upon the globalized production of institutions and the flow of cultural resources made possible through the onslaught of modernity (see Huber 2001; McLagan 1997; see also Shakya 2001). Not only have they embraced modern technologies such as the Internet (see McLagan 1996) to promote their cause[11] but they have also projected their culture as being compatible with universalizing discourses such as environmentalism, (world) peace, and nonviolence. Representations, politicized culture, and an interaction with a Western audience affect the "domestic" and "international" politics of the Tibetan elite in the diaspora. In their search for outside support, the Tibetan elite have been learning the language of international politics dominated by the Western powers (see Frechette 2002; Kolas 1996).

"We live in a nationalised world" and we tend to see the world with a "nationalising eye" (Cubitt 1998, 1). Recognizing the dominance of nationalism as a source of legitimacy in contemporary international politics, for example, the Tibetan government-in-exile has molded its expositions on Tibetan identity accordingly. Though "Old Tibet" had elements of *natio* (Lopez 1998, 197–98), Hobsbawm's protonationalism (Dreyfus 1994), and what Smith calls *ethnie*, a modern sense of nationhood was absent (Ekvall 1960, 382). Tibet as a nation is not a historical reality but a product of post-exilic imagination.[12] The Western influence can also be seen in the evolving cultural and political discourses, including the structure of the government-in-exile. In fact, the Dharamsala establishment has been moving toward democratization (see Boyd 2004) for gaining legitimacy in the West. These developments may be explained in terms of an image-building exercise, steps taken toward keeping up with the times, response to pressures from within the refugee community, and finally, the Dalai Lama's personal initiative.

In complying with dominant representational regimes, Tibetans are following tactics common to many groups who try to counter their relative powerlessness by negotiating within the dominant representational regimes and selectively appropriating favorable aspects. All third world resistance groups have to "negotiate both the post–cold war reframing of global politics and the lingering traces of Western post-colonial fantasies about their country and culture" (Bishop 1998, 123; see also Bishop 2000). Gandhi's adoption of the Orientalist trope of spiritualist Indians, feeding it into a wider political struggle against British imperialism as well as social evils within the Indian society, is a good example.

At the same time, these presentations should not be seen only in terms of a response to Orientalist representations, for often there are elements within the traditional society that facilitate this appropriation. Aris argues that the current predicament of Tibetans seeking Western support against an "Eastern" power (China) can be understood within traditional Tibetan historiography: "All Tibetan chronicles contain a stock chapter which speaks of the key process by which the embers of the doctrine in central Tibet were revived from the west and caused to flame from the east" and therefore "the idea of destruction, whether caused by external attack or internal collapse, is bound up with the idea of flight to a place of refuge and the possibility of return" (BOD MS Or. Aris 14 1990, 65, 67).

The Dalai Lama speaks about spirituality and the peaceful nature of Tibetans. His Strasbourg Proposal of 15 June 1988 is an example: "My country's unique history and profound spiritual heritage render it ideally suited for fulfilling the role of a sanctuary of peace at the heart of Asia" (His Holiness the Dalai Lama 1988). Though some historians argue that there is a strong tradition of warriors among groups of Tibetans (Norbu 1986), this does not undermine the Dalai Lama's claim about a "profound spiritual heritage," for elements of compassion and the principle of nonviolence were present within traditional Tibetan society. Such strategies are more about the selective appropriation of historical narratives for contemporary purposes than about specific historical truths. The specificity of these strategies is shaped by the contemporary vocabulary available for expression. The vocabularies of nationalism and transnationalism are two such discourses that the Tibetans have adopted to make their case.

Transnationalism in the Service of Nationalism

Quite often, diasporas are considered to exist in opposition to nation-states, with diaspora consciousness correspondingly incommensurate with nationalism. Clifford, for example, argues that diasporas can never be exclusively nationalist because they imply multiple attachments (1997, 135–36). However, in the case of the Tibetans, nationalist discourse is a product of the diaspora. Imagining Tibet as a nation is to a large extent a postexilic phenomenon. The most sophisticated articulation of Tibetan national identity thus comes from the more radical sections of the Tibetan diaspora. Western representations and diaspora conditions have also contributed to a shift in emphasis away from ethnicity (Tibetans as *tsampa* eaters) to religion (a "modern" version of Tibetan Buddhism) as the basis of Tibetanness (Lopez 1998, 198). In contrast, Shakya (1993) argues that the shift has been away from "faith" to "flag" as a result of the hegemony of nationalistic discourse.

At the same time, transnationalism, engendered substantially by the transnational Tibet movement, has been an integral part of Tibetan diasporic identity. This is not surprising given that "the Tibet movement represents an emergent form of transnational, intercultural political activism, one that is dependent upon the complex production and circulation of representations of 'Tibetan*ness*' in various arenas that cross cultural and national boundaries" (McLagan 1997, 69; emphasis in original). Tibetan identity has strong constructive elements of transnationalism (Mountcastle 1997), including those that emphasize environment (on "green" Tibetan identity, see Huber 1997), peace, spiritualism, international human rights, universal compassion, and eclectic beliefs. As pointed out earlier, these are distinctly connected to Exotica Tibet. The constituency of Tibetan supporters often overlaps with other transnational social movements. Economically and politically, as well as symbolically, transnational connections feed into the Tibetan diaspora's nationalism. While recognizing the essentially modern aspect of the nationalist and transnationalist discourses prevalent among the Tibet diaspora, it cannot be denied that the traditional Tibetan principles of operating with the external powers have also facilitated this. Working within the framework of a patron-client relationship, Tibetans have managed to construct and reinforce a national identity by drawing upon the patronage of transnational networks and connections. Klieger's analysis of Tibetan nationalism as a modern manifestation of the "patron-client dyad" argues that the Tibetans living in diaspora have been able to retain their status by converting the entire exile community into the client category (1994, 84–120). This is not to argue that a coherent ideology of nationalism accepted by the entire Tibetan diaspora has emerged. The idea of Tibet as a nation is a contested political construct that involves the manufacturing of unity out of tremendous difference and diversity.

Soliciting international support has been one of the main strategies of the Tibetan diaspora elite. The Dalai Lama's well-publicized and frequent trips to various countries are a significant part of this strategy of raising the profile of the Tibetan cause in the international media and mobilizing public opinion in the Western states. Conspicuous avoidance of the Tibet question in the conventional fora of international relations, epitomized by the lack of recognition of Tibetan statehood by any existing state, has forced the Tibetans to seek support through nonconventional means—cultural politics is a part of this. The ultimate goal behind the transnational mobilization remains the assertion of the right to self-determination. Tibetanness thus is a transnational phenomenon, a political practice that transgresses national boundaries but does not question the spatial logic through which these boundaries have come to constitute and frame the conduct of international relations. In a dedication at the beginning of his autobiography, Palden Gyatso reflects a sentiment common to most Tibetans, a hope that international support might help them realize their goal of independence: "And to all of you who inhabit the world who also believe in the virtues of truth, justice and decency. . . . Help to deliver us. Help us to be free, to be independent, to be able to do what we choose—in our own country" (1997).

The imaginative hold and consequent impact of Exotica Tibet is evident in the activities of various Tibet support groups. The support in the form of the "Free Tibet" movement is often based on the image of "Tibet as defenseless underdog, a spiritual society that was minding its own business only to get crushed under the jackboot of an aggressive, materialist overlord" (Schell 2000, 206). However, even the cultivation of this victimization paradigm reflects the agency of Tibetans. Though Tibetan global publicity campaigns consciously portray Tibetans as victims of Chinese oppression, this does not deny them their subjectivity. Instead, they have made conscious and extensive use of Western discourses—whether psychology, philosophy, physics, personal growth, or holistic health—in their attempts both to communicate with Westerners and to reconstitute themselves in conditions of exile (Bishop 1997, 67). Tibetans have colluded with, as well as contested, various Western images of Tibet.

Though many Westerners may like to overrate their own importance in nurturing Tibetan resistance to China, resistance to domination always exists in all societies (Bass 1990, 218), and Tibet is no exception.[13] Dominant cultural and political ideas (in this case Western and Chinese) influence the precise forms that the resistance takes. In the diaspora, it is the preservation of traditional culture and nationalism that is the main dynamic behind the politics of resistance. Within Tibet, this ranges from protest movements demanding independence to forces demanding accommodation of special rights within the Chinese state structure. In either case, it reveals the political agency of Tibetans.

The extent to which the awareness-raising campaigns of the Tibet support groups in the West translate into substantive political support and activism is open to question. In fact, the existing support for the Tibetan cause is based on Exotica Tibet, particular representations of Tibetans as inherently spiritual and peaceful people. This restricts the alternatives available to those Tibetans (see Lazar 1998; Shakya 1991) who might be disillusioned with the Dalai Lama's insistence on nonviolence and his renunciation of the demand for independence. Instead of deriving satisfaction solely from high-profile support for Tibet based on particularized images, many Tibetans are frustrated with the limitations imposed by this on their political struggle. Tsering expresses this sentiment very clearly when he writes, "As for our friends and supporters, while we greatly appreciate their sympathy and support, it is not for them to determine what the goal should be" (1998, 43). The adoption of a human rights model by a Tibetan exile elite, as discussed briefly in the previous chapter, has limitations as in the West this model provided a "language that could be used ambiguously so that the domestic audience would be seen as criticizing China while Chinese officials might be persuaded that the criticisms were sufficiently mild so as not to be threatening to fundamental concerns" (Barnett 2001, 291).

Thus, while molding their identity discourses according to Western exoticized imagery has helped Tibetans in gaining substantial popular support, there is a strong realization among many that this is not an end in itself. As Shakya points out, unlike other international political problems such as the Palestinian one, the Tibetan issue is seen in terms of sentimentality. "If the Tibetan issue is to be taken seriously, Tibet must be liberated from both the Western imagination and the myth of Shangri-la" (1991, 23). It therefore comes as no big surprise that while the international support for Palestinians often comes from other third world countries, Tibet support groups are more common in the civil society of the first world.[14] This has partly to do with the limited success of the Tibetan government-in-exile in establishing networks in the third world. The Tibetan exiles turned for support to former colonizers rather than to the formerly colonized and chose public relations rather than political alliance as their form of politics (Barnett 2001, 279).

TIBETAN (TRANS)NATIONAL IDENTITY: THE TENSIONS WITHIN

The institutional as well as the symbolic practices of the Dalai Lama–led Dharamsala establishment encourage people to act socially and cohesively as Tibetans in an "alien" environment.[15] The emphasis on constructing a unity does not mean an elision of differences within the community. As in any other vibrant society, one can find here differences based on generation, socialization, gender, religiosity, region, sect, period of departure from Tibet, class, and political opinions (see Ardley 2002; Diehl 1998). The popular tendency within the media, Tibet support groups, and many Tibetans themselves, is to represent the Tibetan diaspora community as united under the leadership of the Dalai Lama. However, significant differences can be seen within the diaspora between the Tibetans coming from the U-Tsang region and Khampas and Amdowas. Difference is definitely witnessed in religious matters, as in the Shugden affair[16] or the Rumtek monastery controversy,[17] or, for that matter, in less-publicized differences within the monasteries in South Asia between the old arrivals and the newcomers (see Strom 1997, 39–42). Significant generational differences are also found within the diaspora on matters such as the role of religion in society (is it an end in itself or a cultural resource?); outmigration from South Asia (whether to stay in the region close to the community or move out to Western countries for improvement in individual standard of living); influence of popular Indian and Western culture (should one assimilate with the dominant culture or retain separation?); and political priorities (whether to emphasize preservation of traditional Tibetan culture or focus primarily on the explicitly political demands).[18] In political matters too the diaspora is divided. Study of statements by the Tibetan government-in-exile reveals an ambiguity in their primary political demands (at http://www.tibet .com). While the right of Tibetans to self-determination is asserted, often it is argued in terms of significant and real autonomy within China, sometimes on the model of "One Country, Two Systems" as has been followed in the case of Hong Kong. On the other hand, there are more radical intellectuals and activists within the Tibetan diaspora who make a strong and unambiguous case for struggling toward complete independence (see Lazar 1998).[19] There are several other opinions on this matter. A middle ground is expressed in the Hear Tibet! campaign calling for a United Nations–backed referendum within Tibet allowing the Tibetan people themselves to choose their own political future (see Hear Tibet! 2001).

Thus, a unified Tibetan-in-exile identity espoused on behalf of the Tibetan diaspora is a rhetorical device and an imaginary construct. At the same time, it would be naive to dismiss considerations of the identity question on this ground only, for all the identities are in the last instance a product of the imagination. Following Butler:

> To take the construction of the subject as a political problematic is not the same as doing away with the subject; to deconstruct the subject is not the same as doing away with the concept . . . but to call into question and, perhaps most importantly, to open up a term, like the subject, to a reusage or redeployment that previously has not been authorized. (1992, 15)

Though Tibetanness is an imagined and contested construct, it has its own truth effects on those who consider themselves Tibetans.

Recognition of Tibetans as an "imagining community" problematizes simplistic interrogations of Tibetanness. It does not undermine the quest of a people for self-determination.

CONCLUSION

Tibetan national identity both inside and outside Tibet is a product of constant negotiation and renegotiation. Personal experience mediates national identity. The "transnational" element is as significant a part of Tibetan nationalism as is the "indigenous element." Tibetanness among those living in exile is as much a discursive product of displacement (conditions of diaspora) as of sense of belonging (to a "distinctive nation"). It is a productive process of creative negotiation with Exotica Tibet. My analysis of the poetics and politics of Exotica Tibet seeks to blur the distinctions between the cultural and the political and to underline the constitutive relations between identity and representation within world politics in the postcolonial world. In order to carry on a postcolonial examination of the politics of Exotica Tibet, we have to move beyond the conventional sense of the term "political" and challenge the boundaries between the political and the cultural. This is what I do in the next chapter, where I offer new ways of theorizing Tibetanness through postcoloniality-inspired symbolic geography and a discursive approach that foregrounds the constitutive and performative role played by representation in identity. This should be seen as underlining a postcolonial analytical approach that will help provide a critical reading of world politics, taking into account the centrality of representation.

6

Postcoloniality and Reimag(in)ing Tibetanness

The fish which lives in water
Pray do not draw it up on dry land!
The stag which grazes on the hills
Pray do not lure it down to the vale
—TIBETAN VERSE (TRANSLATED BY W. Y. EVANS),
WENTZ, *MODERN POLITICAL PAPERS*

Tibetanness, or Tibetan identity, is a contingent product of negotiations among several complementary and contradictory processes. These processes may be looked at in terms of different pairs of contrastive dynamics, such as the imperatives of a culture-in-displacement and the need to present an overarching stable identity; interaction with host societies and an avoidance of cultural assimilation into hegemonic cultural formations there; emphasis on tradition as the defining characteristic and the presentation of exiled Tibetans as "modern"; the desire to represent Tibetan culture as unique while at the same time highlighting its universal features; interaction with a sympathetic Western audience and emphasizing difference from Western cultures; and finally, the wish to project a sense of continuity with the past while distancing oneself from oppressive elements of history. These dynamics impact the theory and praxis of Tibetanness at several overlapping and hierarchical levels.[1]

By putting the symbolism of Dharamsala/*dharmashala/dharam-shala* (note the difference in the placing of the "a," highlighting different pronunciations) under a postcolonial critical scrutiny, I offer a deconstructive reading of the Tibetan identity problematic that, instead of jettisoning Tibetan agency, affirms it. The politics of Exotica Tibet—this politics is about the effect of representations on the represented and questions the arbitrary boundary between the cultural and the political—is evident both in the symbolic geography of Dharamsala and in Tibetanness. In the course of this inquiry, I emphasize the symbolism of Dharamsala/*dharmashala/dharamshala* as contested, put forward the dominant story of Tibetanness before offering an alternative reading, and finally, propose a new way of theorizing Tibetanness as discursively constituted by both roots and routes.

Before moving further, let me elaborate on Dharamsala/*dharmashala/dharamshala*. Dharamsala is a place in north India that is currently the residence of the Dalai Lama and the seat of the Tibetan government-in-exile. The place-name Dharamsala comes from the Sanskrit word *dharmashala* composed of two parts—*dharma* (religion) and *shala* (house). So *dharmashala* means "abode of the gods" and "house of religion." But in everyday Hindi language, often pronounced as *dharamshala*, it means a "temporary station," a "guesthouse," lying usually on routes of pilgrimage. An important feature of *dharamshala* is that it provides free or sometimes inexpensive temporary accommodation to travelers. So Dharamsala is the place, *dharmashala* means "house of religion," and *dharamshala* stands for "guesthouse."

I examine the symbolic geography of Dharamsala.[2] Why Dharamsala and not any other, even bigger Tibetan refugee settlement elsewhere? Why symbolic geography and not cultural geography? I focus on Dharamsala since it plays a very crucial role as a symbolic nerve center from which articulations of Tibetanness emerge. These articulations affect the perception of the international media. But even more important, they are reabsorbed into the exile community's self-perception. Thus, instead of representations as merely reflective of identity, they are constitutive of the very entity they seek to represent. The Department of Information and International Relations of the government-in-exile self-consciously presents Dharamsala as "Little Lhasa in India" (1999).

A focus on Dharamsala as a place will be complemented by an interrogation of the root words *dharmashala/dharamshala* in order to tease out the various possible alternative narratives of Tibetanness. My contention is that the symbolic geography of the place, along with a particular implication of the words *dharmashala* and *dharamshala,* supports the dominant story preferred by the exile elite and their non-Tibetan supporters. This story is consonant with Exotica Tibet, which has the effect of fostering a "salvage mentality," a strong preservation ethos (see Michael 1985). Here the emphasis is on the projection of Dharamsala as the "Little Lhasa in India,"[3] a temporary home preserving a historical culture in its pure form before an inevitable return to the original homeland.

However, an alternative reading of Dharamsala/*dharmashala/ dharamshala* provides a different story, one that affords a theoretically sophisticated conceptualization of Tibetanness and therefore challenges the dominant story. Such a reading not only looks at identity as always already in process but also affirms the diaspora experience as something more than a temporary aberration. The two different narratives of diasporic Tibetan identity I posit are not strictly contradictory since they can be retheorized together productively, through postcolonial IR theory, by combining a "deconstructive attitude" with an "agential politics of identity," which, as Radhakrishnan points out, "makes it possible for movements to commit themselves simultaneously to the task of affirming concrete projects of identity on behalf of the dominated and subjugated knowledges and to the utopian or long-term project of interrogating identity-as-such" (1996, xxiii). My alternative reading highlights several things within discourses of Tibetanness at once—the politics of place and the place of politics; the social construction of space and the spatialized social relations; and the rhetoric of essentialism and the practice of strategic essentialism.

SYMBOLISM OF DHARAMSALA: A CONTESTED TERRAIN

Conventionally, identity has been seen as primordial and natural, culture as organically rooted in a particular geographical space, and place as an inert space over which history is enacted. Place is held as providing "an inert, fixed, isotropic back-drop to the real stuff of politics and history" (Keith and Pile 1997, 4; see also Gupta and Ferguson 1997). On this view, Dharamsala is only a static stage for the theatrics of Tibetan diasporic culture and politics. However, this notion of fixity hides the fact that the geography of Dharamsala has had a changing symbolic role for the Tibetan diaspora. A transformation from a poor refugee settlement to one of the most popular tourist destinations in India, a change from a small, dilapidated village to a cosmopolitan small town—these are indicative as well as constitutive of changes within the Tibetan exile community. The questioning of the edifice of the conventional geographical imagination by a "cultural turn" within the field influenced by poststructuralism and postcolonialism makes it possible to study Dharamsala's symbolic geography. For place and space are now seen in social terms—not only do they shape social relations but, more important, they themselves are discursively constituted by social forces.

Spatialities, a term that recognizes the social construction of space and place, can be invoked to study how landscapes themselves are laden with multiple meanings. "Spatialities have always produced landscapes that are loaded with ethical, epistemological and aestheticized meanings" (Keith and Pile 1993, 26). That Dharamsala has come to acquire multiple layers of not always harmonious meaning is therefore not surprising. While for some (the Tibetan refugees) it is a place of refuge from oppression, for others (the Chinese government) it is a center of seditious activities. For some (local Indians) it is a vital opportunity for material advancement; for others (many Western tourists) it is a spiritual refuge from the crass materialism of modern Western societies. For some (the Tibetans as well as non-Tibetan Buddhists) it is a center of pilgrimage; for others (many Indian tourists) it is merely a site of curiosity. All these ascribed meanings, some complementary and some contradictory, problematize any simplistic and holistic reading of the symbolic geography of Dharamsala. Rather than treating such tensions and contradictions as regrettable, we should rather see them as productive of the wider Tibetan diasporic identity-in-process.

Postcolonial criticality stresses the importance of recognizing the complexly intertwined and mutually constitutive relationship between imaginary and material geography. "Imaginary and material geographies are not incommensurate, nor is one simply the product, a disempowered surplus, of the other" (Jacobs 1996, 158). Instead of treating the symbolic in opposition to the material, a richer conceptualization recognizes that there is no "actual" that can be accessed independently of intersubjectivity, that there is no category of the "natural" that is not mediated through culture. This would facilitate an understanding of the spatialized politics of identity as well as the identity politics of space. The former might include a consideration of how particular imaginings of a unified homeland of Tibet shape the discourses of Tibetanness. A discussion of the identity politics of space might, on the other hand, consider how different groups, including the Tibetan government-in-exile, ordinary Tibetan refugees, Tibetans inside Tibet, the Chinese government, Western sympathizers, and the local Himachalis ascribe their own meanings to the place of Dharamsala.

Recognition that all geographies have acquired contested meanings through continuous processes of individual and collective imagination does not preclude a consideration of the physical and structural factors at work. For instance, though the residence of the Dalai Lama and the existence of a government-in-exile are among the more important factors, the physical location of Dharamsala in the hills of the Indian state of Himachal Pradesh has also facilitated its projection and promotion as a "Little Lhasa." Given the reputation of Lhasa as lying on the "roof of the world," it is difficult to imagine a place in the plains (rather than the hills) of India being promoted in the same way. Travel writings that emphasize the relative inaccessibility of Dharamsala are quite common.[4] This resonates with the reputation of Lhasa as the "Forbidden City" at the "roof of the world." In a certain sense, Dharamsala acts as an accessible substitute for those travelers (often white and Western)[5] whose imaginations have been influenced by the earlier writing of imperialist adventurers, "the trespassers on the roof of the world" (to evoke the title of Hopkirk's 1983 book). Thus, the mountainous terrain of McLeod Gunj and its distance from any big city contribute to the symbolic geography of Dharamsala.

The most important structural factor shaping the symbolic geography of Dharamsala is the imperative of refugee status. The locations of Tibetan settlements have been decided entirely by Indian central and state governments. For instance, the Dalai Lama shifted from Mussorie to Dharamsala on Indian Prime Minister Jawaharlal Nehru's advice in 1960. An abandoned British hill station, McLeod Gunj was offered as a suitable quiet place for the Dalai Lama.[6] The transfer of the Central Tibetan Administration (the government-in-exile) followed soon after. Unlike in Lhasa, where the three big monasteries of the Gelugpa order were close to the Dalai Lama's seat, in India these monasteries have been reestablished in far-off places, due to the limitations of land available for settlement. The refugee status of Tibetans in South Asia prohibits them from owning immovable property unless offered by the host government. So any consideration of the symbolic geography of Dharamsala needs to keep these physical and structural factors in mind.

Before dwelling more on Dharamsala and the politics of identity, it should be pointed out that the place commonly designated as the Little Lhasa is actually McLeod Gunj (Upper Dharamsala). As the Himachal Pradesh Tourism Department board reads: "Welcome to Mcleodganj, the little Lhasa in India." The multilayered meanings in this name (McLeod Gunj) may be explored further (something not feasible within the space of this chapter)—British imperialism, the development of hill stations as places of refuge for the imperial class, the indigenization of names, and so on.[7] It can be read as indicating the important role played by British imperial practices in framing the various aspects of the Tibetan question. The distinction between Lower and Upper Dharamsala also reflects a gap between the local population and the refugees. While Tibetans here have generally managed to create their own niche in the wider society, the assertion of difference also leaves the potential open for conflict if the locals perceive the refugees to be a source of problems.[8] The government-in-exile promotes the name Dharamsala, and not McLeod Gunj, as the "Little Lhasa." This may be because Tibetan institutions and establishments are spread throughout the vicinity of Dharamsala. But how far the name "Dharamsala" itself may have inspired it is an open question, for the literal meaning of *dharmashala*—"the house of god/religion/dharma"—resonates well with the location of the Dalai Lama's residence and several religious institutions. Indirectly, the choice of name, with its association with spiritualism and faith, makes it more appealing to Western tourists too.

DHARAMSALA AS A TEMPORARY HOME: THE DOMINANT STORY

What are the specific ways in which the politics of place as embodied in Dharamsala inform the discourses of Tibetan identity? By drawing upon the usage of the words *dharmashala/dharamshala*, we can theorize Tibetan identity discourse in two broad ways—one offering the dominant story and the other allowing an alternative reading. *Dharamshala* in popular Hindi usage refers to a "temporary home," a "guesthouse." The dominant theorization, which has a wide currency among the Tibetan government-in-exile and nationalists as well as non-Tibetan supporters of the Tibetan cause, interprets the experience of diaspora as a temporary and regrettable phenomenon. And indeed, the place Dharamsala is seen as a temporary home with the final destination being the original homeland of Tibet. The exile is seen as a break in the evolution of an ancient civilization in Tibet, a time when it is vital to preserve a pure form of this civilization since it is under erasure in the original home. As my discussion of Exotica Tibet has shown, in journalistic and travel writings one often comes across eulogies to a lost Shangri-la in Tibet (particularly Lhasa) and observations on how the forces of modernization infused under the Chinese rule have spelled doom for the Tibetan culture. Such observations stand in contrast to those about the Tibetan communities living in South Asia, particularly in the area surrounding Dharamsala. In this case, though the cosmopolitan and eclectic cultural scene of McLeod Gunj is recognized, often the emphasis is on the success story of Tibetans in *preserving* their culture. "Working hard to rebuild their lives and preserve their distinctive and timeless culture and lifestyle, these people . . . have become arguably the most successful refugee community in the world whilst continuing the non violent struggle for Tibet's freedom in exile" (Barker 1999). The maintenance of Tibetan identity is seen as a functional expression of this culture.

If we are to identify one crucial theme running through the collective discourses and practices of the Tibetan diaspora, it is the preservation of tradition and culture. When some Tibetans, following the Dalai Lama in 1959, left their country as refugees, a need to preserve the traditional religion and culture in the diaspora was felt. This became particularly acute as markers of Tibetan life came under attack during the Cultural Revolution in China and then, since the 1980s, as the Chinese authorities sought to follow a dual policy of political repression and economic liberalization. The acute fear that Tibetan culture would become extinct in its homeland underlines the predominance of a "salvage mentality," a preservation ethos in the Tibetan diaspora. This also provides legitimacy to the diaspora's claim to be a true representative of Tibet, the custodian of an endangered culture.

It is thus not surprising that Dharamsala is projected as the Little Lhasa in India, and several dynamics support such a depiction. Not only is this the residence of the Dalai Lama and (therefore) a place of pilgrimage for many Tibetans and non-Tibetan Buddhists, but it is also the focus for the individual, communal, and institutional practices of Tibetan culture. Earlier pilgrims used to visit Lhasa, which for them was a source of refuge from the everydayness of life with hope of good in the next life. Now refugee status is itself often seen as a sort of pilgrimage during which a *darshan* (sight) of the Dalai Lama in Dharamsala provides compensation for hardship. As a result, new refugees are first stationed in Dharamsala, helped to meet the Dalai Lama, and only then sent to resettlement camps.

This projection also provides legitimacy to the claims that the Central Tibetan Administration is a government-in-exile, a continuation of the pre-1959 Lhasa government, and therefore the rightful representative of all Tibetan people. It provides added validation to the political struggle for self-determination in Tibet. Dharamsala is perceived as the temporary capital of the entire Tibetan world and the Tibet movement. Conscious efforts have been made to recapture what has been called the spirit of "Old Tibet," for example, the re-creation in Dharamsala of Tsuglakhang (Central cathedral) as an equivalent of Lhasa's Jokhang temple.

The symbolic representation of Dharamsala as Little Lhasa, as Thupten Samphel of the government-in-exile's Department of Information and International Relations (DIIR) pointed out, is to convey that what has been destroyed is being re-created (personal interview 2000). This idea of the re-creation of a civilization and the preservation of culture is the single most important strand of Tibetan identity discourse and is conspicuously evident in Dharamsala's geography.

The institutionalized expression of this theme of the saving of culture is best found at the Norbulingka Institute, dedicated explicitly to the preservation of Tibetan culture in both literary and artistic forms that might otherwise become extinct. For instance, in the Norbulingka's Center for Arts, the skills preserved and passed on through training and apprenticeship include statue making, *thangka* painting, appliqué and tailoring, woodcarving, carpentry, and metal craft. It is emphasized that the practice of making traditional works of art such as religious statues and *thangkas* only in response to the customer's order is a continuation of earlier practices in which patrons would personally commission artists to do such work. Norbulingka is keen "to preserve the relationship between patron and artist free from the taint of commercialisation" (Norbulingka Institute 1995).

Even the Dalai Lama considers preservation to be the single most important achievement of the exile community. He points out that the pure form of culture is now found outside rather than inside Tibet (Powell 1992, 384). This is similar to Richardson's argument that the only hope of "keeping Tibetan characteristics and values alive" is in the refugee population, given that the new generations of Tibetans living inside Tibet are divorced from past ways of thinking; even though the nomadic population maintains old ways of life, they are rough and primitive (1998, 707–8). The idea that Tibetan culture in diaspora is more authentic than the one prevalent in Chinese-controlled Tibet is supported by a few factors. One of them is the passing down of cultural authority though the practice of reincarnation. A significant part of Tibetan culture and religion has been embodied within reincarnate lamas, the most important being the Dalai Lama himself. And many of them left Tibet to become a part of the diaspora. The struggle between the Dalai Lama and Beijing over the reincarnation of the Panchen Lama[9] reinforces the Dharamsala establishment's desire to prevent this process from getting into the wrong and "inauthentic" hands. While outside (read Chinese) influence is resisted, there have been instances where the practice has been deployed to incorporate ethnically non-Tibetan individuals as *nang-pa* (the Buddhist "insider").[10]

The idea of true cultural authority as existing in exile rather than within Tibet is also validated by the presence of some great master craftsmen[11] who had been trained in their art in the "Old Tibet" and then moved to exile. These artists are regarded as "precious" since they are seen as having direct experience of "authentic Old Tibet."[12] Moreover, because of Exotica Tibet and a desire to gain Western support, the exile elite has tended to favor certain strands of Tibetan culture as more authentic and therefore worthy of patronage. For instance, cultural aspects highlighting sectarian differences are often underemphasized in favor of pan-Tibetan identity markers. Here, the ultimate cultural authority has come to be associated with the Dalai Lama himself (see Harris 1999).

An interrelated thematic aspect of the symbolic geography of

Dharamsala is the role of memory in housing a distinct Tibetan identity. Exotica Tibet has directly influenced how Tibetans have constructed their memories of a lost homeland. The names of many establishments in Dharamsala—of not only Tibetan governmental and nongovernmental institutions but also commercial establishments—resonate with specifically Tibetan idioms. For instance, if one walks up the Jogibara Road from the Amnye Machen Institute to the right and Gaden Choeling Nunnery to the left, one finds names such as Amdo Cha-Chung Restaurant, Lhasa Tailors, Café Shambhala, Tsongkha Restaurant, Drepung Loseling Guest House, Tibet Lhoka Café, and so on. Similarly, on the Bhagsu Road starting from the bus stop, one comes across Potala Tours and Travels, Dhompatsang Boutique and Handicraft, Rangzen Café, Tara Café, and Tashi Kangsar Travel Lodge, to mention just a few. Other names, more directly influenced by Exotica Tibet, specifically deploy the ideas of loss and longing, such as the Tibet Memory Restaurant, Lhasa Tailors, Lhasa Hotel, and Hotel Tibet (the hotel belongs to the government-in-exile). It may be possible that an important factor influencing the naming practice could be the nostalgia for Tibet and the desire to create familiarity in strange places. If you don't find Tibetan names in Little Lhasa, where else can you expect to find them?

CULTURE AND THE POLITICS OF PLACE:
SOME CONCEPTUAL PROBLEMS WITH THE DOMINANT STORY

However, this dominant story of Little Lhasa as a temporary station where Tibetan culture is being preserved is highly problematic, both practically and theoretically. While in practical terms this simple story is complicated by the experiences of living as refugees, it is also open to serious theoretical challenges because of the unproblematic acceptance of a stylized understanding of the basic concepts of identity and culture.

Let us first take the theme of the preservation of Tibetan culture. Though the predominant emphasis remains on preserving tradition, the impact of drastic change in the context of cultural production is evident even in traditional areas. Unlike in Tibet, where monastic institutions were the sole custodian of religion, in the diaspora the task of preserving the culture is shared by modern institutions established by the exile administration (see Kolas 1996). Museums, libraries, and institutes established by the government-in-exile are considered repositories of authentic Tibetan culture. These are modeled on Western ideas of cultural preservation. The "culture of Tibet" is in a sense being constructed and objectified through the new institutions and through the ideas of "culture" itself. Particular ideas of Tibet, influenced by Exotica Tibet, are created and embedded in the exhibitionary forms of a range of cultural practices and institutions. A relatively fluid mixture of traditions is being bounded, fixed, and recorded much more efficiently than ever before. Maintaining and recreating a Tibetan identity in exile involves a self-conscious display of Tibetan Buddhist religion and an organized construction of Tibetan culture. As Kolas argues, "Contained within secular institutions, religious expressions have become the objects of Tibetan culture, which represent Tibetan identity to the outside world" (1996, 58–59). This attempt to preserve traditional culture in the modern world has inevitably led to a secularization and objectification of it.[13] Capturing the spirit of "Old Tibet," after all, involves a selective construction of traditions. For instance, when discussing the various styles of Tibetan painting, Harris points out that the dominant style is *new Menri* whose purity is at best "a series of re-inventions" (1999, 69; emphasis in original). The traditional cultural practices are often laden with contemporary political meanings.[14]

Without belittling these attempts at maintaining distinctive traditions of creative and artistic expression, at a theoretical level this overemphasis on preservation should also be seen as being conceptually problematic because it takes a sanitized view of what culture means. Culture is seen as a thing out there that can be identified, mapped, practiced, and preserved. Such a conceptualization of culture essentializes and naturalizes what is socially and politically constructed and contested. It ignores the fact that culture is a "dynamic mix of symbols, beliefs, languages and practices which people create, not a fixed thing or entity governing humans" (Anderson and Gale 1992, 3). Cultural identities, far from being eternally fixed in some essentialized past, are actually subject to the continuous play of history, culture, and power. Tibetan culture is as much a process as it is a product of particular historical processes. An explicit recognition of this would certainly challenge the dominant tendency to make exilic "Tibet" fit Exotica Tibet.

The effect of commodification and tourism on particular expressions of "authentic" Tibetan culture is also important. As Wood argues, tourism affects not only the ways in which ethnic identities are asserted but also which ethnic markers are chosen to symbolize group membership and culture (1998, 222). The desire to attract tourists has played a significant role in the depiction of Dharamsala as the Little Lhasa.

Even the names of many establishments in McLeod Gunj, particularly the commercial ones, highlight the importance of tourism and the desire to appeal to outsiders' idea of Tibet as a Shangri-la. For instance, on the Jogibara Road this is exemplified in names such as Yak Restaurant, Snow Land Restaurants, Hotel Shangri-la, Snow Lion complex (hotel, restaurant, and medical store), and Travel Tibet Tailoring Shop. The fact that many such establishments are owned by local Indians goes to show that a primary motive for such naming practices is to appeal to tourists. In fact, this dynamic is also underlined by the presence of other shops with names that are unabashedly Orientalist, such as Dreaming Oriental Carpet Cottage Handicrafts, Royal Asia Art, Heaven Art, and Rising Horizon Café. It is hard to imagine the old city of Lhasa having place-names such as Shangri-la, Dreaming Oriental, or Yeti before its incorporation into the international tourism networks. My hypothesis is that while Tibetan names such as Amnye Machen Institute, Gangchen Kyishong, and lhagyal-ri reflect a desire to re-create a familiar environment, other more Orientalist names such as Shangri-la and Travel Tibet pander to exoticized representations of Tibet. This is supported by the fact that while the former are predominantly used in Tibetan governmental and nongovernmental institutions, the latter are found exclusively in commercial establishments.

The preservation ethos is not hegemonic in the Tibetan diaspora. Counterhegemonic spaces are available in Dharamsala for innovative and more contemporary practices of culture. Even these practitioners are not in opposition to traditional culture but complementary to it. For instance, though Norbulingka's catalogs and brochures fail to mention this, the institute has a section where young artists work on contemporary themes. Moreover, even the traditional cultural practices are often laden with contemporary political meanings. The Namgyalma Stupa[15] in the center of McLeod Gunj, erected during the 1960s as a memorial to the Tibetans who lost their lives fighting against the Chinese, is a good example of this combination of traditional religion with modern politics. Similarly, the dolls made in the traditional style at Norbulingka carry "Free Tibet" badges.

The political context of occupation and coercion is always present even in the space provided for traditional art and crafts. Despite the dominance of the preservation ethos, the focus of identification has now shifted from local contexts to a national one—instead of individual localities and regions, all of Tibet is collectively imagined as the homeland to which the refugees hope one day to return.

Rather than seeing culture as informing politics and vice versa, the entire category of culture has to be understood as political. For instance, both the desire and the attempt to preserve a culture under threat are acts of resistance to dominant forces of modernization and to the Chinese occupation. Therefore, we must consider not only the way in which politics affects the works of art but in what sense an artwork may itself constitute a political act or statement rather than being conceived merely as the result of a political intention (Millon and Nochlin 1978). It is difficult to miss the centrality of the Tibetan political cause in McLeod Gunj's landscape—"Free Tibet," "Boycott Chinese Goods," and similar stickers and posters are glaringly visible. The symbolic geography of Dharamsala in this sense is a *geography of resistance* as much as it is a *geography of regeneration*. In other words, the cultural is political.

An integral part of Dharamsala's geography is the festivals and various other events occurring throughout the year. Rather than seeing the festivals as merely reflecting religious beliefs or political rituals, we can examine the techniques and dynamics through which the narratives, symbolic spaces, and collective fantasies of communal identities are reproduced and regulated among the Tibetans and their supporters. Examples of such festivals that are replete with multiple meanings are Losar (February 12), Tibetan Uprising Day (March 10), the Dalai Lama's birthday (July 6), Democracy Day of Tibet (September 2), and the commemoration of the awarding of the Nobel Peace Prize to the Dalai Lama (December 10). Connerton's observation that "the ritual performances and commemorative ceremonies are important in building up collective memory, which in turn is crucial for the development of a sense of home" (in Kong and Yeoh 1997, 217) is also applicable in the case of the Tibetan diaspora.

Though the focus is on the preservation of culture, a visible feature of the symbolic geography of Dharamsala is hybridity. In their everyday life, Tibetan refugees in Dharamsala and elsewhere in South

Asia negotiate with the popular culture of India; it should come as no surprise, then, that Bollywood has a very significant influence on the identity of many Tibetans (see Diehl 2002). Everywhere I went, I found a striking similarity between Tibetan songs and songs from both popular Hindi films and Western pop music.

However, such observations, while complicating the notion of preservation of a "pure" culture, do not militate against a more sophisticated conception of Tibetan culture. The new generation may not practice "authentic" versions of culture, but, as evidenced from the activities of the Tibet Youth Congress, their creative negotiations with dominant cultures around them do not hamper their politicization. On the contrary, the ability simultaneously to negotiate and resist varied cultural practices makes the diasporic Tibetans well placed to carry forward their political movement in a rapidly changing world. The simultaneous negotiation, appropriation, and resistance are key features of postcoloniality.

CHALLENGING THE DOMINANT PARADIGM: READING CULTURAL IDENTITY IN TERMS OF ROOTS AND ROUTES

What does a postcolonial reading strategy look like? How can it seek to contextualize a politics of place and identity that takes into account the politics of representation? Here I wish to make six interrelated points relating to Tibetan identity—*roots* and *routes* of culture are complementary; identity is discursively produced; Exotica Tibet plays a productive role; the Dalai Lama's role is vital; an image of the "homeland" is crucial; and, finally, Tibet is a *re-imag(in)ing construct*.

First, the space for a different reading is afforded by the word *dharamshala* itself. As pointed out earlier, the word indicates a temporary home and this temporariness has been a central motif in Tibetan diasporic identity discourses. Tibet, the original homeland, is foregrounded as the final destination in these discourses and it also permeates the material as well as the performative cultural expressions of the Tibetans in diaspora. While focusing on the starting and finishing stations, such a reading ignores the crucial element of the travel itself. *Dharamshala* is not only a temporary home but also a temporary stop on the way to somewhere else. It is a house offering temporary hospitality to travelers on their way. One does not travel from home to *dharamshala* to return back to the home. Travel is transformative and constitutive. Rather, *dharamshala* is a temporary shelter to facilitate travel from one place to some other new place. If instead of focusing solely on the theme of return, we look at the process and experience of journey itself, we may be better placed to appreciate the conundrum of Tibetan identity politics.

As Clifford points out in a different context, "Practices of displacement might emerge as constitutive of cultural meanings rather than as their simple transfer or extension" (1997, 3). Instead of concentrating solely on the essence, the roots of Tibetan identity, we should look at the processes that constitute the routes traveled, including the creation of a pan-Tibetan exilic identity. Adoption of such a view allows us to appreciate the ambiguities involved in the project of cultural preservation as well as the changes that come about in the life of a community of people. While understanding the need to espouse one's cause in terms of an essential identity,[16] the contingency of such claims is not papered over—and herein lies the strength of the alternative theorization. Therefore, instead of framing an artificial opposition between the roots of culture and the routes of culture, we may look at them as complementary, for this false dichotomy is sustained only by the conventional view of culture as rooted in a particular place. If we look, on the other hand, at the roots as contingent foundations that are always already contested, we can begin to appreciate the complementarity.

Second, recognition of the contingent nature of identity does not delegitimize identity claims marshaled by Tibetans for their cause. It simply draws attention to the strategic nature of such claims. This position is possible if one adopts a discursive approach to identity that sees identification not as an artifact or an outcome but as a construction, as something *always in process*. Though not without its determinate conditions of existence, including the material and symbolic resources required to sustain it, identification is in the end conditional, inevitably lodged in contingency. "Identification is, then, a process of articulation, a suturing, an over-determination not a subsumption" (Hall 1996b, 3). We need to recognize that its popular usage notwithstanding, the concept does not signal a stable core of self, unfolding from beginning to end through all the vicissitudes of history without any substantial change (see Kaul 2007). On the contrary, we should accept that identities are always and already fragmented and fractured; they are never singular but multiply constructed across different, often intersecting and antagonistic discourses, practices, and positions.

Butler's idea of performativity is helpful here. As she succinctly puts it, "Identity is performatively constituted by the very 'expressions' that are said to be its results" (1990, 25).[17] The production of the (gendered) subject is not a singular or deliberate "act," but rather the "reiterative and citational practice by which discourse produces the effects that it names" (Butler 1993, 2). Applying this idea to the Tibetan case, we may see Tibetan identity as constituted by particular processes and practices and not as some universal, timeless fixed thing. Tibetan nationalism is conjured up by the anticipation of an essential Tibetanness, and to be effective, it needs to be repeated again and again; it is a process, not a product. It is this "anticipation" of the essence of Tibet, an essential Tibetanness, that is constitutively linked up with Exotica Tibet and Tibetanness.

Rather than seeing the identity question as a matter of simple historical investigation, we can deal with it in terms of the deployment of resources of history, language, and culture in the process of becoming rather than being. The idea of symbolic geography encapsulates such a discursive approach since instead of considering the ideas of locality and community as naturally given, it focuses on social and political processes of place making in Dharamsala. A discursive approach does not deny acts of communal political activism. It only reveals it as contingent, as strategic rather than as something unambiguously natural. The Tibetan claims to "an essential identity, while understandably deployed to serve as foundational identity claims" (Venturino 1997, 108), must be seen as always already imaginary, reified, constructed, and teleological and problematic.

Third, connected to the issue of a discursive approach to identity questions is an explicit recognition of the constitutive role played by Exotica Tibet. Representations, especially Western ones, have had a significant impact on the symbolic geography of Dharamsala and Tibetan identity discourses. The desire to secure patronage from sympathetic outsiders, elicit support for the Tibetan political cause, and make a living through commercial processes—all these forces have contributed to a self-reflexive adoption of Western representations of Tibetans as a part of Tibetanness. Image has been translated into identity. The representation of Tibetans as inherently religious and spiritual has certainly contributed to the mushrooming of yoga classes, retreat centers, and meditation schools in Dharamsala. At the same time, we must keep in mind the fact that the Tibetan exiles are not unique in that Western representations have a major effect on identity practices. As Huber (2001) argues, recent reflexive notions of Tibetan culture and identity witnessed in exile should be understood as products of a complex transnational politics of identity within which populations such as the Tibetan exiles are increasingly representing themselves and being represented by others. One such identity discourse, which Huber (1997) highlights, is connected to environmentalism. The presence within Dharamsala of the Green Hotel and Green Cyber Café, Vegetarian Health Food, and the like may be understood as a conscious desire to appropriate this particular discourse as a part of identity formation. The symbolic geography of Little Lhasa questions the premise that Tibetans are innocent victims—"prisoners of Shangri-la." Instead, even while acknowledging the unequal power relations, one must recognize that the Tibetan exiles possess agency and subjectivity (Klieger 2002a, Klieger 2002b; Korom 1997a, 1997b). This "agency is *always and only a political prerogative*" and "the constituted character of the subject is the very precondition of its agency" (Butler 1992, 13, 12, 17; emphasis in original).

Fourth, an integral part of Dharamsala as well as Tibetan diasporic identity is the crucial role played by the personality as well as the figure of the Dalai Lama. His smiling face adorns almost every establishment in the town, including the shops owned by non-Tibetans.[18] More than anything else, it is his residence here that contributes to the transformation of Dharamsala into Little Lhasa. He has a central position as the symbol of Tibet among Tibetan refugees and in the international media. Within discourses of Tibetanness, the Dalai Lama is "neither wholly transcendent (and thereby out of this world) nor wholly immanent (enmeshed in temporalities like the rest of us), but an ambiguous symbol imbued with the qualities of both" (Nowak 1984, 30). The fourteenth Dalai Lama has come to acquire an unprecedented position. He combines the role of the supreme leader of the entire Tibetan Buddhist community with the role of the chief spokesperson of Buddhist modernism. He is as much a world spiritual leader as the undisputed leader of the Tibetan political cause (Lopez 1998, 181–207). This mix of uniqueness with universalism and of a national cause with transnationalism is also underlined within Dharamsala's symbolic geography.

Fifth, though for the Tibetans the memory, the ideal, and the image of the land from which they have been exiled have been a vital force in the struggle for national recognition, the notion of return to the homeland is problematic. This problematization should not be seen in terms of a pessimistic scenario in which original Tibet has been destroyed and can never be retrieved. Instead, it guards against any naive imagination of a particularized space-time projection of Tibet as a timeless construct. Of course, this theme of return to the homeland is common to many exiled communities. The Palestinians are a good comparative example. In both cases one sees how the longing for home has changed over time from return to specific villages and particular dwellings to an emphasis on a collective national return to "the homeland" conceived more abstractly. Writing specifically about the Palestinians, Bisharat (1997) points out that in exile there occurs a displacement of a community, once understood as being rooted in particular localities, to the level of the nation (see also Bowman 1994). Homeland is conceived as a moral as well as a geographical location.

Last, the adoption of a different reading strategy also foregrounds the idea of Tibet as a *reimag(in)ing construct*. Following Anderson's theory of nations as imagined communities (1983), Tibet can be seen as an imagined construct. However, the use of the form *imagining* rather than *imagined* indicates that the process of imagination is a continuous one. And then, since the Dharamsala establishment plays a crucial role in shaping this imagining process according to some particular images and representations, I put the "in" within parenthesis. The process is as much one of imaging as it is of imagining. The prefix "re" is to counter any sense of simplistic linearity associated with the process of imagining Tibet as a nation.

However, this theorization of Tibet as a discursive reimag(in)ing does not deny the real desires and feelings of the people toward it. Instead, it promotes a historicization and politicization of such desires and feelings. It calls for special attention to be given to the ways spaces and places are made, imagined, contested, enforced, and reimagined. One needs to accept that given the limited vocabulary available to Tibetans to espouse their cause in the international arena, the use of the somewhat old-fashioned concept of nationalism is perfectly understandable. As Kibreab points out, in a world where rights such as equal treatment, access to resources, and freedom of movement are apportioned on the basis of territorially anchored identities, the identity people gain from their association with a particular place is an indispensable instrument (1999). Though a reimag(in)ing construct, Tibet has a *real* impact on the lives of many people, and this itself provides legitimacy to those struggling for the self-determination of Tibetans. My discursive theorization does not render this struggle problematic. At the theoretical level it calls for a reconceptualization of basic themes involved in the articulation of a Tibetan identification process as encapsulated within Dharamsala's symbolic geography. And at the level of political praxis, it simply warns against any naive ideas about nationalism, return to homeland, and the like.

CONCLUSION: AFFIRMING TIBETANNESS THROUGH ITS PROBLEMATIZATION

By way of a conclusion, I would like to clarify that this postcolonial reading based on a different understanding of the words *dharamshala/dharmashala* should not be seen as a simple alternative to the more common story discussed earlier in the chapter, for the political practices embedded within Dharamsala's symbolic geography defy any clear categorization in either of the two conceptual frameworks. My approach appreciates the practical need for espousing Tibetan identity as a strategic essentialism. At the same time, it highlights the need to recognize at a theoretical level the contingent character of these claims. The clear emphasis in my approach is on the "strategic" in the strategic essentialism. A sophisticated postcolonial theorization of Tibetanness in terms of symbolic geography facilitates such a two-pronged approach, while at the same time recognizing the arbitrariness involved in any distinction between theory and practice or between cultural and political identity discourses. Apart from other things, it also recognizes the politics of Exotica Tibet—the constitutive relation between Western representations and Tibetan identity discourses, that is, between Exotica Tibet and Tibetanness.

Conclusion

To "forget IR theory" (Bleiker 1997) is not to ignore it, for any such attempt will leave intact a disciplinary endeavor that has significant purchase on the understanding and construction of world politics. Rather, this forgetting involves *unprivileging* the dominant modes of analysis of world politics and learning to *think differently*. From an IR perspective, the learning process within this book has involved journeying into the *exotic* thoughtscape of social theory, postcolonialism, diaspora studies, cultural theory, colonial discourse analysis, and Tibetology. The journey led to a shedding of old baggage and picking up of new; it had temporary halts but only an arbitrary beginning and an even more contingent end. The book is, in this sense, a journal of a theoretical and empirical journey.

My analysis has involved three "*de-*"s (deparochializing, deconstructive analysis, and description) and three "*re-*"s (representation, reimagining, and retheorizing). After introducing the Tibet question, I set up the argument for a postcolonial IR that seeks to reveal the ethnocentrism and lack of concern for the issues central to the lives of peoples in the non-West of mainstream (and sometimes even critical) IR and to *deparochialize* them. The rest of my endeavor does not always "use" insights from postcolonialism and IR theory but is inspired by postcoloniality (a postcolonial critical attitude). The examination of the theme of *representation* in chapter 1 foregrounds my theoretical belief in the discursive constitution

129

of reality. Representation, especially the Western representation of the non-West, is central to the study of IR as it is a crucial dynamic of world politics, often supporting the dominant truth regimes and structures of power. Critical IR has focused mainly on the constitutive function of representation in generating and sustaining particular foreign policy regimes and on the identity politics of the representer. What about the impact of Western representations on the represented? By ignoring this, critical IR leaves itself open to the charge of West-centrism. This work seeks to rectify this and through the empirical study of Western representations of Tibet highlights its productive and restrictive effects on the non-West. Exotica Tibet is theorized in terms of its poetics and politics.

Chapter 2 offers a *deconstructive analysis* of Western representational practices by studying some common rhetorical strategies of representation. Chapter 3 is a *description* of how Western interaction, seen as imperial encounter, has a constitutive relation with the imagination of Tibet. Chapter 4 charts the formation of Tibet as a geopolitical entity within the wider context of Western theory and praxis of sovereignty, imperialism, and foreign policy. Finally, the next two chapters *retheorize* Tibetanness and argue that Tibet is a *reimag(in)ing* construct. Thus, a postcolonial analysis of the poetics and the politics of Exotica Tibet underlines the importance of critically studying Western representations of the non-West within a deparochialized IR.

My effort here has been to challenge the geographical parochialism of both the mainstream and critical IR endeavors. "Tibet" here stands not only for those who identify with it (the Tibetans) but also as a challenge to critical endeavors in IR as well as to postcolonial theorizing. My attempt has been not only to promote a dialogue between postcolonial theory and IR theory but, more important, to adopt a postcolonial critical attitude—that is, postcoloniality—to offer new, innovative ways of doing IR analyses. Here I am aware that I am deploying "Tibet" to critique certain ways of thinking, in a manner somewhat similar to Orientalists for whom "Tibet" has been only a category to be used, to be deployed for self-serving purposes. My *Orientalizing* gesture reflects partly my failure to break out of the pernicious mode of thought set up by the dominant West and partly a failure of postcolonial thinking that is forced to respond to the West and its knowledge in its own language, on terms set by it. Where my use is different is in a self-consciousness and reflexivity about it, in a strategic deployment that seeks to write back at dominant modes of analyses and challenge the provincialism-in-the-guise-of-universalism characterizing these modes. An awareness of ethnocentrism leads to greater self-reflexivity, sensitivity for the Other, and an openness to alternative theoretical perspectives. My own position as a non-Tibetan interested observer is acknowledged.

This work is a call for a postcolonial IR theoretical approach, the space for which has been cleared by the postpositivist debates. It challenges the commonplace ignorance of the history of imperialism and colonialism in the analysis of supposedly "intractable" political problems in the postcolonial world. It highlights the centrality of the concept of representation to the Western enterprise of knowledge production about its Others. It bares the "real" impact of rhetorical utterances and practices. *Geopolitical Exotica* explores asymmetrical power relations in the discursive production of "Tibet" as a specific site of West–non-West encounter in and beyond the twentieth century. It emphasizes the (re)productive relation between representation and identity and performs a deconstructive cultural analysis of Western images of Tibet by looking at the poetics of representation, which entails recognition of the contingency of identity without giving up the notion of agency. It theorizes Tibetan identity discourses as constitutively and performatively produced in relation to Western imaginaries and imageries, the politics of representation. Though Orientalism finds itself "constantly appropriated, reworked, and re-accentuated in the utterances of others" (Ha 2000, xii), the asymmetrical operation and effect of the power-knowledge nexus remains its chief characteristic.

Postcolonial IR thus offers an effective understanding of the political and productive effect of Western representational practices, especially on non-Western people. The poetics (the "how" question) and politics ("what impact" question) of Western representations are legitimate and vital areas of inquiry for IR because these support particular foreign policy regimes and have a productive effect on the identities of political actors. Postcolonial IR appreciates the importance of popular culture for our understanding of world politics. It alerts us to the fact that what we accept as real is a "changeable and revisable reality. . . . Although this insight does not in itself constitute a political revolution, no political revolution is possible without a radical shift in one's notion of the possible and the real" (Butler 1999, xxiii).

How can we understand more effectively the ways in which Western representations of the Other ("the Exotic") generate vexing political problems in the contemporary postcolonial world? In order to get at this question, I have utilized resources from International Relations, postcolonial and cultural theory, and Tibetan studies to interrogate Exotica Tibet in terms of its poetics (how Tibet is represented) and its politics (what impact these representational regimes have on the represented). I have sustained an empirical study of one specific geopolitical exotica—Exotica Tibet—to substantiate theoretical arguments about the role of representation and identity in the theory and praxis of world politics.

The poetics and politics of Exotica Tibet mark a new way of enculturing political analysis and politicizing cultural criticism, one that seeks to open the endeavor of IR to new vistas. Hybrid endeavors such as postcolonial international relations theory contribute to changing IR from being a "discourse of limits" (Walker 1995, 34) to what I would like to call a *discourse of empowering criticality.*

Notes

INTRODUCTION

1. I use the term "Tibet question" to refer to Tibet as an issue in world politics. By using the interrogative word, I foreground the Tibetan issue as a "problem," in line with the "Palestine question" or the "Irish question." It is more than "the conflict over the political status of Tibet vis-à-vis China" (Goldstein in Goldstein and Kapstein 1998, 14; see also Heberer 1995). Crucially, it includes an examination of the very categories of "Tibet" and "Tibetans."

2. One other reason for this could be what Chan argues is IR's paucity in understanding matters of religions and religious values contributing to the fact that it "has nothing to say about the contest between China and Tibet to ordain and maintain Lamas" (2000, 566). The most famous of these contests is over the reincarnation of the Panchen Lama, usually considered as second in religious hierarchy within Tibetan Buddhism (at least within the dominant Gelugpa sect), next only to the Dalai Lama.

3. The International Commission of Jurists (http://www.icj.org) in Geneva brought out two early reports on Tibet—"The Question of Tibet and the Rule of Law" (1959) and "Tibet and the Chinese People's Republic" (1960)—and continues to issue reports. The UN General Assembly has passed three resolutions on Tibet: 1353 (XIV) 1959; 1723 (XVI) 1961; 2079 (XX) 1965. For details on these as well as other international resolutions on Tibet, see Department of Information and International Relations (1997).

4. Apart from Tibet and the West, the main actor involved is China. In this book, the focus of research is on Western representations and their

impact on the identity of Tibet and Tibetans. This is done as an opening gesture without denying the importance of other aspects, including the Chinese representations. Analysis of Chinese representations of Tibet deserves more space than can be afforded within this study.

Knowledge production about Tibet, especially since the mid-twentieth century when the Chinese communists consolidated their political control, is no longer the preserve of Europeans. Very much in the tradition of Orientalist scholarship and British imperialist writings, the manufacturing of scholarly truths about Tibet within the Chinese academies is implicated in the service of the political regime. Chinese representations of Tibetans as essentially backward, primitive, and barbaric are witnessed not only at the popular level (Wei Jingsheng 1998) but more dangerously within state discourse too (see Heberer 2001; Hillman and Henfry 2006; Kolas 1998; Makley 1997, 1999; Shakya 2002; for Han Chinese representations of minorities in general, see Blum 2000, 2002; Dikotter 1992; Gladney 1994, 2004). Analysis of the Chinese representations of Tibet will show how Tibetans, like most of the non-Han Chinese, are seen as an exotic but backward people requiring Chinese leadership to help them progress. The notion of Tibet's lack of development due to "cultural backwardness" has been very strong in Chinese state policies since the 1951 Seventeen Point Agreement (see Shan 2001; Zugui and Zuji 1996). Development as a rationale for Chinese control is also found in the writings of those sympathetic to the communist regime (see Gelder and Gelder 1964; Suyin 1977) and of many Chinese dissidents (see Xu Mingxu 2000) and creative intellectuals (for exceptions see Cao Changching and Seymour 1998; Yue 2004). Unfortunately this has resonance with the self-justificatory tone of the civilizing mission within Western imperialism. This patronizing tone is also evident in Wang Lixiong, who in the name of recognizing Tibetan agency tends to erase it by tracing the roots of the "intense religiosity" of the Tibetans to "the terrors of their natural environment" (2002, 91).

1. POSTCOLONIALITY, REPRESENTATION, AND WORLD POLITICS

1. For exceptions, see Agathangelou 2004; Chowdhry and Nair 2002; Darby 1997, 1998; Darby and Paolini 1994; Krishna 1993, 1999; Ling 2002; Muppidi 2004; Paolini 1999; Ramakrishnan 1999.

2. Amin rightly argues that though Eurocentrism is anti-universalist, "it does present itself as universalist, for it claims that imitation of the Western model by all peoples is the only solution to the challenges of our time" (1988, vii).

3. It is not surprising that Brown et al. (2002) in *International Relations in Political Thought* focus exclusively on the Western canon. The excuse

they offer is symptomatic of IR in general. For instance, they argue that the relevant criteria for the canon can change on the basis of "current fashions" (such as the current criticism that the canon usually consists of white male Europeans), but this should not deny the "fact" that some "thinkers clearly have produced more significant work than others" (3) (not surprisingly, these are the same as the canonical thinkers). This seems to be a dismissive gesture of relegating those who challenge the Eurocentrism and misogyny of the Western canon as "current fashion."

Brown et al. go on to argue that the "modern global international order developed out of the European states-system, which emerged in the sixteenth and seventeenth century CE from the wreckage of the medieval order which was constructed on the ruins of the Roman empire, in turn the product of the Roman republic and the inheritor of the thought of classical Greece" (14). This buys into the dominant autobiography of modern Western thinking. It misses the crucial constitutive role of the "rest of the world" in the change from the medieval to the modern period. Ironically, the editors stop at the gate of classical Greeks—once again ignoring the question of where the Greeks came from. In such stories, classical Greeks seem to have descended from "heaven," without "impure" influences of nearby cultures, especially the Egyptians (cf. Bernal 1987, 1991). My argument is not against a compilation of the writings of Western political thinkers but against passing it off as global/international thought.

4. The justification Rosenau provides for ignoring "Third world analysts" is "space limitations." But this does not lead him to title the book as *Western Voices* instead of *Global Voices*. On the other hand, Waever (1998) is conscious of his noninvestigation of non-Western cases and does not conflate "American and European developments in international relations" with wider global developments.

5. Sylvester not only includes a "Western feminist (Westfem)" but also ventriloquizes for "Her Third World Alter Ego/Identity (Tsitsi)" (Sylvester 1993; see also Agathangelou and Ling 2004).

6. Some argue that since IR as a discipline is closely linked with the rise of the United States as a "superpower" and because of intellectual predisposition, political circumstances, and institutional opportunities, it is mainly an "American social science" (Hoffman 1977; see also Crawford and Jarvis 2000; Smith 2000). Hence a better term might be "Americentrism." However, Eurocentrism's main feature has been the explaining away of parochialism (European Enlightenment thinking) as superior, progressive, and hence universal. Americentrism does not challenge this. Instead, it reinforces the powerful myth that the West is the best.

7. This term, formerly reserved for communist-ruled Eastern Europe and the USSR, is often used interchangeably for the South following the end of communist regimes there. This goes back to an older distinction

usually made in European thought between the West and the East. For an interesting analysis of the use of the "East" as the Other in the European identity formation, see Neumann 1999.

8. See Ashcroft et al. 1989, 1995; Barker et al. 1994; Chambers and Curtis 1996; Chaturvedi 2000; Gandhi 1998; Hall 1996a; Loomba 1998; Mongia 1996; Moore-Gilbert 1997; Moore-Gilbert et al. 1997; Prakash 1995; Williams and Childs 1997; Young 1990.

9. Though within IR theory significant debates have taken place, including the third debate between "rationalism" and "reflectivism," as Smith points out, the wider discipline of IR "is far more realist, far more state-centric and far more unquestioning of the dominance of realism and positivism than is the case within IR theory" (2000, 379).

10. For a different view on imperialism and IR, see Long and Schmidt 2005.

11. At an institutional level, the unequal relations are exemplified in almost every international body. One of the best examples, of course, is the UN Security Council and its five permanent members with veto power. Grovogui highlights two paradoxes of decolonization. First, only the rights sanctioned by the former colonialists were accorded to the colonized, regardless of the needs and demands of the latter. Second, "the rules and procedures of decolonization were determined and controlled by the former colonial powers to effect specific outcomes" (1996, 6).

12. Some writers put the blame for U.S. interventions in the third world on the third world itself. For instance, Snyder (1999), in his analysis of U.S. relations with Cuba, Iran, Nicaragua, and Zimbabwe, argues that it is their provocation that leads to a U.S. reaction. It reflects the phenomenon of blaming the victims and absolving the victimizer (for interesting views on this phenomenon as witnessed in the case of the Palestinian question, see Said and Hitchens 1988).

13. One interesting divide within the discipline is between those who draw upon poststructuralist thought, represented by the so-called holy trinity (Moore-Gilbert 1997) of postcolonial theory—Edward Said, Homi Bhabha, and Gayatri Spivak—and those who consider poststructuralism to be a retrogressive move that ignores the material deprivation of the peoples in the third world (see Ahmad 1994; Parry 1996; Shohat 1992). For a range of views on the relationship between postcolonialism and poststructuralism, see Adam and Tiffin 1991.

14. See Enloe 2000; Jabri and O'Gorman 1999; Parpart and Zalewski 1998; Peterson and Runyan 1999; Pettman 1996; Steans 1998; Sylvester 2002; Tickner 1992.

15. Feminists have taken the lead over others in their expositions on negotiating between essentialisms and antiessentialisms. One recalls here

Butler's "contingent foundations" (1992), Ferguson's "mobile subjectivities" (1993), and Fuss's strategy of "deploying essentialism" (1989).

16. Here one may point out Said's method of *contrapuntal reading*, which involves a way of reading texts (of literature) so as to reveal their deep implication in dominant systems (imperialism and colonial process). Examples are found in Said 1993.

17. This is linked to the frequent criticism of poststructuralism that it kills off the subject of knowledge and leaves no room for agency. As Spivak clarifies, the poststructuralists "situate subjecting rather than kill the subject or pronounce it dead" (1999, 322). It recognizes that "I am not outside the language that structures me, but neither am I determined by the language that makes this 'I' possible" (Butler 1999, xxiv).

2. IMAGINING THE OTHER

1. Interestingly, since 2002 British supermarkets have sold a "Tibet" line of haircare products (with names such as "Rebirth" and "Balance"), promising "beauty through balance" (http://www.tibetbeauty.com). Indeed, Tibet has come a long way from being a "country of the great unwashed."

2. For Tibetophiles such as Heinrich Hensoldt and Madame Helena Blavatsky (theosophists), the veil was an important metaphor too. But for them it was the Tibetans, especially the Dalai Lama, who lifted the veil, the other veil, the mystical veil of Isis (Bishop 1989, 182).

3. Sociologically, most of the European travelers to Tibet were men operating with specific notions of masculinity. British officials explicitly discouraged female travelers, who were seen as a threat to British prestige. Basil Gould, the political agent in Sikkim and later head of the 1936 Lhasa mission, decreed that women were not permitted to travel in Tibet without a male escort (McKay 1997, 172–73).

4. *Daily Mail*, 12 September 1904, gave the following description of the signing of the Lhasa Convention at the culmination of the Younghusband mission: "The monks wandered about the hall, smiling and laughing in the faces of the British officers and eating nuts" (in IOR: MSS EUR/ F197/523). It is not too far-fetched to see the description of the monks as similar to that of monkeys.

3. POETICS OF EXOTICA TIBET

1. Representations also differed slightly among Western states. For instance, in the first half of the twentieth century (except during the Younghusband mission in 1903–4), American perceptions of Tibet tended to be

less positive than the British representations of Tibet (for American popular perceptions of Tibet before the Second World War, see Miller 1988).

2. One aspect of the story of Tibet as a blank space is the denial of any quintessential Tibetan civilization, especially before the twentieth century. Many commentators opined that what passes as "Tibetan" is merely a mix of "great" neighboring civilizations (Chinese and Indian). Rockhill is typical: "Present advanced degree of civilization is entirely borrowed from China, India, and possibly Turkestan, and Tibet has only contributed the simple arts of the tent-dwelling herdsmen" (1895, 673).

3. Who would count as competitors in this race was of course to be decided by the Europeans. Native explorers and spies (known as pundits) like Sarat Chandra Das who managed to reach Lhasa and made possible the geographical mapping of Tibet (see Das 1902; Waller 1990; Rawat 1973) were ineligible, even though they too had to travel in disguise. Observers cited multiple possible reasons: native surveyors "become so engrossed with the details of their work that they forget to use their eyes and make those general observations on the people and the scenery about them which is a most important objective of their journeying" (Holdich 1906, 233); or "though very intelligent, [they] had no special qualifications for observing those facts of natural science which would be observed by Englishmen" (Delmar Morgan in Walker 1885, 25); or "suffering from the limitations of disguise and the need to move principally among the lower orders of society, [they] produced more valuable reports on topography and communications than on social, economic, and political conditions in Tibet" (Richardson 1962, 74); or "it was easier for the Asiatics and therefore the race was among the Europeans" (Hopkirk 1983, 157). This comes as no surprise because in the imperialist imagination, exploration was a possession of "civilised man." In his 1963 biography of Richard Francis Burton, Farwell begins by stating that "the explorer is always a civilized man; exploration is an advanced intellectual concept" and therefore exploration is "a concept unknown to primitive peoples, and one that remains incomprehensible to women" (see Kabbani 1986, 86).

4. Today "Shangri-la" is the name of a chain of resort hotels. Shangri-La hotels advertise that although mythical in origin, their name epitomizes "the serenity and highly personalised service" for which it is renowned (Shangri-La Media Centre 2001).

5. Interestingly, while the Chinese state has always insisted that "Old Tibet" was feudal and oppressive, in recent times there have been moves by some Tibetan regions to compete to be represented as Shangri-la for tourism. On the use of the Shangri-la myth for ethnic tourism, see Hillman 2003; Kolas 2004.

6. An example of this can be seen in Lonely Planet's (2002) introduction

to Tibet: "Locked away in its Himalayan fortress, Tibet has long exercised a unique hold on the imagination of the West: 'Shangri-La,' 'the Land of Snows,' 'the Rooftop of the World,' Tibet is mysterious in a way that few other places are. Tibet's strategic importance, straddling the Himalayas between China and the Indian subcontinent, made it irresistible to China who invaded in 1950." No mention is made of the British imperial invasion to "open" Tibet.

7. Within the Orientalist frame of thinking, expertise in cultures of the Other lies with the imperialists, not the natives of the culture. Young-husband's mission had "scientific" staff consisting of surveyors, naturalists, geologists, anthropologists (Younghusband in Hayden 1927, vii); their military and scientific roles overlapped. For instance, Waddell was an authority on Tibetan Buddhism, a medical officer, as well as a collector of texts, plants, and birds. Waddell, along with Captain Walton, is credited with "discovering" the Lhasa poppy (see Fletcher 1975, xxi). Similarly, the blue poppy's scientific name is *Meconopsis baileyi*, after its "discoverer," Lieutenant Colonel F. M. Bailey; the wild sheep argali and Tibet antelope chiru are *Ovis ammon hodgsoni* and *Pantholops hodgsoni* after Brian Hodgson, the British resident at the Nepalese court. This practice reflects the view of the Orient as a passive object to be discovered and appropriated by the West. Tibetans (and maybe many non-Tibetans too) were of course familiar with the poppy. But it required a Western man to name it, taxonomize it in a "universal" scheme of things, and thus become its discoverer. Interestingly, in the movie *The Face of Fu Manchu* (1965), the eponymous villain learns how to distill a vicious poison from the "Black Hill poppy" of Tibet thanks to the papers of the Younghusband expedition, where the complete secret of the plant is meticulously laid down. In some instances scientific names of Tibetan flora and fauna are hybrids, such as *Ovis ammon dalailamae przevalskii* (1888) (named after the Dalai Lama and the Russian explorer Nikolai Przhevalsky) for one variant of argali, the wild sheep.

8. In fact, after his Lhasa expedition Younghusband involved himself in nonconventional mystical activities. In an obituary for Younghusband, the *New York Times* merged the man who had led the British invasion with the Hollywood myth: "If as James Hilton strongly suggests in Lost Horizon, Shangri-La is somewhere in Tibet rather than merely somewhere— anywhere . . . then Sir Francis Younghusband probably came closer than anyone else to being Robert Conway" (French 1995, 202).

9. Missionaries had their own romantic vision of Tibet, often emphasizing the darker aspects of Tibetan culture in order to highlight the country's need for Christian enlightenment. Petrus and Susie Rijnhart expressed the goal of their missionary travel as "perpetuating and deepening the

widespread interest in the evangelization of Tibet" for "much has [been] written of the heathen in other countries . . . but the Tibetans with their monstrous butter Buddha occupy a unique place in the world's idolatry" (1901, 1, 119). After all, Lhasa is not "only a city of metaphysical mysteries and the mummery of idol-worship; it is a secret chamber of crime; its rock and its road, its silken flags and its scented altars, are all stained with blood" (Carey 1902, 58). Monastic rapacity and domination along with criticisms of Tibetan sexual morality were common themes in missionary writings. Missionaries saw themselves as "soldiers of Christ" and Tibet as a citadel under siege (Bray 2001, 28). However, by the late twentieth century, missionary accounts show much greater empathy and sometimes a deep cultural understanding.

10. Though Tibet is mainly associated with a variant of Buddhism or "Lamaism," there were quite a few practicing Muslims living in Lhasa. In most of the studies on Tibetan culture, the contribution of Tibetan Muslims is largely ignored. For exceptions, see Sheikh 1991; Siddiqui 1991; *Tibet Journal* 1995.

11. Waddell even purchased a "Lamaist temple with its fittings; and prevailed on the officiating priests to explain . . . in full detail the symbolism and the rites as they proceeded" (1972, viii).

12. Yet the lama is not totally convinced about British control over knowledge, for he says that there are still things that Western scholars do not know, have not sought—things relating to spiritual wisdom. Later, the lama introduces Kim to new art forms and says, chuckling, "The Sahibs have not *all* this world's wisdom" (Kipling 1976, 209; emphasis in original).

13. Wilson surmises why Kipling used the character of a Tibetan lama and not any other Indian religious figure: it was essential to the spiritual relation that was to develop between the lama and Kim that, for Kim, his master be an exotic novelty, for the boy's curiosity about everything new is what marks him out as someone who is likely to learn from life (Wilson 1987, 53). The lama provides exactly this. His simplicity and novelty allowed Kim to claim that "the lama was his trove, and he proposed to take possession" (Kipling 1976, 19). And it was also necessary that the master should be entirely dependent upon Kim for guidance in the real world. The Tibetan lama symbolized radical "otherworldliness."

14. Interestingly, Kipling had borrowed the term "Teshoo Lama" from earlier British accounts of the limited interaction with Tibetans at the end of the eighteenth century. George Bogle (see Markham 1876) as well as Samuel Turner (Turner 1971/1800), representatives of the East India Company, had both interacted with Tashi Lama/Teshoo Lama (later known as Panchen Lama).

15. Naturalization is another theme that operates within Western representational practices, as "natives" are often associated with nature. Here, nature is opposed to culture and civilization: primitive people live in a state of nature and, similarly, those who live close to nature are primitive, uncivilized. Riencourt contends that the "psychic knowledge of the lamas" is caused by the "awe-inspiring landscape, severity of the climate and remoteness of its valleys, the majestic silence and peace of the roof of the world" (1950, 263).

16. For a critical take on David-Neel's travel writing, see Mills 1991. See also Foster and Foster 1987.

17. A secret memorandum dated 22 August 1922 mentions her as a "lady of somewhat doubtful antecedents" (IOR: L/P&S/10/1012 1921, 145).

18. Lopez, for example, praises Rampa's books as having "brought the plight of Tibet to an otherwise indifferent audience of hundreds of thousands of Westerners, who would remain unconcerned were it not for the trappings of astral travel, spiritualism, and the hope of human evolution to a new age" (1998, 107).

19. Fascination with gold has been a part of Western imagination of Tibet since ancient times when the Greeks wrote of gold-digging ants. In the early twentieth century, the British Foreign Office reports: "Even though gold is not produced much in early 20th century, it has little bearing over future possibilities" and approvingly quotes Holdich: 'Tibet is not only rich [in gold] in the ordinary acceptance of the term; she must be enormously rich—possibly richer than any country in the world. For thousands of years gold has been washed out of her surface soil by the very crudest of all processes. . . . From every river which has its source in the Tibetan plateau, gold is washed" (1920, 61).

20. Tibet as a mere playground for Westerners' adventure is more clearly visible in Davidson's *The Rose of Tibet* (1995), originally published in 1962. Its most defining feature is an abundance of sexual motifs. Here we come across priestesses who are not allowed to have sex, but they still do it "like rattlesnakes," often with outsiders, as there are only a hundred monks to "take care" of them (336). We encounter the she-devil who was "not old, and she was not cold; and she was far from being a virgin" (399); instead, she was "delicious and delectable and always unknowable" (407). And she possessed "green tears—emeralds"—half of which she later gives to the hero, an Englishman, Charles Houston, as a sign of her love. Houston not only has sex with her but also insists on her being monogamous. He fails in this as she indulges in the "particularly, vilely horrible" custom of having sex with the main abbot. He now saw her as an object lovely but diseased, a rank thing growing unhealthily on top of a dunghill (441).

4. THE WEST AND THE IDENTITY OF "TIBET"

1. For a comprehensive collection of different perspectives on the Tibet question, see Sautman and Dreyer 2006.

2. Focusing on the constructedness of Tibet does not mean that China or any other geopolitical entity is less constructed. For a contested notion of "China," see Gladney 2004; Liu 2004; Shih 2003.

3. The reasoning of Bogle, an East India Company official in the 1770s, for the need to establish commercial relations with Tibet (and other states in the cis-Himalayan region) reflects the expansionary imperative within the colonizing regime of the East India Company. He says, "The constant drain of money from these provinces [in the Gangetic plains] is a consequence naturally arising from the relative situation in which this country is placed with respect to Great Britain. . . . It is impossible to prevent this drain—all that can be done, is to endeavor to supply it by opening new channels of commerce" (IOR: H/219 1768–84, 375).

4. As Shaumian points out, "Russian authorities never contemplated direct military intervention in Tibet, nor did they nurture plans to conquer India, but skilfully and often successfully exploited the Tibetan question to exert pressure on Great Britain and thereby obtain concessions in other regions that were more germane to their military-strategic and other political interests" (2000, viii).

5. Curzon's fear of Russia in the Great Game was now seen as unimportant in comparison to the bigger game being played in Europe with shifting alliances. "Tibet was a pawn to be manipulated according to the requirements of big power politics. The Game, a strategic one rather than a tactical one, was suddenly being played in the chanceries of Europe, not in the deserts of trans-Himalaya" (MacGregor 1970, 351).

6. A protest by an unknown bureaucrat is prescient: "To omit the line is of course the line of least resistance; but it leaves an ambiguity just when we were striving for precision—and a dangerous ambiguity of wh. the Chinese will continue to avail themselves" (IOR: L/P&S/10/265 1912, 47).

7. Formally known as the "Agreement of the Central People's Government and the Local Government of Tibet on Measures for the Peaceful Liberation of Tibet," it was signed in Beijing on 23 May 1951.

8. Even though religion and politics did not exist as separate categories, a genre of open political and social criticism existed in the form of "street songs" (see Goldstein 1982).

9. Knaus further points out that the Americans operated with a frontier mentality, assuming the Tibetan situation to be the theatrical scene of a "frontier drama with the good guys trying to get rid of bad guys" (1999, 61). According to him, "The CIA men viewed their Tibetan pupils as Oriental versions of self-reliant, straight-shooting American frontiersmen who

were under attack and seeking only the means to fight for their own way of life" (216). Ironically, this sentiment ignored that while in the American case frontiersmen were the invaders, in the Tibetan case the "Oriental frontiersmen" were the ones who suffered from Chinese invasion.

5. THE POLITICS OF TIBETAN (TRANS)NATIONAL IDENTITY

1. This approach is exemplified in Ekvall's (1960) pioneering work in which he identified five common cultural traits through which Tibetans define themselves: religion, folkways, language, race (human lineage), and land.

2. While most commentators consider Tibetans to be victims of forces of modernization and Chinese oppression, scholars like Lopez (1998) consider them victims of the Western perception of Tibetans as inherently religious, peaceful, and spiritual. In contrast, this chapter recognizes the need to consider Tibetans as agents in their own right. Interestingly, Neilson even argues that the Shangri-la myth itself is significant for facilitating "a critical utopianism that allows a reassessment of the Tibetan question outside the politics of territory" (2000, 95).

3. Anderson's categorization of nations as imagined communities (1983) does not fully convey the sense of continuous imagination that goes into the making and existence of a nation, so I prefer to use "imagining." In the next chapter, I retheorize this as "re-imag(in)ing community."

4. None of the prominent experts on nationalism speaks about Tibet, except Hobsbawm, who mentions Tibet only in passing as a possible exception to his theory: "It is difficult to judge how far purely divine authority may have nation-making possibilities. The question must be left to the experts in the history of Mongols and Tibetans" (1990, 72).

5. Their role may be seen as that of the disgruntled traditional intelligentsia described by Gellner (1983, 14).

6. Though some observers such as Grunfeld are of the opinion that "independence is an abstract notion which most Tibetans do not seem to think about very much" (quoted in Sperling 2004), others have provided a convincing rebuttal of such views (see Schwartz 1996; see also Barnett and Akiner 1996).

7. Tibetans have been successful in avoiding assimilation with the host society by following a policy of limited acculturation. In Nepal and in parts of north India, Tibetans contribute substantially to the tourism industry, especially in the regions in which they live. Elsewhere, they concentrate more on specialized craft industries (see Methfessel 1996). Rather than competing with local Indians or Nepalese over scarce resources, they have

established new enterprises, which also benefit locals with their spill-over effects. This does not mean that the relationship between refugees and locals is totally harmonious. As 1999 riots against Tibetans in Manali (India) show, there are potential trouble spots that need to be addressed by community leaders as well as the Indian establishment. Since isolation is hardly a viable choice for most migrant communities (and individuals) when faced with the problems of adjusting in the host society, the Tibetan establishment opted for a policy of limited acculturation as opposed to assimilation. While influences of popular Indian cultures including Bollywood are marked among the lay Tibetans, a sense of separate and distinct identity is prevalent (see Diehl 2002). Both in rhetoric as well as in practice, the Tibetan refugee community has largely avoided the assimilative process of *sanskritisation* that affects most minority groups in India.

8. A particular space-time projection of "homeland" is another constitutive factor in fostering Tibetan identity in the diaspora. Diasporic longing for the homeland is reflected in material as well as artistic production among exile communities. Images of Tibet, such as the Potala Palace, are favorite motifs. This nostalgia for space is complemented by nostalgia for time. It is not contemporary Tibet but pre-1959 Tibet, frozen in time, that defines the longing. As Harris points out, many Tibetan refugee craftspeople and artists are involved in "a nostalgic recreation of *temps perdus*; an inevitable process of conscious archaism" (1993, 112; see also Ahmed 2006). In the diaspora, the role of memory is central to imagining Tibet as a nation, since re-creating and preserving the memories of Tibet is crucial for maintaining the vision of "Free Tibet" as a common cause. These memories also provide the tools of expression, the language and the idioms of Tibetan unity and identity.

9. "The Tibet cause has attracted an exceptionally diverse group of people, some of whom see their activities on behalf of the cause as connected with Buddhist belief and practice, while others are concerned with human rights, opposing communism, and a range of other motivations" (Powers 2000, 3). Among this range of other motivations, New Age Orientalism is prominent. Though often New Age and Western Buddhism are conflated, mostly by their critics, they are quite distinct. Even when criticizing the Western states for betraying Tibet, some supporters adopt a haughty view of a superior Western way of being. For example, Berkin in his book "about a lost state" mentions British imperial policy and weak and market-hungry Western states as part of the cause, but then talks about how the question of Tibet is also about "a clash of values; between western democracy and oriental absolutism" (2000, xv).

10. Klieger further argues that diasporic Tibetan identity formation is a result of ideological convergence between the Western Shangri-la image

and the self-perception of Tibetans: "[a] collision has occurred between the Occidental paradigm of an Eastern paradise, Shangri-La, and an indigenous utopia which constructs a distanced, sacred Tibetan homeland upon the established Shambhala, Mt. Meru, Mt. Potala and divine rule mythology" (1997, 61).

11. Though the odds are stacked against Tibetans in the real world, in the virtual world the situation is radically different . An overwhelming number of Web sites on Tibet are pro-Tibetan. I searched for "Tibet" on 15 February 2001 using Google.com/. Out of the first one hundred links, only three were not connected to the Tibet movement. A similar search on 6 August 2006 yielded thirty-eight out of the first fifty links that were directly connected with the Tibet movement (the rest were either travel-related sites or pro-China sites). To a certain extent, Tibet Online, which claims to serve as a virtual community space for the Tibet movement, succeeds in its aim of leveling the playing field by leveraging the Internet's ability to harness grassroots support for Tibet's survival (*About Tibet Online* 2006).

12. This is not to deny that elements of modern nationalism had started to emerge inside Tibet as early as 1913 when the thirteenth Dalai Lama's proclamation upon his return from exile showed a clear "awareness of Tibet as a distinct country, defined by its culture and history" (Dreyfus 2002, 40). Further, popular movements against the Chinese during the 1950s, including the "Four Rivers, Six Ranges" *(chu bzhi gang drug),* asserted distinct nationalism defined in opposition to Chinese occupation (see Shakya 1999).

13. Contrary to the commonly held assumption on all sides, even in the theocratic, conservative, and "feudal" society of "Old Tibet" resistance to authority was never completely absent. For instance, Bell recalled theater performances in Lhasa in which actors did not hesitate to ridicule certain aspects of their religion and even less so of their officials (IOR: MSS EUR/ F80/217 n.d., 11). He further mentions a "Sun body" play by Kyor-mo Lung-nga troupe in which there was an explicit anti-Chinese political allusion, with "a kick for the Emperor of China" (18–19). Going back even earlier, Aris discusses an eighteenth-century writing by a Tibetan in which positive sympathy can be detected for the undefeated Marathas and their long stand against both the Mughals and the British (1994, 12). All this challenges the image of a passive Tibetan society.

14. There is another explanation for this difference in the support bases for the Palestinian and the Tibetan causes. The former is looked at as a case of European imperialism and settler colonialism on the part of Israel (see Beit-Hallahmi 1993; Finkelstein 1995; Lilienthal 1978). Therefore, decolonization demands the recognition of Palestinian statehood. On the

other hand, as the "colonizer" in the case of Tibet is another postcolonial state, the matter is looked at as an internal issue of a minority nationality, a problem that raises uncomfortable questions within many postcolonial states. This discomfort also reveals the refusal of the international community to follow the logic of decolonization to allow the right of self-determination to all peoples, not only those under European imperialism.

15. The connection between the symbolism implicit in Tibetan government-in-exile structure and the homeland of Tibet is evident in the evolving democratic system with a National Assembly at the top (see Magnusson 1997). Here, a quota system operates according to which there are an equal number of representatives for three principal regions of Tibet, the same number of representatives from each of five major religious sects, a few representatives from outside South Asia, and finally a few nominated members. The Tibetans in diaspora therefore vote to make a symbolic claim to Tibet rather than represent their own interests.

16. Dorje Shugden is an important protector deity of the Gelugpas, the politically dominant Tibetan sect headed by the Dalai Lama. The fierce Shugden protects the purity of the Gelug way, especially against contamination by the sometimes rival Nyingma sect. Early in the twentieth century, a charismatic "revival" movement grew up around Shugden, strongly influencing later generations of Gelug monks and increasing tension with the Nyingma. But in 1976, on the advice of the Nechung oracle, the Dalai Lama banned the worship of Shugden, sparking a controversy that has lately become quite bitter and occasionally violent. This controversy received significant publicity in the international media. Though some media accounts paint Shugden supporters as fundamentalists clinging to Tibet's shamanic past, Lopez (1998) argues that the struggle may actually represent a desire to reassert regional and specifically Tibetan culture. In contrast, the Dalai Lama, in order to constitute Tibet as a unified nation and avoid sectarian tensions, is focusing on universalistic Buddhism.

17. The Kagyupa sect has its headquarters-in-exile at Sikkim's Rumtek Dharma Chakra Center. The Rumtek monastery has been wracked by controversy over who is the "real incarnate" of its founder, the sixteenth Gyalwa Karmapa, who died in 1991.

18. Magazines including *Tibetan Review* often provide space for the dissenting voices of younger generations. An interesting difference is seen when it comes to assessing the assimilative influence of dominant culture on Tibetan life—while the new refugees' "Sinicization" is ridiculed and considered as unpatriotic, elements of "Indianization" and "Westernization" are often tolerated as necessary strategies of survival.

19. Tibetan intellectuals, while demanding independence, also reveal an awareness of the need to learn from historical experiences of decolonization.

For instance, Tsarong (1997) suggests possible ways in which the Tibetan struggle may learn from the decolonization in most of Asia and Africa during the twentieth century.

6. POSTCOLONIALITY AND REIMAG(IN)ING TIBETANNESS

1. My contention is that drawing upon critical social and cultural theories and deploying them contextually is a better approach than shying away from them out of a fear of theoretical imperialism. Often well-intentioned scholars avoid using Western theoretical ideas in the case of the non-West in general and Tibet in particular since history is replete with examples of similar moves to the detriment of local people. However, moving toward a purely empirical study is not the right solution since this idea of pure empiricism is the most hegemonic of Western paradigms. It is complicit with dominant regimes of patriarchal and racialized power. So in my opinion it is better to adopt the critical theory–inspired idea of theorizing everything since it reveals all practices as political and therefore contestable. Even though these themes have originated in the West, they question the assumption of the superiority of the West and thus leave room for alliances with "progressive" ideas from the non-Western world. Approaches that deny a role to theory often operate on unconscious theoretical assumptions that are left uninterrogated.

2. Though the "government" (in exile) in Dharamsala is not recognized by any state in the international community, for Tibetan people themselves, especially those living in diaspora, it is a legitimate representative. The place-name is spelled either Dharamsala or Dharamshala, but the government-in-exile, following Indian government surveys, uses the former spelling.

Dharamsala is a common name used for Dharamsala proper (the Kotwali Bazaar area) or the Lower Dharamsala, McLeod Gunj (also spelled Mcleodganj and McLeod Ganj), or Upper Dharamsala and Gangchen Kyishong (the complex of Central Tibetan Administration). Lower Dharamsala is a predominantly Indian area. While most Tibetan establishments are located in McLeod Gunj, there are some important ones in the vicinity of Lower Dharamsala (for instance the Norbulingka Institute). Dharamsala is used as a generic name for all of these. In terms of location, it can be characterized as a hill station in the north Indian state of Himachal Pradesh.

3. There is a further issue of temporality in the projection as Little Lhasa. Though Little Lhasa was put on the map of global tourism mostly after the mid-1980s, the name had come to be associated with McLeod Gunj from the 1960s (see the passing reference in Avendon 1984, 103).

4. Unlike most other hill stations in India, Dharamsala has no direct railway connection to any major city. The nearest railhead is eighty-five kilometers away.

5. There seems to be a difference of motive for traveling to Dharamsala between (white) Westerners and other visitors. The influence of Exotica Tibet is less noticeable in the case of Japanese and Korean visitors (for whom Dharamsala is often only one part of a Buddhist pilgrimage circuit in India) or Indian tourists (for whom it is a replacement for crowded hill stations like Simla). This is not to say that all the Westerners who come here are affected by the Shangri-la myth (since many come for the same reasons as they visit Kullu, Manali, or Goa—the "hippy trail") or that all non-Western tourists are immune to it.

6. The crucial role played by the Nowrojee family (the biggest proprietor here) in encouraging the development of Little Lhasa needs to be kept in mind. The Nowrojee store's pivotal location at the McLeod Gunj bus stop stands as a silent symbol of this role.

7. The place is named after Sir Donald Friel McLeod, lieutenant governor of Punjab in the mid-nineteenth century.

8. Though it is rare for such tensions between Tibetans and local Indians to erupt in full-fledged rioting, the resentment of the locals against Tibetans, who are perceived as wealthier, is evident. I say this from my personal experience of talking to many Indian taxi drivers and shopkeepers. Since for them I was an insider (with Indian nationality), they often expressed their anxiety about the Tibetan "Others."

9. The Panchen Lama's importance within Tibetan Buddhism is next only to the Dalai Lama's. To undermine the child who was recognized as the reincarnation of the Panchen Lama (and therefore the eleventh in the line) by the Dalai Lama, the Chinese government imprisoned him and recognized another child as the true reincarnation. For an account of this struggle, see Hilton 2000.

10. The most (in)famous instance of this is the recognition by Penor Rinpoche of the Hollywood actor Steven Segal as a reincarnation of the seventeenth-century hidden treasure revealer Chungdrag Dorje of Palyul Monastery.

11. The emphasis in "crafts*men*" is deliberate in order to highlight the gendered character of traditional cultural practices and their reinforcement by preservation ethos. For instance, in the Norbulingka I was told that statue making is not meant for women. Not surprisingly, most women were concentrated in sections such as tailoring. But I also came across women artists in some other sections, including painting.

12. One such artist is Penpa Dorje, confirmed as a "master statue maker" in 1973 by the Dalai Lama.

13. As Thargyal (1997) points out, this process of secularization, which is an epiphenomenon of societal forces, should not be confused with secularism, which is an ideology. He argues that Tibetan Buddhism *(chos)* has potent democratic principles that are leading to secularization, and therefore any simplistic reading of this process, as indicative of a separation of religion and politics, is wrong. While one can appreciate his anxiety to legitimize changes toward democracy in terms of traditional religion, it does not comport very comfortably with frequent statements of the Dalai Lama himself that he wishes to retire from political life once Tibetans get to exercise their right of self-determination.

14. As Nowak points out, Tibetan youths in diaspora use three types of ideological strategies: a less devotional, more politically motivated reconsideration of Buddhist traditions; a neopuritanical concern for maintaining the purity of essential Tibetan symbolic forms; and a sometimes conventional, sometimes extended interpretation of the metaphorical concept of *rangzen* (translated roughly as "self-power, independence") (1984, 139).

15. This Buddhist stupa (monument) is surrounded by prayer wheels and has a statue of Sakyamuni Buddha enshrined in a small chamber.

16. For a different view on the ethics of appreciating the claims to essentiality as being integral to Tibetan identity, see Venturino 1997. Unlike Venturino, I do not seek to recognize Tibetan claims to essentiality on their own terms simply because they are at the foundational level of Tibetan identity. I adopt a more processual view of identity with little patience for claims to essentiality.

17. Performativity is not to be confused with performance. As Butler clarifies, a performative act "is not primarily theatrical; indeed, its apparent theatricality is produced to the extent that its historicity remains dissimulated" (1993, 12).

18. Apart from Indian banks, the only exception to the prevalence of the Dalai Lama's picture that I came across was a shop selling *Desi Sharaab* (country alcohol) on the Jogibara Road.

Bibliography

Abbots, A. 1997. *Naked Spirits: A Journey into Occupied Tibet*, London: Canongate Books.

About Tibet. 2006. Available at http://www.tibet.org (accessed 24 March 2006).

Adam, I., and H. Tiffin, eds. 1991. *Past the Last Post: Theorizing Post-Colonialism and Post-Modernism*, London: Harvester Wheatsheaf.

Adams, V. 1996. "Karaoke as Modern Lhasa, Tibet: Western Encounters with Cultural Politics." *Cultural Anthropology* 11, no. 4: 510–46.

———. 1998. "Suffering the Winds of Lhasa: Politicized Bodies, Human Rights, Cultural Difference, and Humanism in Tibet." *Medical Anthropology* 12, no. 1: 74–102.

Addy, P. 1984. *Tibet on the Imperial Chessboard: The Making of British Policy towards Lhasa, 1899–1925*. Calcutta: Academic Publishers.

Agathangelou, A. 2004. *Global Political Economy of Sex: Desire, Violence, and Insecurity in Mediterranean National State*. Basingstoke, England: Palgrave Macmillan.

Agathangelou, A., and L. H. M. Ling. 2004. "The House of IR: From Family Power Politics to the Poisies of Worldism." *International Studies Review* 6, no. 4: 31–49.

Ahmad, A. 1994. *In Theory: Nations, Classes, Literatures*. London: Verso.

Ahmed, S. J. 2006. "Tibetan Folk Opera: Lhamo in Contemporary Cultural Politics." *Asian Theatre Journal* 23, no. 1: 156–78.

Allen, C. 1999. *The Search for Shangri-La: A Journey into Tibetan History*. London: Abacus.

Amin, S. 1988. *Eurocentrism*. London: Zed.

Anand, D. 2000. "(Re)Imagining Nationalism: Identity and Representation in Tibetan Diaspora in South Asia." *Contemporary South Asia* 9, no. 3: 271–87.

———. 2002a. "A Guide to Little Lhasa in India: The Role of Symbolic Geography of Dharamsala in Constituting Tibetan Diasporic Identity." In *Tibet, Self, and the Tibetan Diaspora: Voices of Difference,* ed. P. C. Klieger. Leiden, Netherlands: Brill.

———. 2002b. "A Story to Be Told: IR, Postcolonialism, and the Tibetan (Trans)Nationalism." In *Power, Postcolonialism, and International Relations: Reading Race, Gender, and Class,* ed. G. Chowdhry and S. Nair. London: Routledge.

———. 2003. "Travel-Routing Diaspora . . . Homing on Tibet." *Diaspora* 12, no. 3: 211–29.

———. 2006a. "The West and the Tibetan Issue." In B. Sautman and J. T. Dreyer, eds., *Contemporary Tibet: Politics, Development and Society in a Disputed Region.* Armonk, N.Y.: M. E. Sharpe.

———. 2006b. "Archive and the Poetics of 'Exotica Tibet.'" In *Tibetan Borderlands: Proceedings of the Tenth Seminar of the IATS, 2003,* ed. P. C. Klieger. Leiden, Netherlands: Brill.

Anderson, B. 1983. *Imagined Communities: Reflections on the Origin and Spread of Nationalism.* London: Verso.

Anderson, K., and F. Gale, eds. 1992. *Inventing Places: Studies in Cultural Geography.* Melbourne: Longman Cheshire and Wiley Halsted Press.

Ardley, J. 2002. *The Tibetan Independence Movement: Political, Religious, and Gandhian Perspectives.* London: RoutledgeCurzon.

Aris, M. 1994. "India and the British According to a Tibetan Text of the Later Eighteenth Century." In *Tibetan Studies: Proceedings of the 6th Seminar of the International Association for Tibetan Studies, Fagernes 1992,* ed. P. Kvaerne. Oslo: Institute for Comparative Research in Human Culture.

Ashcroft, B., G. Griffiths, and H. Tiffin. 1989. *Empire Writes Back: Theory and Practice in Post-Colonial Literatures.* London: Routledge.

———, eds. 1995. *The Post-Colonial Studies Reader.* London: Routledge.

Ashley, R. K., and R. B. J. Walker. 1990a. "Speaking the Language of Exile: Dissident Thought in International Studies." *International Studies Quarterly* 34, no. 3: 259–68.

———. 1990b. "Conclusion: Reading Dissidence/Writing the Discipline: Crisis and the Question of Sovereignty in International Studies." *International Studies Quarterly* 34, no. 3: 367–416.

Avendon, J. F. 1984. *In Exile from the Land of Snows.* London: Michael Joseph.

Bailey, F. M. 1957. *No Passport to Tibet.* London: Travel Book Club.

Balakrishnan, G., ed. 1996. *Mapping the Nation.* London: Verso.

Barber, N. 1969. *From the Land of Lost Content: The Dalai Lama's Fight for Tibet.* London: Collins.

Barker, D. 1999. "Free Spirits: Tibet in Exile." Photo exhibition. Available at http://www.friendsoftibet.org/diane.html (accessed 2 October 2001).

Barker, F., P. Hulme, and M. Iversen, eds. 1994. *Colonial Discourse, Postcolonial Theory.* Manchester, England: Manchester University Press.

Barnett, R. 1991. "The Effectiveness of Parliamentary Initiatives." In *The Anguish of Tibet,* ed. P. K. Kelly, G. Bastian, and P. Aiello. Berkeley, Calif.: Parallax Press.

———. 1999. "Essay." In *The Tibetans: A Struggle to Survive,* ed. S. Lehman. London: Virgin Books.

———. 2001. "'Violated Specialness': Western Political Representations of Tibet." In *Imagining Tibet: Perceptions, Projections, and Fantasies,* ed. T. Dodin and H. Rather. Boston: Wisdom.

———. 2006. "Beyond the Collaborator-Martyr Model: Strategies of Compliance, Opportunism and Opposition within Tibet." In *Contemporary Tibet: Politics, Development, and Society in a Disputed Region,* ed. B. Sautman and J. T. Dreyer. London: M. E. Sharpe.

Barnett, R., and S. Akiner, eds. 1996. *Resistance and Reform in Tibet.* Delhi: Motilalbanarsidass.

Bartelson, J. 1995. *Genealogy of Sovereignty.* Cambridge: Cambridge University Press.

Bass, C. 1990. *Inside the Treasure House: A Time in Tibet.* London: Victor Gollancz.

Bataille, G. 1992 [1949]. "Lamaism: The Unarmed Society." *Lungta* 6: 33–40.

Baumann, M. 1997. "Shangri-la in Exile: Portraying Tibetan Diaspora Studies and Reconsidering Diaspora(s)." *Diaspora* 6, no. 3: 377–404.

Baylis, J., and S. Smith, eds. 2005. *Globalization of World Politics: An Introduction to International Relations.* 3rd ed. Oxford: Oxford University Press.

Beit-Hallahmi, B. 1993. *Original Sins: Reflections on the History of Zionism and Israel.* New York: Olive Branch Press.

Bell, C. 1924. *Tibet: Past and Present.* Oxford: Clarendon Press.

———. 1928. *The People of Tibet.* Oxford: Clarendon Press.

Bennett, T. 1995. *The Birth of the Museum: History, Theory, Politics.* London: Routledge.

Berkin, M. 2000. *The Great Tibetan Stonewall of China.* Chichester, England: Barry Rose Law Publishers.

Bernal, M. 1987. *Black Athena: The Afroasiatic Roots of Classical Civilization.* Volume I: *The Fabrication of Greece, 1785–1985.* London: Free Association.

————. 1991. *Black Athena: The Afroasiatic Roots of Classical Civilization*. Vol. 2, *The Archaeological and Documentary Evidence*. London: Free Association.

Bernbaum, E. 2001. *The Way to Shambhala: A Search for the Mythical Kingdom beyond the Himalayas*. Boston: Shambhala Publications.

Bhabha, H. K. 1983. "The Other Question—The Stereotype and Colonial Discourse." *Screen* 24, no. 6: 18–36.

————. 1994. *The Location of Culture*. London: Routledge.

————, ed. 1990. *Nation and Narration*. London: Routledge.

Biersteker, T. J., and C. Weber, eds. 1996. *State Sovereignty as Social Construct*. Cambridge: Cambridge University Press.

Billig, M. 1995. *Banal Nationalism*. London: Sage.

Bisharat, G. E. 1997. "Exile to Compatriot: Transformations in the Social Identity of Palestinian Refugees in the West Bank." In *Culture, Place, Power: Explorations in Critical Anthropology*, ed. A. Gupta and J. Ferguson. Durham, N.C.: Duke University Press.

Bishop, P. 1989. *The Myth of Shangri-La: Tibet, Travel Writing, and the Western Creation of a Sacred Landscape*. Berkeley: University of California Press.

————. 1993. *Dreams of Power: Tibetan Buddhism and the Western Imagination*. London: Athlone Press.

————. 1997. "Glimpsing Tibet: A Landscape of Closure and Loss." *Literature and History* 6, no. 2: 56–71.

————. 1998. "To Raise the Tibetan Flag? The Dalai Lama as News." *Australian Journal of Communication* 25, no. 1: 111–25.

————. 2000. "Caught in the Cross-Fire: Tibet, Media, and Promotional Culture." *Media, Culture, and Society* 22, no. 5: 645–64.

————. 2001. "Not Only a Shangri-La: Images of Tibet in Western Literature." In *Imagining Tibet: Perceptions, Projections, and Fantasies*, ed. T. Dodin and H. Rather. Boston: Wisdom.

Biswas, S. 2001. "'Nuclear Apartheid' as Political Position: Race as a Postcolonial Resource?" *Alternatives* 26, no. 4: 485–522.

Blavatsky, H. P. 1892. *From the Caves and Jungles of Hindostan*. London: Theosophical Publishing Society.

Bleiker, R. 1997. "Forget IR Theory." *Alternatives* 22, no. 1: 57–85.

Blum, S. D. 2000. *Portraits of "Primitives": Ordering Human Kinds in the Chinese Nation*. London: Rowman and Littlefield.

————. 2002. "Margins and Centers: A Decade of Publishing on China's Ethnic Minorities." *Journal of Asian Studies* 61, no. 4: 1287–310.

Blunt, A., and G. Rose, eds. 1994. *Writing Women and Space: Colonial and Postcolonial Geographies*. New York: Guilford Press.

BOD MS Asquith 93. 1913. "Asquith Papers." Modern Political Papers. Oxford: Bodleian Library.

BOD MS Eng.misc.C.843. n.d. "WY Evans-Wentz (d.1965) Papers." Modern Political Papers. Oxford: Bodleian Library.

BOD MS Or. Aris 14. 1990. "Aris Collection: Harvard Lectures." Department of Oriental Collections. Oxford: Bodleian Library.

BOD MS Or. Aris 15. n.d. "Aris Collection." Department of Oriental Collections. Oxford: Bodleian Library.

BOD MS Or. Aris 18. n.d. "Aris Collection: Last Winter on the McMahon Line." Department of Oriental Collections. Oxford: Bodleian Library.

Bonnington, C., and C. Clarke. 2000. *Tibet's Secret Mountain: The Triumph of Sepu Kangri*. London: Phoenix.

Bourdieu, P. 1977. *Outline of a Theory of Practice*. Trans. R. Nice. Cambridge: Cambridge University Press.

Bowman, G. 1994. "'Country of Words': Conceiving the Palestinian Nation from the Position of Exile." In *The Making of Political Identities*, ed. E. Laclau. London: Verso.

Boyd, H. R. 2004. *The Future of Tibet: The Government-in-Exile Meets the Challenge of Democratization*. New York: Peter Lang.

Bradley, H. 1999. "The Seductions of the Archive: Voices Lost and Found." *History of the Human Sciences* 12, no. 2: 107–22.

Brah, A. 1996. *Cartographies of Diaspora: Contesting Identities*. London: Routledge.

Bray, J. 2001. "Nineteenth- and Early Twentieth-Century Missionary Images of Tibet." In *Imagining Tibet: Perceptions, Projections, and Fantasies*, ed. T. Dodin and H. Rather. Boston: Wisdom.

Brown, C., T. Nardin, and N. Rengger, eds. 2002. *International Relations in Political Thought: Texts from the Ancient Greeks to the First World War*. Cambridge: Cambridge University Press.

Burman, B. R. 1979. *Religion and Politics in Tibet*. Delhi: Vikas Publishing House.

Buruma, I. 2000. "Found Horizon." *New York Review of Books*, June 29. Available at http://www.nybooks.com/articles/26 (accessed 22 August 2006).

Butler, J. 1990. *Gender Trouble: Feminism and the Subversion of Identity*. New York: Routledge.

———. 1992. "Contingent Foundations: Feminism and the Question of 'Postmodernism.'" In *Feminists Theorize the Political*, ed. J. Butler and J. Scott. London: Routledge.

———. 1993. *Bodies That Matter: On the Discursive Limits of "Sex."* London: Routledge.

———. 1999. *Gender Trouble: Feminism and the Subversion of Identity*. Rev. ed. New York: Routledge.

Buzan, B., and R. Little. 2000. *International Systems in World History:*

Remaking the Study of International Relations. Oxford: Oxford University Press.

Cammann, S. 1951. *Trade through the Himalayas: The Early British Attempts to Open Tibet*. Princeton, N.J.: Princeton University Press.

Campbell, D. 1998a. *National Deconstruction: Violence, Identity, and Justice in Bosnia*. Minneapolis: University of Minnesota Press.

———. 1998b [1992]. *Writing Security: United States Foreign Policy and the Politics of Identity*. Rev. ed. Minneapolis: University of Minnesota Press.

Campbell, D., and M. Dillon, eds. 1993. *The Political Subject of Violence*. Manchester, England: Manchester University Press.

Candler, E. 1905. *Unveiling of Lhasa*. London: Edward Arnold.

Cao Changching, and J. D. Seymour, eds. 1998. *Tibet through Dissident Chinese Eyes: Essays on Self-Determination*. New York: M. E. Sharpe.

Carey, W. 1902. *Travel and Adventure in Tibet including the Diary of Miss Anne R Taylor's Remarkable Journey*. London: Hodder and Stoughton.

Carlson, A. 2004. *Beijing's Tibet Policy: Securing Sovereignty and Legitimacy*. Washington: East-West Center. Available at http://www.eastwestcenter.org/stored/pdfs/PS004.pdf (accessed 2 August 2006).

———. 2005. *Unifying China, Integrating with the World: Securing Chinese Sovereignty in the Reform Era*. Stanford, Calif.: Stanford University Press.

Carrington, M. 2003. "Officers, Gentlemen, and Thieves: The Looting of Monasteries during the 1903/4 Younghusband Mission to Tibet." *Modern Asian Studies* 37, no. 1: 81–109.

Chakrabarty, D. 2000. *Provincializing Europe: Postcolonial Thought and Historical Difference*. Princeton, N.J.: Princeton University Press.

Chambers, I., and L. Curtis, eds. 1996. *The Post-Colonial Question: Common Skies, Divided Horizon*. London: Routledge.

Chan, S. 2000 "Writing Sacral IR." *Millennium* 29, no. 3: 565–89.

Chan, S., and A. J. Williams, eds. 1994. *Renegade States: The Evolution of Revolutionary Foreign Policy*. Manchester, England: Manchester University Press.

Chapman, F. S. 1992 [1940]. *Lhasa the Holy City*. Delhi: Bodhi Leaves Corporation.

Chatterjee, P. 1986. *Nationalist Thought and the Colonial World: A Derivative Discourse?* London: Zed Books.

———. 1993. *The Nation and Its Fragments: Colonial and Postcolonial Histories*. Princeton, N.J.: Princeton University Press.

Chaturvedi, V., ed. 2000. *Mapping Subaltern Studies and the Postcolonial*. London: Verso.

Chay, J. ed. 1990. *Culture and International Relations*. New York: Praeger.

Chiu, Hungdah, and J. T. Dreyer. 1989. *Tibet: Past and Present*. Occasional Papers/Reprints Series in Contemporary Asian Studies, no. 1. Baltimore: University of Maryland School of Law.

Chow, R. 1993. *Writing Diaspora: Tactics of Intervention in Contemporary Cultural Studies*. Bloomington: Indiana University Press.

Chowdhry, G., and S. Nair, eds. 2002. *Power in a Postcolonial World: Race, Gender, and Class in IR*. New York: Routledge.

Clapham, C. 1996. *Africa and the International System*. Cambridge: Cambridge University Press.

Clifford, J. 1988. *The Predicament of Culture: Twentieth-Century Ethnography, Literature, and Art*. Cambridge, Mass.: Harvard University Press.

———. 1997. *Routes: Travel and Translation in the Late Twentieth Century*. Cambridge, Mass.: Harvard University Press.

Clifford, J., and G. Marcus, eds. 1986. *Writing Culture: The Poetics and Politics of Ethnography*. London: University of California Press.

CNN.com. 2001. "Dalai Lama and Bush Meet 'Like Old Friends.'" 23 May. Available at http://archives.cnn.com/2001/WORLD/asiapcf/east/05/23/dalai.bush.02/index.html (accessed 20 August 2006).

Cocker, M. 1992. *Loneliness and Time: British Travel Writing in the Twentieth Century*. London: Secker and Warburg.

Cohen, R. 1997. *Global Diasporas: An Introduction*. London: UCL Press.

Conboy, K., and J. Morrison. 2002. *The CIA's Secret War in Tibet*. Lawrence: University Press of Kansas.

Connolly, W. E. 1991. *Identity/Difference: Democratic Negotiations of Political Paradox*. Ithaca, N.Y.: Cornell University Press.

Constantinou, C. 1998. "Before the Summit: Representations of Sovereignty on the Himalayas." *Millennium* 27, no. 1: 23–53.

Crawford, R. M., and D. S. Jarvis, eds. 2000. *International Relations: Still an American Social Science? Toward Diversity in International Thought*. Albany: State University of New York Press.

Cubitt, G. 1998. Introduction to *Imagining Nations*, ed. G. Cubitt. Manchester, England: Manchester University Press.

Dalby, S. 1988. "Geopolitical Discourse: The Soviet Union as Other." *Alternatives* 13, no. 4: 415–42.

Darby, P. 1997. "Postcolonialism." In *At the Edge of International Relations: Postcolonialism, Gender, and Dependency*, ed. P. Darby. London: Pinter.

———. 1998. *The Fiction of Imperialism: Reading between International Relations and Postcolonialism*. London: Cassell.

Darby, P., and A. Paolini. 1994. "Bridging International Relations and Postcolonialism." *Alternatives* 19, no. 3: 371–97.

Das, S. C. 1902. *Journey to Lhasa and Central Tibet.* London: John Murray.

David-Neel, A. 1936 [1931]. *With Mystics and Magicians in Tibet.* London: Penguin.

———. 1991 [1927]. *My Journey to Lhasa.* New Delhi: Time Books International.

Davidson, L. 1995 [1961]. *"The Night of Wenceslas" and "The Rose of Tibet."* London: Wenlam.

De Filippi, F. 1932. *An Account of Tibet: The Travels of Ippolito Desideri of Pistoia, S.J., 1712–1727.* London: George Routledge and Sons.

Deasy, H. H. P. 1901. *In Tibet and Chinese Turkestan.* London: T. Fisher Unwin.

Department of Information and International Relations. 1997. *International Resolutions and Recognitions on Tibet (1959 to 1997).* Dharamsala: Central Tibetan Administration.

———. 1999. *Dharamsala: A Guide to Little Lhasa in India.* Dharamsala: DIIR.

Der Derian, J., and M. J. Shapiro, eds. 1989. *International/Intertextual Relations: Postmodern Readings of World Politics.* Lexington, Mass.: D. C. Heath.

Diehl, K. 2002. *Echoes from Dharamsala: Music in the Life of a Tibetan Refugee Community.* Berkeley: University of California Press.

Diken, B., and C. B. Laustsen. 2001. "Postal Economies of the Orient." *Millennium* 30, no. 3: 761–84.

Dikotter, F. 1992. *The Discourse of Race in Modern China.* Stanford, Calif.: Stanford University Press.

Dodin, T., and H. Rather. 2001a. "Imagining Tibet: Between Shangri-La and Feudal Oppression." In *Imagining Tibet: Perceptions, Projections, and Fantasies,* ed. T. Dodin and H. Rather. Boston: Wisdom.

———, eds. 2001b. *Imagining Tibet: Perceptions, Projections, and Fantasies,* Boston: Wisdom.

Doty, R. L. 1993. "Foreign Policy as Social Construction: A Post-Positivist Analysis of U.S. Counterinsurgency Policy in the Philippines." *International Studies Quarterly* 37, no. 3: 297–320.

———. 1996a. "Immigration and National Identity: Constructing the Nation." *Review of International Studies* 22, no. 3: 235–55.

———. 1996b. *Imperial Encounters: The Politics of Representation in North-South Relations.* Minneapolis: University of Minnesota Press.

———. 2001. "Desert Tracts: Statecraft in Remote Places." *Alternatives* 26, no. 4: 523–43.

Dreyfus, G. 1994. "Proto-Nationalism in Tibet." In *Tibetan Studies: Proceedings of the 6th Seminar of the International Association for Tibetan*

Studies, Fagernes 1992, ed. P. Kvaerne. Oslo: Institute for Comparative Research in Human Culture.

———. 2002. "Tibetan Religious Nationalism: Western Fantasy or Empowering Vision?" In *Tibet, Self, and the Tibetan Diaspora: Voices of Difference,* ed. P. C. Klieger. Leiden, Netherlands: Brill.

Du Halde, P. J. B. 1738. *A Description of the Empire of China and Chinese-Tartary, Together with the Kingdoms of Korea, and Tibet: Containing the Geography and History (Natural as well as Civil) of those Countries.* 2 vols. London: T. Gardner.

Ekvall, R. A. 1960. "The Tibetan Self-Image." *Pacific Affairs* 33, no. 4: 375–81.

Eley, G., and R. G. Suny, eds. *Becoming National: A Reader.* Oxford: Oxford University Press.

Engelhardt, I. 2002. "The Closing of the Gates: Tibetan-European Relations at the End of the Eighteenth Century." In *Tibet, Past and Present,* ed. H. Blezer. Leiden, Netherlands: Brill.

Enloe, C. 2000 [1989]. *Bananas, Beaches, and Bases: Making Feminist Sense of International Politics.* Rev. ed. Berkeley: University of California Press.

Escobar, A. 1995. *Encountering Development: The Making and Unmaking of the Third World.* Princeton, N.J.: Princeton University Press.

Evans-Wentz, W. Y. 1949. *The Tibetan Book of the Dead, or, The After-Death Experiences of the "Bardo" Plane, according to Lama Kazi Dawa-Samdup's English Rendering.* London: Geoffrey Cumberlege/Oxford University Press.

Fabian, J. 1990. "Presence and Representation: The Other and Anthropological Writing." *Critical Inquiry* 16, no. 4: 753–72.

Feigon, L. 1996. *Demystifying Tibet: Unlocking the Secrets of the Land of the Snows.* Chicago: Ivan R. Dee.

Ferguson, K. E. 1993. *The Man Question: Visions of Subjectivity in Feminist Theory.* Berkeley: University of California Press.

Fergusson, W. N. 1911. *Adventure, Sport, and Travel on the Tibetan Steppes.* London: Constable and Co.

Finkelstein, N. G. 1995. *Image and Reality of the Israel-Palestine Conflict.* London: Verso.

Fleck, G. 1995. "Tibet and the Universal Postal Union." *Tibetan Review* (March): 16–18.

Fleming, P. 1961. *Bayonets to Lhasa: The First Full Account of the British Invasion of Tibet in 1904.* London: Rupert Hart-Davis.

Fletcher, H. R. 1975. *A Quest of Flowers: The Plant Explorations of Frank Ludlow and George Sheriff Told from Their Diaries and Other Occasional Writings.* Edinburgh: Edinburgh University Press.

Forbes, A. A. 1989. *Settlements of Hope: An Account of Tibetan Refugees in Nepal*. Cambridge, Mass.: Cultural Survival.

Foreign Office. 1920. *Tibet* (Number 70). London: H. M. Stationary Office.

Forman, H. 1936. *Through Forbidden Tibet: An Adventure into the Unknown*. London: Jarrolds Publishers.

Foster, B. M., and M. Foster. 1987. *Forbidden Journey: The Life of Alexandra David-Neel*. San Francisco: Harper and Row.

Foucault, M. 1970. *The Order of Discourse: An Archaeology of the Human Sciences*. London: Tavistock.

———. 1972. *The Archaeology of Knowledge*. London: Tavistock.

———. 1980. *Power/Knowledge: Selected Interviews and Other Writings, 1972–1977*. Ed. C. Gordon. London: Harvester Wheatsheaf.

———. 1984. *The Foucault Reader*. Ed. P. Rabinow. London: Penguin.

———. 1986. *Language, Counter-Memory, Practice*. Ed. D. Bouchard. Ithaca, N.Y.: Cornell University Press.

Frechette, A. 2002. *Tibetans in Nepal: The Dynamics of International Assistance among a Community in Exile*. New York: Berghahn Books.

French, P. 1995. *Younghusband: The Last Great Imperial Adventurer*. London: Flamingo.

Freshfield, D. W. 1905. "The Gates of Tibet." *Journal of the Society of Arts* 53, no. 2724: 264–73.

Frontline. 1998a. Interview with Martin Scorsese. *Dreams of Tibet: A Troubled Country and Its Enduring Fascination*. Available at http://www.pbs.org/wgbh/pages/frontline/shows/tibet/interviews/scorsese.html (accessed 20 August 2006).

———. 1998b. Interview with Richard Gere. *Dreams of Tibet: A Troubled Country and its Enduring Fascination*. Available at http://www.pbs.org/wgbh/pages/frontline/shows/tibet/interviews/gere.html (accessed 20 August 2006).

———. 1998c. Interview with Steven Segal. *Dreams of Tibet: A Troubled Country and Its Enduring Fascination*. Available at http://www.pbs.org/wgbh/pages/frontline/shows/tibet/interviews/segal.html (accessed 22 October 2006).

Fuss, D. 1989. *Essentially Speaking: Feminism, Nature, and Difference*. London: Routledge.

Gaddis, J. L. 1987. *The Long Peace: Inquiries into the History of the Cold War*. New York: Oxford University Press.

Gallagher, E. J. 1997. *America by Johannes Stradanus*. Available at http://www.lehigh.edu/~ejg1/ed/strad1.html (accessed 20 August 2006).

Gandhi, L. 1998. *Postcolonial Theory: A Critical Introduction*. Edinburgh: Edinburgh University Press.

Geddie, J. 1882. *Beyond the Himalayas: A Story of Travel and Adventure in the Wilds of Thibet*. London: T. Nelson and Sons.

Gelder, S., and R. Gelder. 1964. *The Timely Rain: Travels in New Tibet.* London: Hutchinson.

Gellner, E. 1983. *Nations and Nationalism.* Oxford: Blackwell.

General Assembly of the United Nations. 1959. "Question of Tibet." United Nations General Assembly Resolution 1353 (XIV), 21 October. Available at http://daccessdds.un.org/doc/RESOLUTION/GEN/NR0/141/76/IMG/NR014176.pdf?OpenElement (accessed 2 August 2006).

General Assembly of the United Nations. 1961. "Question of Tibet." United Nations General Assembly Resolution 1723 (XVI), 20 December. Available at http://daccessdds.un.org/doc/RESOLUTION/GEN/NR0/167/76/IMG/NR016776.pdf?OpenElement (accessed 3 August 2006).

General Assembly of the United Nations. 1965. "Question of Tibet." United Nations General Assembly Resolution 2079 (XX), 18 December. Available at http://daccessdds.un.org/doc/RESOLUTION/GEN/NR0/218/42/IMG/NR021842.pdf?OpenElement (accessed 2 August 2006).

George, J. 1994. *Discourses of Global Politics: A Critical (Re)Introduction to International Relations.* Boulder, Colo.: Lynne Rienner.

———. 1996. "Understanding International Relations after the Cold War: Probing beyond the Realist Legacy." In *Challenging Boundaries: Global Flows, Territorial Identities,* ed. M. J. Shapiro and H. R. Alker. Minneapolis: University of Minnesota Press.

Ghosh, S. 1977. *Tibet in Sino-Indian Relations, 1899–1914.* New Delhi: Sterling Publishers.

Gibbs, D. N. 2001. "Social Science as Propaganda? International Relations and the Question of Political Bias." *International Studies Perspectives* 2, no. 4: 417–27.

Gilman, S. L. 1985. *Difference and Pathology: Stereotypes of Sexuality, Race, and Madness.* Ithaca, N.Y.: Cornell University Press.

Ginsburgs, G. 1960. "Peking-Lhasa-New Delhi." *Political Science Quarterly* 75, no. 3: 338–54.

Gladney, D. C. 1994. "Representing Nationality in China: Refiguring Majority/Minority Identities." *Journal of Asian Studies* 53, no. 1: 92–123.

———. 2004. *Dislocating China: Muslims, Minorities, and Other Subaltern Subjects.* Chicago: University of Chicago Press.

Goldstein, M. C. 1982. "Lhasa Street Songs: Political and Social Satire in Traditional Tibet." *Tibet Journal* 7, nos. 1–2: 56–66.

———. 1995. "Tibet, China, and the United States: Reflections on the Tibet Question." *Occasional Paper Series of the Atlantic Council of the United States.* Available at http://omni.cc.purdue.edu/~wtv/tibet/article/art4.html (accessed 4 August 2006).

———. 1997. *The Snow Lion and the Dragon: China, Tibet, and the Dalai Lama.* Berkeley: University of California Press.

Goldstein, M. C., with Gelek Rimpoche. 1989. *A History of Modern Tibet, 1913–1951: The Demise of the Lamaist State*. Berkeley: University of California Press.

Goldstein, M. C., and M. T. Kapstein, eds. 1998. *Buddhism in Contemporary Tibet*. London: University of California Press.

Gordon, T. E. 1876. *Roof of the World: Being the Narrative of a Journey over the High Plateau of Tibet to the Russian Frontier and the Oxus Sources on Pamir*. Edinburgh: Edmonston and Douglas.

Government of Tibet in Exile. n.d. "The Status of Tibet." *White Paper on Tibet: Proving Truth from Facts*. Online. Available at http://www.tibet.com/Status/statuslaw.html (accessed 12 August 2006).

Grenard, F. 1904. *Tibet: The Country and its Inhabitants*. London: Hutchinson.

Gross, S. L. 1966. "Introduction: Stereotype to Archetype: The Negro in American Literary Criticism." In *Images of the Negro in American Literature*, ed. S. L. Gross and J. E. Hardy. Chicago: University of Chicago Press.

Grovogui, S. N. 1996. *Sovereigns, Quasi Sovereigns, and Africans*. Minneapolis: University of Minnesota Press.

Grunfeld, T. A. 1987. *The Making of Modern Tibet*. London: Zed Books.

Guha, R., and G. C. Spivak, eds. 1988. *Selected Subaltern Studies*. Delhi: Oxford University Press.

Gupta, A., and J. Ferguson, eds. 1997. *Culture, Place, Power: Explorations in Critical Anthropology*. Durham, N.C.: Duke University Press.

Gurr, T. R., and D. Khosla. 2001. "Domestic and Transnational Strategies for Managing Separatist Conflicts: Four Asian Cases." In *Journeys through Conflict: Narratives and Lessons*, ed. H. R. Alker, T. R. Gurr, and K. Rupensinghe. London: Rowman and Littlefield.

Gusterson, H. 1999. "Nuclear Weapons and the Other in the Western Imagination." *Cultural Anthropology* 14, no. 1: 111–43.

Gyatso, P., with T. Shakya. 1997. *The Autobiography of a Tibetan Monk*. New York: Grove Press.

Gyatso, T. 1998 [1990]. *Freedom in Exile: The Autobiography of the Dalai Lama of Tibet*. 2nd ed. London: Abacus.

Ha, M-P. 2000. *Figuring the East: Segalen, Malraux, Duras, and Barthes*. Albany, N.Y.: State University of New York Press.

Hale, C. 2004. *Himmler's Crusade*. London: Bantam Books.

Hall, S. 1990. "Cultural Identity and Diaspora." In *Identity: Community, Culture, Difference*, ed. J. Rutherford. London: Lawrence and Wishart.

———. 1992. "The West and the Rest: Discourse and Power." In *Formations of Modernity*, ed. S. Hall and B. Gieben. Cambridge: Polity.

———. 1996a. "When Was the 'Post-Colonial'? Thinking at the Limit."

In *The Post-Colonial Question: Common Skies, Divided Horizon*, ed. I. Chambers and L. Curtis. London: Routledge.

———. 1996b. "Introduction: Who Needs 'Identity'"? In *Questions of Cultural Identity*, ed. S. Hall and P. Du Gay. London: Sage.

———. 1997a. "The Spectacle of the 'Other.'" In *Representation: Cultural Representations and Signifying Practices*, ed. S. Hall. London: Sage.

———. 1997b. "The Work of Representation." In *Representation: Cultural Representations and Signifying Practices*, ed. S. Hall. London: Sage.

Han Suyin. 1977. *Lhasa, the Open City: A Journey to Tibet*. London: Cape.

Hannum, H. 1990. *Autonomy, Sovereignty, and Self-Determination: The Accommodation of Conflicting Rights*. Philadelphia: University of Pennsylvania Press.

Hansen, P. H. 1996. "The Dancing Lamas of Everest: Cinema, Orientalism, and Anglo-Tibetan Relations in the 1920s." *American Historical Review* 101, no. 3: 712–44.

———. 1998. "Inventing Virtual Sherpas." Paper Presented at the Workshop on Outdoor Recreation, Urrea, Sweden, September.

———. 2001. "Tibetan Horizon: Tibet and the Cinema in the Early Twentieth Century." In *Imagining Tibet: Perceptions, Projections, and Fantasies*, ed. T. Dodin and H. Rather. Boston: Wisdom.

Harrer, H. 1956. *Seven Years in Tibet*. Trans. R. Graves. London: Pan Books.

———. 1985. *Return to Tibet*. Trans. E. Osers. London: Penguin.

Harris, C. 1993. "Desperately Seeking the Dalai Lama." In *Disrupted Borders: An Intervention in Definitions and Boundaries*, ed. S. Gupta. London: Rivers Oram Press.

———. 1999. *In the Image of Tibet: Tibetan Painting after 1959*. London: Reaktion Books.

Hayden, H. 1927. *Sport and Travel in the Highlands of Tibet*. London: Richard Cobden-Sanderson.

Hear Tibet! 2001. *International Campaign for a UN Referendum on Tibet: Self-Determination*. Available at http://www.heartibet.org (accessed 12 August 2006).

Heberer, T. 1995. "The Tibet Question as a Problem of International Politics." *Aussenpolitik* 3: 299–309.

———. 2001. "Old Tibet a Hell on Earth? The Myth of Tibet and Tibetans in Chinese Art and Propaganda." In *Imagining Tibet: Perceptions, Projections, and Fantasies*, ed. T. Dodin and H. Rather. Boston: Wisdom.

Hedin, S. 1903. *Central Asia and Tibet*. London: Hurst and Blackett.

Hillman, B. 2003. "Paradise under Construction: Myths and Modernity in Northwest Yunnan." *Asian Ethnicity* 4, no. 2: 175–88.

Hillman, B., and L. A. Henfry. 2006. "Macho Masculinity: Masculinity and Ethnicity on the Edge of Tibet." *Modern China* 32, no. 2: 251–72.

Hilton, I. 2000. *The Search for the Panchen Lama.* New York: W. W. Norton.

———. 2006. "Dalai Lama: Buddhist Spiritual Leader." *New Statesman,* 22 May, 29.

Hilton, J. 1933. *Lost Horizon.* London: Macmillan.

———. 1954. *Lost Horizon.* Adapted and modified by E. F. Dodd. London: Macmillan.

———. 1967. *Lost Horizon.* Introduction and notes by M. M. Barber. London: Macmillan.

Hinsley, F. H. 1986 [1966]. *Sovereignty.* 2nd ed. Cambridge: Cambridge University Press.

His Holiness the Dalai Lama. 1988. *Address to Members of the European Parliament.* Available at http://www.tibet.com/Proposal/strasbourg.html (accessed 15 October 2001).

Hobsbawm, E. 1990. *Nations and Nationalism since 1780: Programme, Myth, Reality.* Cambridge: Cambridge University Press.

Hobsbawn, E., and T. Ranger, eds. 1992 [1983]. *The Invention of Tradition.* Rev. ed. Cambridge: Cambridge University Press.

Hoffman, J. 1998. *Sovereignty.* Minneapolis: University of Minnesota Press.

Hoffman, S. 1965. *The State of War: Essays on the Theory and Practice of International Relations.* New York: Praeger.

———. 1977. "American Social Science: International Relations." *Daedalus* 106, no. 3: 41–60.

Holdich, T. 1906. *Tibet, the Mysterious.* London: Alston Rivers.

Holsti, K. J. 1985. *The Dividing Discipline: Hegemony and Diversity in International Theory.* London: Allen and Unwin.

Holte, J. 1991. "Hello Dalai." *New Republic* 205, no. 20: 21–23. Available at http://ccbs.ntu.edu.tw/FULLTEXT/JR-ADM/holte.htm (accessed 20 August 2006).

Hopkirk, P. 1983. *Trespassers on the Roof of the World: The Race for Lhasa.* Oxford: Oxford University Press.

———. 1997. *Quest for Kim in Search for Kipling's Great Game.* Oxford: Oxford University Press.

Houston, S., and R. Wright. 2003. "Making and Remaking Tibetan Diasporic Identities." *Social and Cultural Geography* 4, no. 2: 217–31.

Hovell, L. L. 1993. "Horizons Lost and Found: Travel, Writing, and Tibet in the Age of Imperialism." Ph.D. dissertation, Syracuse University.

Huber, T. 1997. "Green Tibetans: A Brief Social History." In *Tibetan Culture in the Diaspora: Papers Presented at a Panel of the 7th Semi-*

nar of the International Association for Tibetan Studies, Graz, 1995, ed. F. J. Korom. Vienna: Verlag Der Osterreichischen Akademie Der Wissenschaften.

———. 2001. "Shangri-La in Exile: Representations of Tibetan Identity and Transnational Culture." In *Imagining Tibet: Perceptions, Projections, and Fantasies,* ed. T. Dodin and H. Rather. Boston: Wisdom.

Huc, R. 1982 [1851]. *Lamas of the Western Heavens.* Trans. C. de Salis. Introduction by J. Keay. London: Folio Society.

Huggan, G. 2001. *The Postcolonial Exotic: Marketing the Margins.* London: Routledge.

Human Rights Watch. 2005. *Trials of a Tibetan Monk: The Case of Tenzin Delek,* 16, 1. Available at http://hrw.org/reports/2004/china0204/china0204.pdf (accessed 2 August 2006).

Hunt, M. H. 1987. *Ideology and U.S. Foreign Policy.* London: Yale University Press.

Hutt, M. 1996. "Looking for Shangri-La: From Hilton to Lamichhane." In *The Tourist Image: Myths and Myth Making in Tourism,* ed. T. Selwyn. Chichester, England: John Wiley.

Inden, R. 1990. *Imagining India.* Oxford: Blackwell.

India Office Records (IOR): H/219. 1768–84. "Correspondence and Reports Relating to Assam, Bhutan, China, Lhasa, Nepal and Tibet from George Bogle and Lt Samuel Turner, 16 Mar 1768–2 Mar 1784." India Office Records: Home Office Miscellaneous Series. London: British Library.

IOR: L/MIL/17/14/92. 1910. "Military Report on Tibet." India Office Records: Military Department and War Staff Records. London: British Library.

IOR: L/P&S/10/147. 1908. "Tibet: The Dalai Lama, 1904–13." India Office Records: Political and Secret Separate (Subject) Files. London: British Library.

IOR: L/P&S/10/150 2750 5-7. 1908. "Tibet: Infringement of Treaties, Frontier Questions, Chinese Troops, 1904–13." India Office Records: Political and Secret Separate (Subject) Files. London: British Library.

IOR: L/P&S/10/265. 1912. "China and Tibet, 1912." India Office Records: Political and Secret Separate (Subject) Files. London: British Library.

IOR: L/P&S/10/718. 1917. "Tibet: Proposed Revision of 1914 Convention, 1922–30." India Office Records: Political and Secret Separate (Subject) Files. London: British Library.

IOR: L/P&S/10/1012. 1921. "Tibet: Travellers, Including Swedish and Russian Expeditions, 1921-29." India Office Records: Political and Secret Separate (Subject) Files. London: British Library.

IOR: L/P&S/10/1113.1924. "Tibet: Relations with British Government,

1924–31." India Office Records: Political and Secret Separate (Subject) Files. London: British Library.

IOR: L/P&S/11/15 File P 1701. 1912. "Tibet: Parliamentary Questions, Apr–Jul 1912." India Office Records: Political and Secret Annual Files. London: British Library.

IOR: L/P&S/11/64 File P 3937. 1913. "Tibet: Exchange of Presents between the Dalai Lama and King George V, May 1913–Sep 1914." India Office Records: Political and Secret Annual Files. London: British Library.

IOR: L/P&S/11/68. 1913. "Tibet: Representation in Chinese Parliament, Nov 1913–Mar 1917." India Office Records: Political and Secret Annual Files. London: British Library.

IOR: L/P&S/18/B138. 1902. "Note on Tibet." India Office Records: Political and Secret Department Memoranda. London: British Library.

IOR: L/P&S/18/B144. 1903. "Memorandum on Tibet." India Office Records: Political and Secret Department Memoranda. London: British Library.

IOR: L/P&S/18/B157. 1906. "Tibet." India Office Records: Political and Secret Department Memoranda. London: British Library.

IOR: MSS EUR/C270/FL2/E/1/144. n.d. "An undated account of Lhasa and its inhabitants by Brigadier-General Herbert Augustus Iggulden (1861–1937), Chief Staff Officer Tibet Mission Escort, 1903–04." India Office Records: European Manuscripts. London: British Library.

IOR: MSS EUR/D722/18. n.d. "Shuttleworth Collection." India Office Records: European Manuscripts. London: British Library.

IOR: MSS EUR/F157. n.d. "Bailey Collection." India Office Records: European Manuscripts. London: British Library.

IOR: MSS EUR/F197. n.d. "Younghusband Collection." India Office Records: European Manuscripts. London: British Library.

IOR: MSS EUR/F80/217. n.d. "Charles Bell Collection." India Office Records: European Manuscripts. London: British Library.

IOR: V Cd. 1920. [1904]. "Papers Relating to Tibet." India Office Records: V/4 Parliamentary Papers HoC. London: British Library.

International Campaign for Tibet. 2006 [November 1950]."El Salvador's UN Appeal for Tibet." Available at http://www.savetibet.org/advocacy/un/resolutions/elsalvador.php (accessed 10 August 2006).

Jabri, V., and E. O'Gorman, eds. 1999. *Women, Culture, and International Relations*. London: Lynne Rienner.

Jacobs, J. M. 1996. *Edge of Empire: Postcolonialism and the City*. London: Routledge.

James, A. 1986. *Sovereign Statehood: The Basis of International Society*. London: Allen and Unwin.

Kabbani, R. 1986. *Imperial Fictions: Europe's Myths of Orient*. London: Pandora.

Kamenetz, R. 1995. *The Jew in the Lotus: A Poet's Rediscovery of Jewish Identity in Buddhist India*. San Francisco: Harper and Row.

Kaschewsky, R. 2001. "The Image of Tibet in the West before the Nineteenth Century." In *Imagining Tibet: Perceptions, Projections, and Fantasies*, ed. T. Dodin and H. Rather. Boston: Wisdom.

Katz, N. 1991. "A Meeting of Ancient Peoples: Western Jews and the Dalai Lama of Tibet: Searching Out the Jewish Secret for Surviving Exile." *Jerusalem Letters of Lasting Interest VP* 113, March. Available at http://www.jcpa.org/jl/hit20.htm (accessed 10 August 2006).

Kaul, N. 2007. *Imagining Economics Otherwise: Encounters with Identity/Difference*. London: Routledge.

Keal, P. 2003. *European Conquest and the Rights of Indigenous Peoples: The Moral Backwardness of International Society*. Cambridge: Cambridge University Press.

Keith, M., and S. Pile, eds. 1993. *Place and the Politics of Identity*. London: Routledge.

——, eds. 1997. *Geographies of Resistance*. London: Routledge.

Kewley, V. 1990. *Tibet: Behind the Ice Curtain*. London: Grafton Books.

Kibreab, G. 1999. "Revisiting the Debate on People, Place, Identity, and Displacement." *Journal of Refugee Studies* 12, no. 4: 384–428.

Kipling, R. 1976. [1901]. *Kim*. London: Pan Books.

Klein, B. S. 1990. "How the West Was One: Representational Politics of NATO." *International Studies Quarterly* 34, no. 3: 311–25.

——. 1994. *Strategic Studies and World Order*. Cambridge: Cambridge University Press.

Klieger, P. C. 1994. *Tibetan Nationalism: The Role of Patronage in the Accomplishment of a National Identity*. Meerut: Archana Publications.

——. 1997. "Shangri-La and Hyperreality: A Collision in Tibetan Refugee Expression." In *Tibetan Culture in the Diaspora: Papers Presented at a Panel of the 7th Seminar of the International Association for Tibetan Studies, Graz, 1995*, ed. F. J. Korom. Vienna: Verlag Der Osterreichischen Akademie Der Wissenschaften.

——. 2002a. *Tibet-O-Rama: Self and Other in a Tale from the Edge of Tibet*. San Francisco: Green Arrow Press.

——, ed. 2002b. *Tibet, Self, and the Tibetan Diaspora: Voices of Difference*. Leiden, Netherlands: Brill.

——. 2006. "Riding High on the Manchurian Dream: Three Paradigms in the Construction of the Tibetan Question." In *Contemporary Tibet: Politics, Development, and Society in a Disputed Region*, ed. B. Sautman and J. T. Dreyer. London: M. E. Sharpe.

Knaus, J. K. 1999. *Orphans of the Cold War: America and the Tibetan Struggle for Survival*. New York: Public Affairs.

Knight, E. F. 1894. *Where Three Empires Meet*. London: Longman, Green.

Knight, G. E. O. 1930. *Intimate Glimpses of Mysterious Tibet and Neighbouring Countries*. London: Golden Vista Press.

Kolas, A. 1996. "Tibetan Nationalism: The Politics of Religion." *Journal of Peace Research* 33, no. 1: 51–66.

———. 1998. "Chinese Media Discourses on Tibet: The Language of Inequality." *Tibet Journal* 23, no. 3: 69–77.

——— 2004. "Tourism and the Making of Place in Shangri-La." *Tourism Geographies* 6, no. 3: 262–78.

Kolas, A., and M. P. Thowsen. 2005. *On the Margins of Tibet: Cultural Survival on the Sino-Tibetan Frontier*. Seattle: University of Washington Press.

Kong, L., and B. S. A. Yeoh. 1997. "The Construction of National Identity through the Production of Ritual and Spectacle: An Analysis of National Day Parades in Singapore." *Political Geography* 16, no. 3: 213–39.

Korom, F. J., ed. 1997a. *Constructing Tibetan Culture: Contemporary Perspectives*. Quebec: Heritage Press.

———. 1997b. *Tibetan Culture in the Diaspora: Papers Presented at a Panel of the 7th Seminar of the International Association for Tibetan Studies, Graz, 1995*. Vienna: Osterreichischen Akademie Der Wissenschaften.

Krasner, S. D. 1999. *Sovereignty: Organized Hypocrisy*. Princeton, N.J.: Princeton University Press.

Krishna, S. 1993. "The Importance of Being Ironic: A Postcolonial View on Critical International Relations Theory." *Alternatives* 18, no. 3: 385–417.

———. 1999. *Postcolonial Insecurities: India, Sri Lanka, and the Question of Nationhood*. Minneapolis: University of Minnesota Press.

Kvaerne, P. 2001. "Tibet Images among Researchers on Tibet." In *Imagining Tibet: Perceptions, Projections, and Fantasies*, ed. T. Dodin and H. Rather. Boston: Wisdom.

Laird, T. 2002. *Into Tibet: The CIA's First Atomic Spy and His Secret Expedition to Lhasa*. New York: Grove Press.

Lamb, A. 1960. *Britain and Chinese Central Asia: The Road to Lhasa, 1767 to 1905*. London: Routledge and Kegan Paul.

———. 1986. *British India and Tibet, 1766–1910*, rev. ed. London: Routledge and Kegan Paul.

Landon, P. 1905. *Lhasa: An Account of the Country and People of Central Tibet and of the Progress of the Mission Sent There by the English Government in the Year 1903–04*. London: Hurst and Blackett.

Landry, D., and G. MacLean, eds. 1996. *The Spivak Reader: Selected Works of Gayatri Chakravorty Spivak*. London: Routledge.

Lapid, Y. 1989. "The Third Debate: On the Prospects of International Theory in a Post-Positivist Era." *International Studies Quarterly* 33, no. 3: 235–54.

Lapid, Y., and F. Kratochwi, eds. 1996. *The Return of Culture and Identity in IR Theory*. Boulder, Colo.: Lynne Rienner.

Lazar, E., ed. 1998. *Tibet: The Issue Is Independence*. Delhi: Full Circle.

Lebow, R. N. 1976. *White Britain and Black Ireland: The Influence of Stereotypes on Colonial Policy*. Philadelphia: Institute for the Study of Human Issues.

LePage, V. 1996. *Shambhala: The Fascinating Truth behind the Myth of Shangri-La*. Wheaton: Quest Books.

Lewis, M. W., and K. E. Wigen. 1997. *The Myth of Continents: A Critique of Metageography*. Berkeley: University of California Press.

Lewis, R. 1996. *Gendering Orientalism: Race, Feminity, and Representation*. London: Routledge.

Li, Tieh-tseng. 1954. *Tibet: Today and Yesterday*. New York: Bookman Associates.

Liao Zugui, and Zhang Zuji, eds. 1996. *Theses on Tibetology in China*. Beijing: China Tibetology Publishing House.

Lillienthal, A. M. 1978. *The Zionist Connection: What Price Peace?* New York: Dodd, Mead.

Liming, S. 1994. "The Younghusband Expedition and China's Policy towards Tibet, 1903–1904." In *Tibetan Studies: Proceedings of the 6th Seminar of the International Association for Tibetan Studies, Fagernes, 1992*, ed. P. Kvaerne. Oslo: Institute for Comparative Research in Human Culture.

Ling, L. H. M. 2002. *Postcolonial International Relations: Conquest and Desire between Asia and the West*. Basingstoke: Palgrave.

Liu, L. H. 2004. *The Clash of Empires: The Invention of China in Modern World Making*. London: Harvard University Press.

Lonely Planet. 2002. *Tibet*. Available at http://www.lonelyplanet.com/destinations/north_east_asia/tibet (accessed 1 July 2002).

Long, D., and B. Schmidt. 2005. *Imperialism and Internationalism in the Discipline of International Relations*. Albany: State University of New York Press.

Loomba, A. 1998. *Colonialism/Postcolonialism*. London: Routledge.

Lopez, D. S. Jr. 1998. *Prisoners of Shangri-La: Tibetan Buddhism and the West*. Chicago: University of Chicago Press.

———, ed. 1995. *Curators of the Buddha: The Study of Buddhism under Colonialism*. Chicago: University of Chicago Press.

Macaulay, C. 1972. *Report of a Mission to Sikkim and the Tibetan Frontier, 1884*. Kathmandu: Ratna Pustak Bhandar.

Macdonald, D. 1929. *The Land of the Lama*. London: Seeley, Service.

MacGregor, J. 1970. *Tibet: A Chronicle of Exploration*. London: Routledge and Kegan Paul.

Magnusson, J. 1997. "How Tibetans Deal with Political Conflicts in Exile: The National Democratic Party of Tibet Enters Exile Politics." Paper Presented at the 5th Conference of the Nordic Tibetologists, Moesgard, 5–7 September. Available at http://www.hum.au.dk/etno/Arbejdspapir/ 5magnusson.htm (accessed 31 July 2006).

———. 2002. "A Myth of Tibet: Reverse Orientalism and Soft Power." In P. C. Klieger, ed., *Tibet, Self, and the Tibetan Diaspora: Voices of Difference*. Leiden, Netherlands: Brill.

Makley, C. E. 1997. "The Meaning of Liberation: Representations of Tibetan Women." *Tibet Journal* 22, no. 2: 4–29.

———. 1999. "Embodying the Sacred: Gender and Monastic Revitalization in China's Tibet." Ph.D. dissertation, University of Michigan.

Malkki, L. 1992. "Citizens of Humanity: Internationalism and the Imagined Community of Nations." *Diaspora* 3, no. 1: 41–68.

Margolis, E. S. 2000. *War at the Top of the World: The Struggle for Afghanistan, Kashmir, and Tibet*. London: Routledge.

Markham, C. R. 1876. *Narratives of the Mission of George Bogle to Tibet and of the Journey of Thomas Manning to Lhasa*. London: Trubner and Co.

Matthiessen, P. 1995 [1978]. *The Snow Leopard*. London: Harvill Press.

Mayall, J. 1990. *Nationalism and International Society*. Cambridge: Cambridge University Press.

McClintock, A. 1995. *Imperial Leather: Race, Gender, and Sexuality in the Colonial Context*. London: Routledge.

McCue, G. 1999. *Trekking in Tibet: A Traveller's Guide*. 2nd ed. Seattle: The Mountaineers.

McGranahan, C. 2003. "Empire and the Status of Tibet: British, Chinese, and Tibetan Negotiations, 1913–1934." In *The History of Tibet*, ed. A. McKay, vol. 3. London: RoutledgeCurzon.

McKay, A. 1997. *Tibet and the British Raj: The Frontier Cadre, 1907–1947*. Richmond, Surry, England: Curzon Press.

———. 2001. "'Kicking the Buddha's Head': India, Tibet, and Footballing Colonialism." In *Soccer in South Asia*, ed. P. Dimo and J. Mills. London: Frank Cass.

———. 2003, "Nineteenth Century British Expansion of the Indo-Tibetan Frontier: A Forward Perspective." *Tibet Journal* 28, no. 4: 61–76.

McLagan, M. 1996. "Computing for Tibet: Virtual Politics in the Post-Cold War Era." In *Connected: Engagements with Media*, ed. G. Marcus. London: University of Chicago Press.

———. 1997. "Mystical Visions in Manhattan: Deploying Culture in the Year of Tibet." In *Tibetan Culture in the Diaspora: Papers Presented at a Panel of the 7th Seminar of the International Association for Tibetan*

Studies, Graz, 1995, ed. F. J. Korom. Vienna: Osterreichischen Akademie Der Wissenschaften.

Mearsheimer, J. J. 1990. "Why We Will Soon Miss the Cold War." *Atlantic Online,* August. Available at http://www.theatlantic.com/politics/foreign/mearsh.htm (accessed 14 June 2002).

Mehra, P. 1968. *The Younghusband Expedition: An Interpretation.* London: Asia Publishing House.

———. 1979. *The North-Eastern Frontier: A Documentary Study of the Internecine Rivalry between India, Tibet, and China.* Vol. 1, *1906–1914.* Delhi: Oxford University Press.

———. 2005. "In the Eyes of its Beholders: The Younghusband Expedition (1903–04) and Contemporary Media." *Modern Asian Studies* 39, no. 3: 725–39.

Methfessel, T. 1996. "Socioeconomic Adaption of Tibetan Refugees in South Asia over 35 Years in Exile." In *Tibetan Culture in the Diaspora: Papers Presented at a Panel of the 7th Seminar of the International Association for Tibetan Studies, Graz, 1995,* ed. F. J. Korom. Vienna: Osterreichischen Akademie Der Wissenschaften.

Michael, F. 1985. "Survival of a Culture: Tibetan Refugees in India." *Asian Survey* 25, no. 7: 737–44.

Midgley, C., ed. 1998. *Gender and Imperialism.* Manchester, England: Manchester University Press.

Miller, A. G., ed. 1982. *In the Eye of the Beholder: Contemporary Issues in Stereotyping.* New York: Praeger.

Miller, B. 1988. "American Popular Perceptions of Tibet from 1858–1938." *Tibet Journal* 13, no. 3: 3–19.

Millington, P. 1905. *To Lhassa at Last.* London: Smith, Elder.

Millon, H. A., and L. Nochlin, eds. 1978. *Art and Architecture in the Service of Politics.* London: MIT Press.

Mills, M. A. 2001. *Identity, Ritual, and State in Tibetan Buddhism.* London: Curzon Press.

Mohanty, C. T., A. Russo, and L. Torres, eds. 1991. *Third World Women and the Politics of Feminism.* Bloomington: Indiana University Press.

Mongia, P., ed. 1996. *Contemporary Postcolonial Theory: A Reader.* London: Arnold.

Moore-Gilbert, B. 1997. *Postcolonial Theory: Contexts, Practices, Politics.* London: Verso.

Moore-Gilbert, B., G. Stanton, and W. Maley, eds. 1997. *Postcolonial Criticism.* London: Longman.

Moran, P. 2004. *Buddhism Observed: Travelers, Exiles, and Tibetan Dharma in Kathmandu.* London: Routledge.

Morpurgo, M. 1998. *Escape from Shangri-La.* London: Morpurgo.

Mountcastle, A. 1997. "Tibetans in Exile: The Construction of Global Identities." Ph.D. dissertation, Rutgers University.

———. 2006. "The Question of Tibet and the Politics of the 'Real.'" In *Contemporary Tibet: Politics, Development, and Society in a Disputed Region*, ed. B. Sautman and J. T. Dreyer. London: M. E. Sharpe.

Muppidi, H. 2004. *The Politics of the Global*. Minneapolis: University of Minnesota Press.

Neilson, B. 2000. "Inside Shangri-La/Outside Globalisation: Remapping Orientalist Visions of Tibet." *Communal/Plural* 8, no. 1: 95–112.

Neumann, I. B. 1999. *Uses of the Other: "The East" in European Identity Formation*. Manchester, England: Manchester University Press.

New York Times. 1911. "Tibet's Living Deity Interviewed at Last." 17 May. Available at http://www.nytimes.com/library/world/asia/051711tibet-special.html (accessed 20 October 2001).

Nish, I., ed. 1995. *British Documents on Foreign Affairs: Reports and Papers from the Foreign Office Confidential Print, Part I, Series E (Asia, 1860–1908)*. Vol. 26. Washington: University Publications of America.

Norbu, D. 1990. "The Europeanization of Sino-Tibetan Relations, 1775–1907: The Genesis of Chinese 'Suzerainty' and Tibetan 'Autonomy.'" *Tibet Journal* 15, no. 4: 28–74.

———. 1997. "Tibet in Sino-India Relations: The Centrality of Marginality." *Asian Survey* 37, no. 11: 1078–95.

Norbu, J. 1986. *Warriors of Tibet: The Story of Aten and the Khampa's Fight for the Freedom of Their Country*. London: Wisdom.

———. 1998. "Dances with Yaks: Tibet in Film, Fiction, and Fantasy of the West." *Tibetan Review* (January): 18–23.

———. 2001. "Behind the Lost Horizon: Demystifying Tibet." In *Imagining Tibet: Perceptions, Projections, and Fantasies*, ed. T. Dodin and H. Rather. Boston: Wisdom.

Norbulingka Institute. 1998. Available at http://www.tibet.org/norling (accessed 4 October 2001).

Nowak, M. 1984. *Tibetan Refugees: Youth and the New Generation of Meaning*. New Brunswick, N.J.: Rutgers University Press.

Outside Online. 1999. "The Man Who Knocked the Bastard Off." *Outside Magazine,* October. Available at http://outside.away.com/outside/magazine/1099/199910hillary1.html (accessed 20 August 2006).

Palace, W. 2005. *The British Empire and Tibet, 1900–1922*. London: RoutledgeCurzon.

Paolini, A. J. 1999. *Navigating Modernity: Postcolonialism, Identity, and International Relations*. Boulder, Colo: Lynne Rienner.

Parpart, J., and M. Zalewski, eds. 1998. *The "Man" Question in International Relations*. Oxford, England: Westview Press.

Parry, B. 1996. "Resistance Theory/Theorising Resistance, or Two Cheers for Nativism." In *Contemporary Postcolonial Theory: A Reader*, ed. P. Mongia. London: Arnold.

Parsons, G. 1997. "Another India: Imagining Escape from the Masculine Self." In *At the Edge of International Relations: Postcolonialism, Gender, and Dependency*, ed. P. Darby. London: Pinter.

Pattersdon, G. 1990. *Requiem for Tibet*. London: Aurum Press.

Peissel, M. 1972. *The Secret War in Tibet*. Boston: Little, Brown.

Petech, L. 1950. *China and Tibet in the Early Eighteenth Century*. Leiden, Netherlands: Brill.

Peterson, V. S., and A. S. Runyan. 1999. [1993]. *Global Gender Issues: Dilemmas in World Politics*, 2nd ed. Oxford, England: Westview Press.

Pettman, J. J. 1996. *Worlding Women: A Feminist International Politics*. London: Routledge.

Polo, Marco. 1958. *The Travels of Marco Polo*. Trans. and introduction by R. Latham. Harmondsworth, England: Penguin.

Powell, A. 1992. *Heirs to Tibet: Travels among the Exiles in India*. New Delhi: Bluejay Books.

Powers, J. 2000. "The Free Tibet Movement: A Selective Narrative History." In *Engaged Buddhism in the West*, ed. C. S. Queen. Boston: Wisdom. Available at http://jbe.gold.ac.uk/7/powers001.html (accessed 20 August 2006).

Prakash, G., ed. 1995. *After Colonialism: Imperial Histories and Postcolonial Displacements*. Princeton, N.J.: Princeton University Press.

Pratt, A. E. 1892. *To the Snows of Tibet through China*. London: Longmans, Green.

Pratt, M. L. 1992. *Imperial Eyes: Travel Writing and Transculturation*. London: Routledge.

Prost, A. 2006. "The Problem with 'Rich Refugees': Sponsorship, Capital, and the Informal Economy of Tibetan Refugees." *Modern Asian Studies* 40, no. 1: 233–53.

Radhakrishnan, R. 1996. *Diasporic Mediations: Between Home and Location*. Minneapolis: University of Minnesota Press.

Ramakrishnan, A. K. 1999. "The Gaze of Orientalism: Reflections on Linking Postcolonialism and International Relations." *International Studies* 36, no. 2: 129–63.

Rampa, T. L. 1956. *The Third Eye: The Autobiography of a Tibetan Lama*. London: Secker and Warburg.

———. 1959. *Doctor from Lhasa*. London: Souvenir Press.

———. 1960. *The Rampa Story*. London: Souvenir Press.

Rawat, I. S. 1973. *Indian Explorers of the Nineteenth Century: Accounts of Explorations in the Himalayas, Tibet, Mongolia, and Central*

Asia. New Delhi: Publications Division, Ministry of Information and Broadcasting.

Rhie, M., and R. Thurman. 1991. *Wisdom and Compassion: The Sacred Art of Tibet*. London: Thames and Hudson.

Richards, T. 1992. "Archive and Utopia." *Representations* 37 (Winter): 104–35.

———. 1993. *The Imperial Archive: Knowledge and the Fantasy of Empire*. London: Verso.

Richardson, H. E. 1962. *Tibet and Its History*. London: Oxford University Press.

———. 1988. "Tibetan Lamas in Western Eyes." *Bulletin of Tibetology* 1 (February): 21–33.

———. 1998. *High Peaks, Pure Earth: Collected Writings on Tibetan History and Culture*. Ed. M. Aris. London: Serindia.

Riencourt, A. de. 1950. *Roof of the World: Tibet, Key to Asia*. New York: Rinehart.

Rijnhart, S. C. 1901. *With the Tibetans in Tent and Temple: Narrative of Four Years' Residence on the Tibetan Border, and of a Journey into the Far Interior*. London: Oliphant, Anderson, and Ferrier.

Rockhill, W. W. 1895. *Notes on the Ethnology of Tibet: Based on the Collections in the U.S. National Museum*. Washington, D.C.: Government Printing Office.

Root, D. 1996. *Cannibal Culture: Art, Appropriation, and the Commodification of Difference*. London: Westview Press.

Rose, N. H., and B. Warren. 1995. *Living Tibet: The Dalai Lama in Dharamsala*. New Delhi: Paljor Publications.

Rosenau, J. 1993. *Global Voices: Dialogues in International Relations*. Oxford, England: Westview Press.

Said, E. 1978. *Orientalism: Western Conceptions of the Orient*. New York: Penguin.

———. 1993. *Culture and Imperialism*. London: Chatto and Windus.

Said, E., and C. Hitchens, eds. 1988. *Blaming the Victims: Spurious Scholarship and the Palestinian Question*. London: Verso.

Salter, M. B. 2002. *Barbarians and Civilizations in International Relations*. London: Pluto.

Samuel, G. 1982. "Tibet as a Stateless Society and Some Islamic Parallels." *Journal of Asian Studies* 41, no. 2: 215–29.

———. 1993. *Civilized Shamans: Buddhism in Tibetan Societies*. Washington: Smithsonian Institution Press.

———. 1994. "Tibet and the Southeast Asian Highlands: Rethinking the Intellectual Context of Tibetan Studies." In *Tibetan Studies: Proceedings of the 6th Seminar of the International Association for Tibetan*

Studies, Fagernes, 1992, ed. P. Kvaerne. Oslo: Institute for Comparative Research in Human Culture.

Sandberg, G. 1904. *The Exploration of Tibet: Its History and Particulars from 1623 to 1904*. Calcutta: Thacker, Spink.

San Juan, E. 2000. *After Postcolonialism: Remapping Philippines–United States Confrontations*. Oxford: Rowman and Littlefield.

Sautman, B. 1999. "The Tibet Issue in Post-Summit Sino-American Relations." *Pacific Affairs* 72, no. 1: 7–21.

———. 2002. "Resolving the Tibet Question: Problems and Prospects." *Journal of Contemporary China* 11, no. 30: 77–107.

Sautman, B., and J. T. Dreyer, eds., 2006. *Contemporary Tibet: Politics, Development, and Society in a Disputed Region*. London: M. E. Sharpe.

Sautman, B., and Shiu-hing Lo. 1995. *The Tibet Question and the Hong Kong Experience*. Occasional Papers/Reprints Series in Contemporary Asian Studies, no. 2 (127). Baltimore: University of Maryland School of Law.

Schell, O. 2000. *Virtual Tibet: Searching for Shangri-La from the Himalayas to Hollywood*. New York: Metropolitan Books/Henry Holt.

Schick, I. C. 1999. *The Erotic Margin: Sexuality and Spatiality in Alterist Discourse*. London: Verso.

Schmitz, G. 2004. "Tibet's Position in International Law." In *Exile as Challenge: The Tibetan Diaspora*, ed. D. Bernstorff and H. Von Welck. New Delhi: Orient Longman.

Scholberg, H. 1995. *Tibet!* New Delhi: Indus.

Schroeder, J. E. 1998. "Consuming Representation: A Visual Approach to Consumer Research." In *Representing Consumers: Voices, Views and Visions*, ed. B. B. Stern. London: Routledge.

Schwartz, R. D. 1996. *Circle of Protest: Political Ritual in the Tibetan Uprising*. Delhi: Motilalbanarsidass Publishers.

Scott, D. 1999. *Refashioning Futures: Criticism after Postcoloniality*. Princeton, N.J.: Princeton University Press.

Shakabpa, W. D. 1984. *Tibet: A Political History*. New York: Potala Publications.

Shakya, T. 1991. "Tibet and the Occident: The Myth of Shangri-La." Special issue on Tibetan authors, *Lungta*. (April): 21–28.

———. 1993. "Whither the Tsampa Eaters?" *Himal* 6, no. 5: 8–11.

———. 1996. "Introduction: The Development of Modern Tibetan Studies." In *Resistance and Reform in Tibet*, ed. R. Barnett and S. Akiner. Delhi: Motilalbanarsidass Publishers.

———. 1999. *The Dragon in the Land of Snows: A History of Modern Tibet since 1947*. London: Pimlico.

————. 2000. "Who Are the Prisoners?" *Journal of the American Academy of Religion* 69, no. 1: 183–89.

————. 2002. "Blood in the Snows: Reply to Wang Lixiong." *New Left Review* 15 (May–June): 39–60.

————. 2005. "The Prisoner: Review of Melvyn Goldstein et al., *A Tibetan Revolutionary.*" *New Left Review* 34 (July–August): 153–59.

Shangri-La Media Center. 2001. "New Advertising Campaign for Shangri-La." Press release, 9 April. Available at http://www.shangri-la.com/eng/aboutus/media/press/article_34.htm (accessed 25 October 2001).

Shapiro, M. J. 1988. *The Politics of Representation: Writing Practices in Biography, Photography, and Policy Analysis.* Madison: University of Wisconsin Press.

Shapiro, M. J., and H. R. Alker, eds. 1996. *Challenging Boundaries: Global Flows, Territorial Identities.* Minneapolis: University of Minnesota Press.

Sharma, S. K., and U. Sharma, eds. 1996. *Encyclopaedia of Tibet.* New Delhi: Anmol Publications.

Sharpe, J. 1993. *Allegories of Empire: The Figure of Woman in the Colonial Text.* Minneapolis: University of Minnesota Press.

Shaumian, T. 2000. *Tibet: The Great Game and Tsarist Russia.* Oxford: Oxford University Press.

Sheffer, G. 1986. "A New Field of Study: Modern Diasporas in International Politics." In *Modern Diasporas in International Politics,* ed. G. Sheffer. London: Croom Helm.

Sheikh, A. G. 1991. "Tibetan Muslims." *Tibet Journal* 16, no. 4: 86–89.

Shih, Chih-yu. 2003. *Navigating Sovereignty: World Politics Lost in China.* London: Palgrave Macmillan.

Shinoda, H. 2000. *Re-Examining Sovereignty: From Classical Theory to the Global Age.* London: Macmillan.

Shohat, E. 1992. "Notes on the 'Postcolonial.'" *Social Text* 31/32: 99–113.

————. 1995. "The Struggle over Representation: Casting, Coalitions, and the Politics of Identification." In *Late Imperial Culture,* ed. R. de la Campa, E. A. Kaplan, and M. Sprinker. London: Verso.

Siddiqui, A. 1991. "Muslims in Tibet." *Tibet Journal* 16, no. 4: 71–85.

Sjolander, C. T., and C. T. Cox, eds. 1994. *Beyond Positivism: Critical Reflections in International Relations.* Boulder, Colo.: Lynne Rienner.

Smith, A. D. 1991. *National Identity.* London: Penguin.

Smith, S. 2000. "The Discipline of International Relations: Still an American Social Science?" *British Journal of Politics and International Relations* 2, no. 3: 374–402.

Smith, S., K. Booth, and M. Zalewski, eds. 1996. *International Theory: Positivism and Beyond*. Cambridge: Cambridge University Press.

Smith, W. W. 1996. *Tibetan Nation: A History of Tibetan Nationalism and Sino-Tibetan Relations*. Boulder, Colo.: Westview Press.

Snyder, R. S. 1999. "The U.S. and Third World Revolutionary States: Understanding the Breakdown in Relations." *International Studies Quarterly* 43, no. 2: 265–90.

Sperling, E. 2004. *The Tibet-China Conflict: History and Polemics*. Washington, D.C.: East-West Centre. Available at http://www.eastwestcenterwashington.org/Publications/sperling.pdf (accessed 10 August 2006).

Spivak, G. C. 1988. "Can the Subaltern Speak?" In *Marxism and the Interpretation of Culture*, ed. C. Nelson and L. Grossberger. Urbana: University of Illinois Press.

———. 1990. *The Postcolonial Critic—Interviews, Strategies, Dialogues*. Edited by S. Harasym. London: Routledge.

———. 1993. *Outside in the Teaching Machine*. London: Routledge.

———. 1997. "Poststructuralism, Marginality, Postcoloniality and Value." In *Contemporary Postcolonial Theory: A Reader*, ed. P. Mongia. London: Arnold.

———. 1999. *A Critique of Postcolonial Reason: Towards a History of the Vanishing Present*. Cambridge, Mass.: Harvard University Press.

Spufford, F. 1996. *I May Be Some Time*. London: Faber and Faber.

Spurr, D. 1993. *Rhetoric of Empire: Colonial Discourse in Journalism, Travel Writing, and Imperial Administration*. Durham, N.C.: Duke University Press.

Steans, J. 1998. *Gender and IR: An Introduction*. Cambridge, England: Polity Press.

Steedman, C. 1998. "The Space of Memory: In an Archive." *History of the Human Sciences* 11, no. 4: 65–83.

Strang, D. 1996. "Contested Sovereignty: The Social Construction of Colonial Imperialism." In *State Sovereignty as Social Construct*, ed. T. J. Biersteker and C. Weber. Cambridge: Cambridge University Press.

Strom, A. K. 1997. "Between Tibet and the West: On Traditionality, Modernity, and the Development of Monastic Institutions in the Tibetan Diaspora." In *Tibetan Culture in the Diaspora: Papers Presented at a Panel of the 7th Seminar of the International Association for Tibetan Studies, Graz, 1995*, ed. F. J. Korom. Vienna: Verlag Der Osterreichischen Akademie Der Wissenschaften.

Suleri, S. 1992. *Rhetoric of English India*. Chicago: University of Chicago Press.

Sullivan, Z. T. 1993. *Narratives of Empire: The Fictions of Rudyard Kipling.* Cambridge: Cambridge University Press.

Sylvester, C. 1993. "Reconstituting a Gender Eclipsed Dialogue." In *Global Voices: Dialogues in International Relations,* ed. J. Rosenau. Oxford: Westview Press.

———. 2002. *Feminist International Relations: An Unfinished Journey.* Cambridge: Cambridge University Press.

Thargyal, R. 1997. "Is There a Process of Secularization among the Tibetans in Exile?" In *Tibetan Culture in the Diaspora: Papers Presented at a Panel of the 7th Seminar of the International Association for Tibetan Studies, Graz, 1995,* ed. F. J. Korom. Vienna: Verlag Der Osterreichischen Akademie Der Wissenschaften.

Thupten Samphel. 2000. Tibetan Government-in-Exile's Department of Information and International Relations. Personal interview, January, Dharamsala.

Tibetan Book of the Dead: Liberation through Understanding in the Between. 1998. Trans. R. A. F. Thurman; composed by Padma Sambhava; discovered by Karma Lingpa. New Delhi: HarperCollins.

Tibet Journal. 1995. Special issue, 20, no. 3.

Tickner, J. A. 1992. *Gender in International Relations: Feminist Perspectives on Achieving Global Security.* New York: Columbia University Press.

Tololyan, K. 1991. "The Nation-State and its Others: In Lieu of a Preface." *Diaspora* 1, no. 1: 3–7.

———. 1996. "Rethinking Diaspora(s): Stateless Power in the Transnational Moment." *Diaspora* 5, no. 1: 3–36.

TPPRC (Tibetan Parliamentary and Policy Research Center). 2000. *The Case concerning Tibet: Tibet's Sovereignty and the Tibetan People's Right to Self-Determination.* 2nd ed. New Delhi: TPPRC.

Trungpa, Chogyam. 1995. *Shambhala: The Sacred Path of the Warrior.* Ed. C. R. Gimian. Boston: Shambhala.

Tsarong, P. 1992. "Understanding Decolonization and Its Implications for the Tibetan Movement." *Tibetan Review* (November): 14–19.

Tsering, L. 1998. "The Issue Is Independence." In *Tibet: The Issue Is Independence,* ed. E. Lazar. Delhi: Full Circle.

Turner, S. 1971. *An Account of an Embassy to the Court of the Teshoo Lama in Tibet, 1800.* New Delhi: Manjushri.

Tuttle, G. 2005. *Tibetan Buddhists in the Making of Modern China.* New York: Columbia University Press.

Uncovered Editions. 1999. *The British Invasion of Tibet: Colonel Younghusband, 1904.* London: The Stationary Office.

Van Maanen, J., ed. 1995. *Representation in Ethnography.* London: Sage.

Venturino, S. 1992. "Reading Negotiations in the Tibetan Diaspora." In *Constructing Tibetan Culture: Contemporary Perspectives,* ed. F. J. Korom. Quebec: Heritage Press.

Vertovec, S. 1992. "Three Meanings of 'Diaspora' Exemplified among South Asian Religions." *Diaspora* 6, no. 3: 277–300.

Waddell, L. A. 1905. *Lhasa and Its Mysteries: With a Record of the Expedition of 1903–1904.* London: John Murray.

———. 1972 [1905]. *Tibetan Buddhism with Its Mystic Cults, Symbolism, and Mythology.* New York: Dover Publications.

Waever, O. 1998. "The Sociology of a Not So International Discipline: American and European Developments in International Relations." *International Organization* 52, no. 4: 687–727.

Walker, J. T. 1885. *Four Years' Journeyings through Great Tibet by One of the Trans-Himalayan Explorers of the Survey of India.* London: Wm. Clowes and Sons.

Walker, R. B. J. 1990. "Sovereignty, Identity, Community: Reflections on the Horizons of Contemporary Political Practice." In *Contending Sovereignties: Redefining Political Community,* ed. R. B. J. Walker and S. H. Mendlovitz. Boulder, Colo: Lynne Rienner.

———. 1993. *Inside/Outside: International Relations as Political Theory.* Cambridge: Cambridge University Press.

———. 1995. "From International Politics to World Politics." In *The State in Transition: Reimagining Political Space,* ed. J. A. Camilleri, A. P. Jarvis, and A. J. Paolini. Boulder, Colo.: Lynne Rienner.

Waller, D. 1990. *The Pundits: British Exploration of Tibet and Central Asia.* Lexington: University Press of Kentucky.

Walt van Praag, M. C. 1987. *The Status of Tibet: History, Rights, and Prospects in International Law.* London: Wisdom.

Wang Jiawei, and Nyima Gyaincain, eds. 1992. *The Historical Status of China's Tibet.* Beijing: China Intercontinental Press. Available at http://www.tibet-china.org/historical_status/english/ (accessed 15 August 2006).

Wang Lixiong. 2002. "Reflections on Tibet." Translated by Liu Xiaohong and A. T. Grunfeld. *New Left Review* 14 (March–April): 79–111.

Ward, F. K. 1934. *A Plant Hunter in Tibet.* London: Jonathan Cape.

Weber, C. 1995. *Simulating Sovereignty: Intervention, the State, and Symbolic Exchange.* Cambridge: Cambridge University Press.

———. 1999. "IR: The Resurrection or New Frontier of Incorporation." *European Journal of International Relations* 5, no. 4: 435–50.

Wei Jingsheng. 1998. "A Letter to Deng Xiaoping." In *Tibet through Dissident Chinese Eyes: Essays on Self-Determination,* ed. Cao Changching and J. D. Seymour. New York: M. E. Sharpe.

Weldes, J. 1999. *Constructing National Interests: The United States and the Cuban Missile Crisis*. Minneapolis: University of Minnesota Press.

Weldes, J., M. Laffey, H. Gusterson, and R. Duvall, eds. 1999. *Cultures of Insecurity: States, Communities, and the Production of Danger*. Minneapolis: University of Minnesota Press.

Wellby, M. S. 1898. *Through Unknown Tibet*. London: T. Fisher Unwin.

Wiggins, L. R. 1994. "Sino-Tibetan Relations and Tributary Ideology." *Tibet Journal* 25, no. 1: 63–73.

Wilby, S. 1988. *Journey across Tibet: A Young Woman's 1900-Mile Trek across the Rooftop of the World*. Chicago: Contemporary Books.

Williams, P., and P. Childs. 1992. *An Introduction to Post-Colonial Theory*. London: Prentice Hall, Harvester Wheatsheaf.

Willoughby, M. E. 1924. "The Relation of Tibet to China." *Journal of the Central Asian Society* 11, no. 3: 187–203.

Wilson, A. 1987. "Kipling's Kim." In *Modern Critical Interpretations: Rudyard Kipling's "Kim,"* ed. H. Bloom. New York: Chelsea House.

Wood, R. E. 1998. "Touristic Ethnicity: A Brief Itinerary." *Ethnic and Racial Studies* 21, no. 2: 218–41.

Woodcock, G. 1971. *Into Tibet: The Early British Explorers*. London: Faber and Faber.

World Tibet News. 1999. "Murdoch Brands Dalai Lama a 'Monk in Gucci Shoes,'" 7 September. Available at http://www.tibet.ca/en/wtnarchive/1999/9/7_5.html (accessed 20 August 2006).

———. 1998. "Clinton Urges China to Talk to Dalai Lama," 27 June. Available at http://www.tibet.ca/en/wtnarchive/1998/6/19_2.html (accessed 20 August 2006).

Xu Guangui. 1992. "The United States and the Tibet Issue." *Asian Survey* 37, no. 11: 1062–77.

Xu Mingxu. 2000. "Tibet Question: A New Cold War." Paper Presented at the 18th World Congress of the International Political Science Association, August, Quebec City.

Yegenoglu, M. 1998. *Colonial Fantasies: Towards a Feminist Reading of Orientalism*. Cambridge: Cambridge University Press.

Young, R. 1990. *White Mythologies—Writing History and the West*. London: Routledge.

Younghusband, F. 1910. *India and Tibet: A History of the Relations Which Have Subsisted between the Two Countries from the Time of Warren Hastings to 1910; With a Particular Account of the Mission to Lhasa of 1904*. London: John Murray.

Yue, Gang. 2004. "Echoes from the Himalaya: The Quest of Ma Lihua, a Chinese Intellectual in Tibet." *Journal of Contemporary China* 13, no. 38: 69–88.

Zheng Shan, ed. 2001. *A History of Development of Tibet.* Trans. Chen Guansheng and Li Peizhu. Beijing: Foreign Language Press.

Žižek, S. 2001. *On Belief.* London: Routledge.

FILMOGRAPHY

Kundun (video recording). 1992. Walt Disney Video. Directed by M. Scorsese, produced by B. de Fina.

Lost Horizon (DVD). 1937. Directed and produced by Frank Capra.

Seven Years in Tibet (video recording). 1992. Tristar Pictures and Madalay Entertainment. USA. Directed by Jean-Jacques Annaud, produced by Jean-Jacques Annaud, I. Smith, and J. H. Williams.

The Face of Fu Manchu (video recording). 1965. UK. Directed by D. Sharp.

Publication History

Chapter 2 was published in *New Political Science*. Copyright 2007 Taylor and Francis. Reprinted with permission. *New Political Science* is available online at http://journalsonline.tandf.co.uk.

A portion of chapter 3 was published as "Archive and the Poetics of 'Exotica Tibet,'" in *Tibetan Borderlands: Proceedings of the Tenth Seminar of the IATS, 2003*, ed. P. C. Klieger (Leiden: Brill Academic Publishers, 2006). Reprinted with permission.

Chapter 4 is adapted from "The Tibet Question and the West: Issues of Sovereignty, Identity, and Representation," in *Contemporary Tibet: Politics, Development, and Society in a Disputed Region*, ed. Barry Sautman and June Teufel Dreyer (Armonk, N.Y.: M. E. Sharpe, 2006). Reprinted with permission.

Chapter 4 draws on "A Story to Be Told: IR, Postcolonialism, and the Tibetan (Trans)Nationalism," in *Power, Postcolonialism, and International Relations: Reading Race, Gender, and Class*, ed. G. Chowdhry and S. Nair (London: Routledge, 2002). Reprinted with permission.

Chapter 5 draws on "(Re)Imagining Nationalism: Identity and Representation in Tibetan Diaspora in South Asia," *Contemporary South*

Asia 9, no. 3 (2000): 271–87, and "Travel-routing Diaspora . . . : Homing on Tibet," *Diaspora: A Journal of Transnational Studies* 12, no. 3 (2003): 211–29. Reprinted with permission. *Contemporary South Asia* may be found at http://www.tandf.co.uk/journals.

Chapter 6 was previously published as "A Guide to Little Lhasa in India: The Role of Symbolic Geography of Dharamsala in Constituting Tibetan Diasporic Identity," in *Tibet, Self, and the Tibetan Diaspora: Voices of Difference*, ed. P. C. Klieger (Leiden, Netherlands: Brill Academic Publishers, 2002). Reprinted with permission.

Index

agency, 18, 19, 26, 37, 85, 87, 125, 131, 134, 137; non-Westerners', 4, 12; subjectivity and, 8, 10, 125; Tibetan, 88, 104, 110, 125, 134

Amban, 68, 73

American foreign policy, 13, 21

American social science: international relations as, 135

Amin, S., 134

ancient Greeks, 135, 141

archive, 12, 38, 94; Shangri-La as utopian, 39–42, 43, 46

Aris, M., 70, 101, 145

autonomy, xviii, 5, 66, 67, 79, 82; real, 106; suzerainty and, 67. *See also* Chinese suzerainty–Tibetan autonomy formula

Bell, C., 81, 92, 145

Blavatsky, Madame H., 34, 147

Bogle, G., 68, 69, 140, 142

Bollywood, 122, 144

Bradley, H., 38

British expedition of Tibet of 1903–4, 30; Younghusband's account of the, 21, 43–46. *See also* Invasion of Tibet, British; Tibet mission of 1903–4; Younghusband expedition

British expedition of Tibet of 1922–23, 26

British imperialism, 101, 114; and Tibet, xviii, 42–45, 65–85

Brown, C., 134

Buddhism, 96; spread in the West, 39, 144. *See also* Tibetan Buddhism

Buddhism of Tibet or Lamaism, The, 47

Butler, J., 106, 124, 137, 149. *See also* performativity

Buzan, B., 2

Campbell, D., 13, 14

Candler, E., 24, 29, 30, 31, 72

Chan, S., 133

Chapman, F. S., 26, 32, 75

Chinese nationalism, 80
Chinese representations of Tibet, 134
Chinese suzerainty–Tibetan autonomy formula, 74–76
Cholka-sum, 92
Chos srid gnyis ldan (religion and politics combined), 55, 80, 93, 96. *See also* religion and politics
Christian missionaries, 47, 53, 68, 139–40
chronopolitics, 31–32
civilizing, imperialism as, 20, 33, 46, 134
Clapham, C., 10
classification, 24–25, 47
Clifford, J., 102, 123
Clinton, B., 55
Cold War, xv, 3, 7
constructionist theories, 15
Cultural Revolution, 83, 95, 105
cultural turn, 112
Curzon, Lord, 29, 71–72, 142

Daily Mail, 24, 137
Dalai Lama, 62, 97, 101, 103, 104, 113, 137; dual role as religious as well as political leader, 93, 96, 105, 116; and the emphasis on preservation of culture, 117; the figure of, 53–56, 125; Heinrich Harrer and, 63, 64; Nobel Prize, 121; Shugden affair, 146; as a symbol of peace, 101; as a symbol of Tibetan nation, 96, 117, 122, 146; and Tashi Lama (Panchen Lama), 44, 68, 117, 133, 148; Tibetan government-in-exile, led by, xiv, xix, 89, 90, 92, 97, 100, 105
Dalai Lama, Fifth, 49

Dalai Lama, Fourteenth, 83, 84, 125
Dalai Lama, Thirteenth, 50, 57, 71–73, 115, 143
Dalby, S., 14
Darby, P., 7, 8, 10, 11
Das, S. C., 70, 138
David-Neel, A., 25, 34, 35, 57–59, 60
Davidson, L., 141
Deasy, H. H. P., 57
debasement, xvii, 25–27, 46, 47, 48
decolonization, 6, 7, 79, 97, 136
deconstruct/deconstructive/deconstruction, 8, 12, 106, 110, 111, 129, 130, 131
Desideri, Ippolito, 53, 68
Dharamsala, xix, 54, 92, 97, 105, 109–27, 147, 148
diaspora, xv–xviii, 129; Tibetan, 54, 84, 85, 88–107, 111–22, 144, 146, 147, 149
differentiation, 24–25, 47
disciplinary/disciplinarity/antidisciplinarity, xiv, 5, 8, 129
discipline: IR as, 5–9, 11, 135, 136
Discovery of America, The, 28
displacement, 88, 94, 107
Doty, R., xv, 14, 33, 37
Dreyfus, G., 94
Du Halde, P. J. B., 53

East India Company, 70, 140, 142
Ekvall, R. A., 143
environmentalism, 84, 100, 125
eroticization, xvii, 27–31
essentialism, 19, 46, 47, 61, 87, 111; antiessentialism and, 11, 136–37. *See also* strategic essentialism
ethnocentrism, xv, xvii, 92, 129, 131

Eurocentric, 2, 10
Evans-Wentz, W. Y., 49
exile: conscious adoption of the
    term, 89; cultural survival of
    Tibetan identity in, 109–27;
    Dalai Lama in, 54, 145; home-
    land and, 144; nationalism
    among Tibetans in, 86–107;
    Tibetans in, 21

feminism, 8; as critical IR theory,
    5, 10
feminization, 27, 28
Forbidden City, 39, 57, 63, 113
Foreign Office, 26, 43, 75, 141
Forman, H., 38
Foucault, M., 15
Free Tibet, 84, 99, 104, 120, 121,
    144

Ganden monastery, 50
gaze, 22–24, 46, 47, 56
Gere, R., 36, 99,
gerontification, 34, 47, 61
gold, 40, 62, 69, 141
Goldstein, M. C., 95
Great Game, xv, 71, 142
Grenard, F., 28, 32
Grueber and D'Orville, 53
Grunfeld, T., 143
Guru massacre, 20, 33, 34
Gyatso, Palden, 103

Harrer, H., 36, 63–64
Harris, C., 119, 144
Hastings, W., 43, 70
Hedin, S., 29
hierarchization, 25
Hillary, E., 20
Hilton, J., 39–43, 139
Hobsbawm, E., 94, 100, 143
Hoffman, S., 2

Hollywood, 50, 63, 64, 98, 99,
    139
Holsti, K. J., 2
homeland, 91, 144; diaspora and,
    89, 90, 93; return to, 126, 127;
    Tibetan, 97, 111, 115, 118, 145,
    146; unified/original Tibetan,
    113, 115, 121, 122
Hopkirk, P., 58
Huber, T., 125
human rights, 97, 98, 102, 104,
    144; Dalai Lama and, 96; as a
    tool, xvi, 5, 83–85; violation in
    Tibet, 82, 83
Hunt, M., 21

idealization, xvii, 25–27, 47, 52,
    61, 63; Tibet's, 43, 45, 48, 50
imagining community, 91, 94, 107
imperialism, xviii, 6, 16, 147; and
    IR, xv, 7, 8, 130, 131, 136;
    and Orientalism, 12, 137; and
    postcolonialism, 4; and repre-
    sentation of the non-Western
    Other, 17–36; Western, 5, 134,
    145, 146
India and Tibet, 43, 46
infanitilization, xvii, 33–34, 46, 51
instrumentalist–primordialist
    debate, 93–94
International Commission of
    Jurists, 133
International/Intertextual
    Relations, 10
International Studies Quarterly, 2
invasion of Tibet, British, 19–21,
    24, 29, 33, 44, 46, 48, 52,
    53, 72, 73, 81, 139. See also
    British expedition of Tibet of
    1903–4
invasion of Tibet, Chinese, 42, 73,
    84, 143

Kabbani, R., 18
Kapstein, M. K., 95
Kawaguchi, Ekai, 30
Kibreab, G., 126
Kim and *Kim*, 34, 50–53, 140
Kipling, R., 33. *See also* Kim and
    Kim
Klein, B. S., 14
Klieger, P. C., 99, 103, 144
Knaus, J. K., 142
Knight, G. E., 26
knowledge-power, 15
Kolas, A., 119
Korom, F. J., 55
Krishna, S., 10
Kundun, 64

Lamaism, 45, 47, 48, 81, 144
Lamaist state, 74, 83, 91
Lamb, A., 19
land of snows, 58, 139
Landon, P., 32, 33, 34, 37
Lhasa, 23, 26, 28, 29–32, 41, 43,
    45, 48, 50, 53, 56–59, 63–64,
    68–72, 78, 93; government of,
    44, 97; Lamas of, 21; monks
    of, 25; protests, 95–96; race
    for, 39. *See also* "Little Lhasa
    in India"
Lhasa and its Mysteries, 47
Lhasa Convention, 72–73
Little, R., 2
"Little Lhasa in India," 109–27.
    See also Dharamsala; McLeod
    Gunj
Lonely Planet, 138
Lopez, D., 21, 84, 98, 143, 146
Lost Horizon, 39, 41, 42

Macdonald, D., 30
mahatmas, 48
Malkki, L., 91

Manchu, 67, 68, 77
Manning, T., 26, 53
Marco Polo, 38–39
masculinity, 28, 137
Mathiessen, P., 59
McClintock, A., 29
McGranahan, C., 70, 78
mchod-yon, 77, 78
McLeod Gunj, 113–15,
    120–21, 147, 148. *See also*
    Dharamsala
medieval, 31–32, 64, 135
Millington, P., 29
modernization, 30, 94, 98, 115,
    121, 143
Mongol, 67, 80, 143
Monlam, 55
moralization, 27, 30–31, 46, 47
Moran, P., 99
Mount Everest, 20
Murdoch, Rupert, 55

naturalization, 56, 141
Nazi, 27
Neumann, I., 14, 136
New Age, 32, 141, 144
New Internationalist, 99
New York Times, 139
Noel, Captain J., 20
Norbu, J., 60
Norbulingka Institute, 116–17,
    120, 147, 148
Norgay, T., 20
Nowak, M., 149

objectification, 22, 119
occidental, 2, 12, 35
O'Connor, W. F., 25
Old Tibet, 100, 116–17, 119, 138,
    145
Oriental, 21, 27, 28, 30, 51, 52,
    65, 142, 143, 144

Orientalism, xviii, 12, 13, 51, 131, 144; Tibet and, 16
Orientalist, 99, 101, 120, 130, 134, 139

Palestinians, 4, 99, 105, 126, 136, 145
Panchen Lama, 68, 117, 133, 140, 148
patron-client relations, 80, 99, 103, 117, 124
patron-priest relations, 77–78
performativity, 124, 149
political and ethnographic Tibet, 92–93
positivism, 1, 6, 136
poststructuralism, 5, 10, 112, 136, 137
Potala, 30, 32, 44, 63, 144
preservation ethos, 11, 115, 120, 121, 148
preservation of culture, 97, 116, 121
primitive Buddhism, 52
pro-Tibet lobby, 67. *See also* Save Tibet
proto-nationalism, 55, 94

racialization, 25
Radhakrishnan, 111
Rampa, T. L., 24, 60–62, 141
rangzen, 98, 149
Rawling, Captain Cecil, 19
refugee, 54, 55, 97, 99, 101, 110–17, 125, 144; as a term, 89
religion and politics, 54, 55, 142, 149. *See also Chos srid gnyis ldan*
representational strategies, xvii, 24, 31, 46, 47, 56, 63. *See also* strategies of representation
Richardson, H., 39, 81, 117

Riencourt, A., de., 30, 34, 141
Rijnharts, 30
Rockhill, W. W., 138
romantic paternalism, 82
"rooftop of the world," 56, 139
roots and routes, 110, 122–23
Rosenau, J., 135

Said, E., 17, 20, 136, 137
Samuel, G., 79
Sandberg, G., 25
Save Tibet, 84, 98. *See also* pro-Tibet lobby
Scott, D., 5
Segal, S., 148
self-affirmation, 27, 46, 47, 56, 63
self-criticism, 35, 47, 56, 61, 63
self-determination, 4, 6, 54, 97, 107, 116, 127; right to, 5, 84, 92, 98, 99, 103, 106, 149
Seventeen Point Agreement (1951), 73, 80, 134
Seven Years in Tibet, 63–64
Shakya, T., 77, 102, 105
Shambhala, 40, 145
Shangri-la, 29, 38, 64, 82, 97, 99, 115, 144, 145, 148; James Hilton and, 39–42; myth of, 105, 138–39, 143; Tibetans as prisoners of, 84, 88, 97, 125, 138
Shaumian, T., 142
Sheffer, G., 89
Sherpas, 20, 59
Shigatse, 44
Shugden, 105, 146
Shuttleworth, 81
Simla Talks, 74
Sino-Indian relations, xv, 82
Sino-Western relations, xv
Smith, A., 93, 94, 100
Smith, S., 136

Snow Leopard, The, 59–60
Snyder, R. S., 136
sovereignty, xvi, xviii, 6, 7, 11, 65–83, 85, 130
Sperling, E., 78
Spivak, G. C., 3, 8, 11, 136
stereotype, 19–21, 61
stereotyping, xvii, 35, 46, 47, 56, 61
Strasbourg Proposal, 101
strategic essentialism, 11, 91, 111, 127
strategies of representation, 18, 22, 36, 130. *See also* representational strategies
subjectivity, 8, 10, 11, 16; Tibetan, xv, 104, 125
surveillance, 22–24
suzerainty, xvi, xviii, 66–80
Sylvester, C., 135

Tashi Lama, 40, 144. *See also* Teshoo Lama
Teshoo Lama, 50–53, 69, 140. *See also* Tashi Lama
Thargyal, R., 149
theosophist, 48
third debate, xiv, 11, 136
Third Eye, The, 61
Thurman, R. A. F., 49
Tibetan Books of the Dead, The, 47, 49, 59
Tibetan Buddhism, 32, 45, 47, 55, 78, 98, 102, 133, 139, 140, 146, 148, 149; comparison with classical Buddhism, 47, 81, 93; as idealized Buddhism, 49; as impure Buddhism 47–48, 52
Tibetan Review, 146
Tibet mission of 1903–4, 23, 34,

42, 46. *See also* British expedition of Tibet of 1903–4
Tibetophilia, 39
Tibet question, 13–18, 65, 80, 81, 83–85, 91, 95, 98, 103, 129, 133, 142
Tibet support groups, 91, 98, 103, 104, 105
Tintin in Tibet, 32
transnationalism, 84, 102, 125
truth claims, 15, 16
tsampa, 102
Tsering, L., 104
Turner, S., 69, 140

UN General Assembly, 82, 133
UN Security Council, 136
Unveiling of Lhasa, 29

veil, 24, 28, 29, 137
Venturino, S., 149
"victimisation paradigm," 91

Waddell, L. A., 29, 47–48, 139, 140
Waever, O., 135
Ward, F. K., 79
Weldes, J., 14
Wellby, M. S., 57
white man's burden, 33, 35
Willoughby, M. E., 70
Wilson, A., 140
Wolff, Joesph, 27

yeti, 24, 32, 60, 62, 120
Younghusband expedition, 53, 54. *See also* British expedition of Tibet of 1903–4

Žižek, S., 22, 34

DIBYESH ANAND is a reader in international relations at the Centre for the Study of Democracy at the University of Westminster in England. He has published on postcolonial international relations, the Tibet question, and Hindu nationalism.

BORDERLINES

(continued from page ii)

Volume 19 Cristina Rojas, *Civilization and Violence: Regimes of Representation in Nineteenth-Century Colombia*

Volume 18 Mathias Albert, David Jacobson, and Yosef Lapid, editors, *Identities, Borders, Orders: Rethinking International Relations Theory*

Volume 17 Jenny Edkins, *Whose Hunger? Concepts of Famine, Practices of Aid*

Volume 16 Jennifer Hyndman, *Managing Displacement: Refugees and the Politics of Humanitarianism*

Volume 15 Sankaran Krishna, *Postcolonial Insecurities: India, Sri Lanka, and the Question of Nationhood*

Volume 14 Jutta Weldes, Mark Laffey, Hugh Gusterson, and Raymond Duvall, editors, *Cultures of Insecurity: States, Communities, and the Production of Danger*

Volume 13 François Debrix, *Re-Envisioning Peacekeeping: The United Nations and the Mobilization of Ideology*

Volume 12 Jutta Weldes, *Constructing National Interests: The United States and the Cuban Missile Crisis*

Volume 11 Nevzat Soguk, *States and Strangers: Refugees and Displacements of Statecraft*

Volume 10 Kathy E. Ferguson and Phyllis Turnbull, *Oh, Say, Can You See? The Semiotics of the Military in Hawai'i*

Volume 9 Iver B. Neumann, *Uses of the Other: "The East" in European Identity Formation*

Volume 8 Keith Krause and Michael C. Williams, editors, *Critical Security Studies: Concepts and Cases*

Volume 7 Costas M. Constantinou, *On the Way to Diplomacy*

Volume 6 Gearóid Ó Tuathail (Gerard Toal), *Critical Geopolitics: The Politics of Writing Global Space*

Volume 5 Roxanne Lynn Doty, *Imperial Encounters: The Politics of Representation in North–South Relations*

Volume 4 Thom Kuehls, *Beyond Sovereign Territory: The Space of Ecopolitics*

Volume 3 Siba N'Zatioula Grovogui, *Sovereigns, Quasi Sovereigns, and Africans: Race and Self-Determination in International Law*

Volume 2 Michael J. Shapiro and Hayward R. Alker, editors, *Challenging Boundaries: Global Flows, Territorial Identities*

Volume 1 William E. Connolly, *The Ethos of Pluralization*